Bees in Early Modern Transatlantic Literature

This book examines apian imagery—bees, drones, honey, and the hive—in the seventeenth- and eighteenth-century literary and oral traditions. In England and the New World colonies during a critical period of expansion, the metaphor of this communal society faced unprecedented challenges even as it came to emblematize the process of colonization itself. The beehive connected the labor of those marginalized by race, class, gender, or species to larger considerations of sovereignty. This study examines the works of William Shakespeare; Francis Daniel Pastorius; Hopi, Wyandotte, and Pocasset cultures; John Milton; Hester Pulter; and Bernard Mandeville. Its contribution lies in its exploration of the simultaneously recuperative and destructive narratives that place the bee at the nexus of the human, the animal, and the environment. The book argues that bees play a central representational and physical role in shaping conflicts over hierarchies of the early transatlantic world.

Nicole A. Jacobs teaches in Women's, Gender & Queer Studies and English at California Polytechnic State University in San Luis Obispo. Her articles have appeared in *Studies in Philology, Criticism, The Shakespearean International Yearbook, Appositions,* and the *Routledge Handbook of Shakespeare and Animals.*

Perspectives on the Non-Human in Literature and Culture
Series Editor: Karen Raber, University of Mississippi, USA

Literary and cultural criticism has ventured into a brave new world in recent decades: posthumanism, ecocriticism, critical animal studies, the new materialisms, the new vitalism, and other related approaches have transformed the critical environment, reinvigorating our encounters with familiar texts, and inviting us to take note of new or neglected ones. A vast array of non-human creatures, things, and forces are now emerging as important agents in their own right. Inspired by human concern for an ailing planet, ecocriticism has grappled with the question of how important works of art can be to the preservation of something we have traditionally called "nature." Yet literature's capacity to take us on unexpected journeys through the networks of affiliation and affinity we share with the earth on which we dwell—and without which we die—and to confront us with the drama of our common struggle to survive and thrive has not diminished in the face of what Lyn White Jr. called "our ecological crisis." From animals to androids, non-human creatures and objects populate critical analyses in increasingly complex ways, complicating our conception of the cosmos by dethroning the individual subject and dismantling the comfortable categories through which we have interpreted our existence. Until now, however, the elements that compose this wave of scholarship on non-human entities have had limited places to gather to be nurtured as a collective project. "Perspectives on the Non-Human in Literature and Culture" provides that local habitation. In this series, readers will find creatures of all descriptions, as well as every other form of biological life; they will also meet the non-biological, the microscopic, the ethereal, the intangible. It is our goal for the series to provide an encounter zone where all forms of human engagement with the non-human in all periods and national literatures can be explored, and where the discoveries that result can speak to one another, as well as to scholars and students.

Bees in Early Modern Transatlantic Literature
Sovereign Colony
Nicole A. Jacobs

For more information about this series, please visit: www.routledge.com/Perspectives-on-the-Non-Human-in-Literature-and-Culture/book-series/PNHLC

Bees in Early Modern Transatlantic Literature

Sovereign Colony

Nicole A. Jacobs

Routledge
Taylor & Francis Group

NEW YORK AND LONDON

First published 2021
by Routledge
52 Vanderbilt Avenue, New York, NY 10017

and by Routledge
2 Park Square, Milton Park, Abingdon, Oxon, OX14 4RN

Routledge is an imprint of the Taylor & Francis Group, an informa business

Library of Congress Cataloging-in-Publication Data
A catalog record for this title has been requested

ISBN: 978-0-367-41614-0 (hbk)
ISBN: 978-1-003-12237-1 (ebk)

Typeset in Sabon
by codeMantra

Contents

Acknowledgments

Like the hive, this book has relied upon the support and nurturance of many. To Linda Woodbridge, I owe so much in my development as a scholar and as a person. I am also deeply grateful to Laura Knoppers, Alexa Alice Joubin, Mihoko Suzuki, Garrett Sullivan, and Marcy North for their guidance over the years. I offer my thanks to Jenell Navarro, not only for her friendship but also for her feedback and insights as I developed this project. My gratitude and affection extend to the entire Navarro family, including José, Nayeli, and Joaquin. I have also had wonderfully supportive chairs in Women's, Gender & Queer Studies, including Elizabeth Adan, Jane Lehr, and Jean Williams. For friendship, collegiality, and forbearance in hearing so much about bees, I thank Jen and Dylan Retsek, Cassie Thomas, Jacqueline Campbell, Dan and Linda Manheim, Jonathan and Colleen Zing, John Henry Martin, Jennifer Fuller, Rochelle Zuck, Amy Wiley, Phyllisa Smith Deroze, Kate Pilhuj, Giuseppina Iacono Lobo, Julius Lobo, Lindsey Simon-Jones, Niamh O'Leary, Marcy Blumberg, Anna Kerlek, Gregorio Narvasa, Virginia Lovell, Ana Maria Diaz, Steele Nowlin, and Jeff Pruchnic. For their support, I thank Patricia and Kenneth Jacobs. For unwavering love and guidance, I also thank Jane and Bobby Kenney. I wish that the incomparably loving Joan Jacobs could have seen this volume in print.

I would like to thank Karen Raber for her always outstanding and insightful guidance as an editor. The project has grown productively due to the comments and suggestions of John Morrillo, Richard Grinnell, and an anonymous reader with the press. I appreciate the efforts of Mitchell Manners at Routledge in the publishing process. Holly Dugan, Tiffany Jo Werth, and Reid Barbour also provided fantastic editorial feedback as I developed my earlier work on bees. My thanks to Jennifer Linhart Wood for sharing her expansive knowledge of early modern music and acoustics and to Luz Calvo for her insights about honey in the *Florentine Codex*.

This work has also been shaped by excellent feedback and conversations at various conferences, especially from Ayesha Ramachandran, Joseph Campana, Wendy Wall, Leah Knight, Alan Stewart, Brent Dawson, Crystal Bartolovitch, Erica Fudge, Kat Lecky, and Laura Estill.

I would like to thank the amazingly helpful librarians and archivists at the British Library, the Bodleian Library, the Brotherton Collection at the University of Leeds Library, and the Huntington Library. My thanks extend to Sadada Jackson as well as the staff of the Tozzer, Houghton, and Widener Libraries at Harvard University. I am especially grateful to Brett Bodemer at the Kennedy Library at Cal Poly for securing critical sources, especially during the COVID-19 pandemic, even offering me books from his own collection during the library's closure.

Portions of Chapter 1 were previously published as "Bernardian Ecology and Topsell's Redemptive Bee in *The Tempest*," Copyright © 2020 in *The Routledge Handbook of Shakespeare and Animals*, edited by Holly Dugan and Karen Raber. Reproduced by permission of Taylor and Francis Group, LLC, a division of Informa plc. An abbreviated version of Chapter 4 comes from "John Milton's Bee, from Polemic to Epic" from STUDIES IN PHILOLOGY, Volume 113. Copyright © 2015 by the University of North Carolina Press. Used by permission of the publisher. www.uncpress.org.

I appreciate the guidance and good will of Pete Skarda, who not only set me up with my first hive of bees, but who also helped me inestimably when they continued to swarm. I also extend my gratitude to the Central Coast Beekeepers' Alliance for all of their community work to save swarms, offer education and mentorship for beekeepers, and make our region as bee-friendly as possible. I wish to express my deep affection for my first hive of bees, who were so gentle with me despite my inexperience and from whom I learned so much.

My children Ainsley and Jacob have shared an unbridled enthusiasm in learning about bees and the environment and have joyfully and patiently played in the gardens of every repository I have visited in researching this book. I could never express the full measure of my love and gratitude to my husband Dustin Stegner. He has given me the time and space to write, read every page, and has even risked mixing ladders with saws to catch an errant swarm. He has supported every personal and professional step of my journey, and I dedicate this book to him.

Introduction

Abusing the Hive

Introduction

There is a paradox in humanity's treatment of bees in the early modern period. The hive represented a powerful metaphor of an orderly social structure and the English monarchy itself, but it was commonplace to kill the bees and steal their honey and wax. For centuries, the apian metaphor had been taken up within empires and kingdoms to justify the hegemony of the elite and by the Catholic Church to authorize top-down papal authority. Under the banner of beehive exemplarity, poets, theorists, and beekeepers alike assigned to bees a host of qualities deemed desirable in human society: virtue, chastity, judgment, order, ingenuity, efficiency, obedience, self-sacrifice, valor, ferocity, discernment, shrewdness, cleanliness, respect for elders, organization, offence at foul odors, skill in meteorological prognostication, and, above all, industriousness. Invariably, bees were depicted as working tirelessly for the common good and taking no leisure, a goal to which authorities would aspire in managing what they viewed as a disorderly populace. English monarchs, including Charles II, specifically identified with the sovereign bee, and yet across the kingdom, beekeepers slaughtered hives en masse.

Most beekeepers of the seventeenth century used straw skeps or other containers that required them to burn, poison, or drown hives in order to harvest their honey. In addition, Edmund Southerne in *A Treatise Concerning the Right Use and Ordering of Bees* (1593), recommends that if a hive has not stored approximately five quarts of honey by Bartholomewtide (August 24), then it is best "to kill them and take that which they have" rather than "lose your labour."[1] Shakespeare's King Henry IV renders this commonplace bee-killing practice into a simile that expresses his frustration with his own waning power. On his deathbed, the king laments the ingratitude that "foolish over-careful fathers" face at the hands of their sons:

> For this they have been thoughtful to invest
> Their sons with arts and martial exercises:
> When, like the bee, culling from every flower

> The virtuous sweets,
> Our thighs pack'd with wax, our mouths with honey,
> We bring it to the hive, and, like the bees,
> Are murdered for our pains.[2]

In framing his own experience as akin to that of the honeybee, and placing his son in the role of the beekeeper—who exploits the bee's labor before killing it—Henry IV taps into the potent symbolism of those humans who viewed themselves as facing a specifically creaturely form of disempowerment. Both are compelled by a human master to work toward their own demise and to see the exploitation of their community. If, however, even sovereigns could be "murdered for our pains," then what hope of justice was held for any of the workers?

At the same time that beekeepers were killing their hives, they also realized their value. Although seventeenth-century beekeepers and natural philosophers did not yet fully understand the mechanisms of honeybee pollination, they did perceive that bees' value to humans far exceeded that of their commodities of honey and wax. John Dryden's translation of Virgil's *Georgics* (1697) sums it up best in saying that bees "share with [man] one common Fate / In Health and Sickness, and in Turns of State."[3] It is difficult, then, to reconcile the social value of bees to human culture given their treatment. In *The Reformed Commonwealth of Bees* (1655), Samuel Hartlib laments the destructive practices of seventeenth-century beekeeping,

> The Ancients made a constant revenue of their bees without killing them at any time, and that this so profitable government of bees is now utterly lost, is too much apparent from the common practice of all nations at this day, who generally kill the bees to take the honey.[4]

His solution to rescue the bees from this inglorious fate was to introduce a new box hive favored by Sir Thomas Browne, which—unlike the prevalent straw skep—would allow keepers to harvest bees' products without killing them. Notably, however, the impulse to preserve bees was not generally borne, as it is today, out of the risk of scarcity and consequential negative effects on humankind, but rather out of an economical move that would save the beekeeper from having to hunt for or otherwise procure new colonies. Efforts in the latter half of the century to save the bees were funded in large part by the crown, as this work reinforced the authority of the English sovereign through that of the sovereign bee.

Much discussion about bee culture in early modern England held that their social structure modeled the perfect form of government for sociable creatures, especially humans. Indeed, Gervase Markham called honeybees "this regall race."[5] John Levett's *The Ordering of Bees: or the*

True History of Managing Them (1634) typifies a seventeenth-century representation of honeybee sovereignty as an example for human society. Of the sovereign or "Master Bee," Levett indicates that they

> are absolute in their authorities and commands, and out of a regall power or civil Discipline ... hav[e] a supreame prerogative above all the rest, he overvieweth all that are within the compasse of his squadrons, he administreth Justice unto all, correcting the lazie, sloathfull, and disobedient, and giving honour and incouragement to those which are painfull, laborious, and diligent.[6]

This depiction of a sovereign bee in an orderly hive is built upon the notion that there is a "natural" order ordained by God. Levett's "Master Bee" is an arbiter who may dispense both punishment and reward according to his own standards. Levett's perspective as a beekeeper reflects a largely human conception of sovereignty: its exceptional juridical power. Giorgio Agamben outlines what he calls "a state of exception," or the ability to determine whether and where to apply the law or to act outside of it, as the instantiating premise of sovereignty itself.[7] According to Agamben,

> If the exception is the structure of sovereignty, then sovereignty is not an exclusively political concept, an exclusively juridical category, a power external to law ... it is the originary structure in which law refers to the life and includes it in itself by suspending it.[8]

Importantly, sovereignty witnesses the approach of the human to the animal and the animal to the human. The connection between sovereignty and the ways in which it is built upon relationships with animals has long been a part of the European tradition.[9] Peggy McCracken, for instance, looks to literary uses of Genesis and the ways in which medieval French literature "debate[s] postlapsarian relations of authority and power over animals, and ... imagine[s] models of sovereignty shared among humans and between humans and nonhuman creatures."[10] In seventeenth-century England, Levett's sovereign bee had the power to convey the ultimate authority, both inside and outside the law, while simultaneously negotiating the relationship between the human and the creature.

Even among those theorists who relied upon a conventional reading of the hive's exemplarity to human government, however, there was some variance in the understanding of bee sovereignty. In *Leviathan* (1651), Thomas Hobbes compares the human commonwealth to that of the beehive, noting that in the hive, "the only way to erect such a Common Power ... [is] to conferre all their power and strength upon one Man, or upon one Assembly of men, that may reduce their Wills, by plurality of voices, unto the Will."[11] Hobbes's approach differs from Levett's, however, in his distinction between natural and covenantal commitments to apian and human societies, respectively. The sovereign of the human commonwealth exercises the same influence as the sovereign bee, but for Hobbes the human sovereign is superior to the apian in the language and reason that dictate the contractual basis of the commonwealth. Sovereign power also traverses geography. Hobbes notes that the provinces of Rome or the Virginian settlement ultimately appoint their governors as representatives of the sovereign's force: "for there, if the Sovereign be not Judge, though in his own cause, there can be no Judge at all."[12] Indeed, during English colonization, the *translatio imperii* sought to invest the colonial governors with this power of the English sovereign hive hierarchy abroad. During this period, the English aimed not only to colonize and expand but also to provision this increasing population with the growth of the agricultural revolution. As English colonists sought to encompass greater influence and territory, there were some loyalists who curried favor by endorsing a conventional model of the metaphorical hive.

Beehives also proved essential to the physical colonizing efforts of the English, as they were transported across the Atlantic on ships during diapause (a seasonal period of relative dormancy) in the winter, emerging the next spring as inadvertent tools of English colonization. The honeybee was not native to North America, and before its introduction to Virginia in 1621, the colonies foundered.[13] The English colonial project was reliant on honeybee products and labor for success. And while these early colonists did not understand that many of their European crops were failing due to a lack of bee pollination, they did observe that colonies with hives—from Maine to Virginia—thrived. In fact, in *New English Canaan* (1632), Thomas Morton made the observation that honeybees were the canaries in the mine of New World colonization: If English hives could survive, then the scouting location was deemed *Zona temperata* or "this golden meane" because this climate is the best for "the Bee" and the Englishman.[14] On one side of colonization, the honeybee, in its precariousness, mitigated against the dangers faced by the early colonists. On the other, the English pursuit of a sovereign colony necessarily undercut the autonomy of its creaturely precedent in the hive as well as the already-established sovereignty of the Indigenous nations of North America. This period of conquest coincided with both political and philosophical upheaval in England. The rising republicanism that would erupt into the English Civil War and the regicide of Charles I took place during the Scientific Revolution with its establishment of scientific method and discoveries about physiology, including the confirmation that bees live in a society governed by a queen and run by female worker bees.

Bees in Early Modern Transatlantic Literature: Sovereign Colony examines the literary and cultural output of writers and theorists in England and America who often rejected a masculinized and consolidated hive, instead working to destabilize the sovereign exception through sympathetic or resistant depictions of the worker bee. Increasingly, writers of this era would chip away at the notion that the beehive offered a panacea for human error, sin, greed, and laziness. A significant group of dramatists, poets, and storytellers would break down this model to reveal the connections between the worker bee and the worker human. Both were represented as serving the interests of a human master who ultimately sought their destruction for his own gain. From Shakespeare to Native American storytellers, from Milton to Hester Pulter, writers and theorists reframed the icon of the beehive. In doing so, they revealed the incongruities between the natural order of the hive and the human propensity toward disorder and conflict.

A significant portion of seventeenth-century English and American literary output represents human emulation of the compliant and self-sacrificing worker bee as problematic. Why should entire classes of people be expected to accept an assigned and rigid role in the larger social structure? These critiques, however, are not lodged at honeybee species themselves but rather the anthropocentric metaphors that would perpetuate the notion of a divinely endorsed exemplar of hierarchy. As the writers examined in this book demonstrate, those in power during this period wield the symbol of the beehive as a tool not only to justify their own position but also to punish, oppress, or deceive their less fortunate fellow human and nonhuman beings. One early example to highlight this prevailing trope can be witnessed in Shakespeare's *2 Henry VI*, as Jack Cade bolsters his rebellion. He addresses the irony that the products of domesticated animals like bees and sheep should be the instruments of oppression for the landholders and laborers of England. He says that the bee's sting, its primary means of defense, is not nearly as destructive as human's abuse of the insect's labor. To Cade, the most pernicious use of the honeybee is in the field of law: "'tis the bee's wax; for I did but seal once to a thing, and I was never mine own man since."[15] From Cade's perspective, the product of bees' industry, which on its own is useful and innocuous enough, is leveraged by Henry VI and his government as a symbol to hold the people in a constant state of debt, compelling them to work to the death just as the bees who made the wax would do.

Who performs what labor for whom and at what personal cost operates as a central motif in several works within the early English transatlantic traditions, particularly when it comes to women's labor. In the seventeenth century, when the sex of bee queens, workers, and drones was first hypothesized and then confirmed through microscopic observation, engagements with bees often reflected this upheaval in the tradition of the masculine sovereign hive. The connection between the worker bee and worker human is reinforced by the gender of beekeepers as well. Although those who sought bee-box patents and wrote bee husbandry manuals were men, much of the practical keeping of bees was performed by women. Indeed, as Levett writes in his introduction to *The Ordering of Bees*, "The greatest use of this book will be for the unlearned Country people, especially good women, who commonly in this Country take more care and regard of this kinde of commodity."[16] The good women beekeepers provide necessary labor to the household and the kingdom, but like the worker bee are also dispensable to the sovereign state of exception.

And while bees are only one of many creatures exploited by the elite, they are unique in their contribution to the larger paradigm of interspecies coexistence. Animal studies has explored the ways in which animal characteristics and comparisons are used to designate a host of living beings, including humans, as less worthy of living lives free from oppression due to race, religion, class, gender, or ability. In early modern studies, Erica Fudge and Bruce Boehrer have both examined a range of nonhuman lives in relation to Cartesian reason and rationality as well as regard for animal character that descends with the growing establishment of "the human" as a critical category.[17] The beehive, however, does not fit easily into such paradigms as a result of its unique status as an exemplar to human society that is still subordinate to and exploited by human beings. Karen Raber's concept of "shared embodiment" between human and nonhuman beings is one that applies concretely to the life of the hive.[18] As I will demonstrate, the similar corporeal vulnerabilities of the bee and the human lend to a discussion of precarious lives within animal studies. Laurie Shannon's work treats with a host of "zoo-topian" figures, and her discussions of cosmology and exceptionalism offer valuable insights into the swarm's prerogative and political significance in the period.[19] Although the insect more broadly has typically occupied a marginal position in animal studies, as Eric C. Brown notes, insects' defining characteristic as "entoma" or those that exist "in sections" specifically "marks insects as humanity's Other, even as their swarming, hiving, and colonizing behaviors reproduce various self-identifications in human beings."[20] How the beehive contributes to animal studies, I suggest, is that it represents not only the individual within the greater collective, but it also helps to shape how discussions of labor and use of time and resources factor into polity.

This study contends that the beehive is an invaluable cultural icon that intervenes at the confluence of English colonization, agriculture, and science as a means of considering who has control over these expanding resources and who is excluded from their benefits. The Parliamentarian John Pym reflects on the state of the king's political sovereignty: "I know not what it is. ... I know how to add 'sovereign' to his person, but not to his power."[21] The authors studied here do not necessarily suggest an overthrow of the sovereign, but rather they emphasize the will of the individual worker bee and the strength of her collective swarm. Joseph Campana considers the impact of insects on notions of sovereignty and polity: "The particularity of early modern creatures—their morphologies, scales, milieus, and modalities of life—enable distinctive theorizations of collectivity precisely because variations across life forms alter how we understand the nature of what a political animal might be."[22] Writers on various positions of the political spectrum turned to the apian metaphor not specifically to advocate for one form of government or another, but rather to express the disempowerment faced by the majority, those who, like the worker bee, were expected to subordinate their own pleasures and inclinations to that of the collective.

The critical intervention of this book is that it places the honeybee at the nexus of the human and the nonhuman, particularly within shifting configurations of sovereignty, labor, gender, and race during a pivotal epoch of world ecology. I argue that English, American, and Native American writers' deployment of bees, drones, honey, hives, and swarms have much to tell us about competing perspectives on social structures among and between living beings as well as the role of the individual within the collective. The study's aim is two-fold. First, it explores how the beehive figures both physically and figuratively into the process of colonization, maintenance of the kingdom or commonwealth, and war. Second, it shows how as political and military insurgency ushers in new alignments of power, the beehive offers a sophisticated and contentious paradigm for envisioning the possibilities between the sovereign and the workers of a colony. A central contention of this book is that resistant strains of literary and political treatments of the hive critique the impulse to harness the labor of the masses for the power of the few, thereby imagining alternative configurations of what it means to exercise personal or collective sovereignty.

In this introduction, I first discuss how European understandings of bee society, extending from ancient Greece through early modern England, helped to transform the discourse of honeybees' metaphorical and physical status in the seventeenth century. Second, I outline how the Reformation initiated the basis of challenges to hive exemplarity while simultaneously offering an influential and transgressive set of ecological world views. Third, I highlight the ways in which English knowledge of the honeybee colony helped to shape the rhetoric of New World colonization. Finally, I apply a posthumanist reading to demonstrate the ways in which the beehive stands as a unique model of precariousness, ultimately offering a generative paradigm for interspecies coexistence.

The Idealized Labor of the Hive

Before delving into how the literary and oral traditions of the early transatlantic posed specific challenges to the tradition of the English sovereign hive, it is worthwhile to explore how the beehive metaphor developed into a foundational tenet of European political formation.

The gathering storehouse of apian knowledge, which stretched back to ancient Greece, was aimed toward justifying the continued subordination of the majority of people to the will of the sovereign. Nevertheless, the seventeenth century marks an important shift in the ways that this knowledge was distributed and perceived. Frederick R. Prete, in addressing the treatment of bees in England, asserts that there is "a historically important rift developed in literature about the bee" between "scholarly or academic books" and "practical works on beekeeping directed to the ordinary person."[23] Although there are several contributing factors in the emergence of this rift, I would suggest that the result of this disparity has further consequences. Several writers in England and America relied upon the increasingly popular wisdom about beehive structure and labor in order to question codified social hierarchies.

Early modern beekeepers recognized that there were three distinct classes of bees within the hive that were differentiated by size, appearance, and role. Moreover, their descriptions of these ranks of bees within the hive were clearly anthropomorphic. At the top of the hierarchy was placed the single sovereign bee, which had historically been mistaken as a king. This bee, it was believed, ruled over all other members of the hive, a notion that was supported by the sovereign bee's large physical stature, distinctly different treatment and diet from other pupae, and centrality to overall hive activity.[24] At the beginning of the seventeenth century, Charles Butler, in *The Feminine Monarchie* (1609), was responsible for popularizing the notion that this ruler bee was the queen of an "Amazonian or feminine kingdom," doing so based upon long-held beekeeping knowledge and observations.[25] Definitive proof of the queen bee's sex would arrive in the early 1670s when Jan Swammerdam viewed the insects under a microscope. After the queen, all other bees in the hive descended in order and were expected to dispatch their delegated tasks without hesitation.

Second in the hierarchy was the female worker bee that was responsible for all of the practical work within the social structure. Even within this rank, however, there were further divisions of degree, as different assignments garnered varying levels of respect, at least among their keepers. Butler, for instance, believed those worker bees who directly fed and served the queen enjoyed a more privileged role as lieutenants and advisors. Moreover, there appeared to be a possibility for some social advancement, as it was widely accepted that worker bees' assigned roles might shift as they matured. The revered role of defending the hive, beekeepers believed, was reserved for the most seasoned veterans. Other hive duties included collecting honey, feeding pupae, scouting new hive locations, and building and maintaining honeycombs. Worker bees were viewed as individuals who would sacrifice, even to the death, for the survival and well-being of the collective hive, a quality that would particularly resonate among the human elite, who believed the sacrifices of the masses ultimately served the greater good.

The last and only derided class within the hive consisted of drone bees, which to the early modern understanding were the epitome of laziness. We now know that these male bees are responsible for procreating with the queen to ensure the future generations of the hive, a supposition considered in Butler's work but not fully accepted in most beekeeping manuals until the eighteenth century. Bees had long been thought to generate spontaneously without sexual reproduction.[26] Drones were thus viewed largely as a liability, in that they depleted the hive's resources by consuming far more than their smaller female counterparts without offering any labor or contribution in return. As Aristotle outlines in *Historia animalium*, a perceived positive quality of bee society is that it has no tolerance for such laggards: "The bees drive out all that are idle or wasteful."[27] In addition, Southerne indicates of the autumn expulsion of drones by worker bees that there is little reason for a beekeeper to intervene in managing the drone population, as "the Bees of themselves will kill so many as they thinke good" until the hive enters diapause in the winter with only its female queen and workers.[28] In other words, any perceived pilferers were seen by beekeepers as getting their comeuppance for their failure to prepare the community for times of hardship.

Several early modern writers contributed to the prolific literature of bee husbandry, which had two main goals: (1) to disseminate knowledge about extracting the greatest yields of honey and wax from hives, and (2) to promote an apian model of collectivity for human society. Dedicated beekeeping manuals included Thomas Hill's *A Profitable Instruction of the Perfect Ordering of Bees* (1568), Southerne's *A Treatise Concerning the Right Use and Ordering of Bees*, Samuel Purchas' *A Theatre of Political Flying Insects Wherein especially the Nature, the Worth, the Work, the Wonder, and the Manner of Right-Ordering of the Bee is Discovered and Described* (1657), and John Worlidge's *Apiarium: or a Discourse of Bees* (1676). In the dedication to Levett's *The Ordering of Bees*, the author's son (also named John Levett) outlines the conventional view of bees by natural philosophers who

> observe the nature, working, policy, thrift, and exquisite perfection of this little Flie, in all affayres of war or peace, at home or abroad: and yet have they all been rather brought to height of admiration, than made fit for full explication of the wisdome which (surpassing their own wisdome) they have found in the Bee.[29]

Butler's *The Feminine Monarchie* stands out as the most influential and enduring due to the extensive knowledge of beekeeping and apian behavior that would guide his manual through additional printings in

1623, 1634, and a Latin translation in 1673. Bees were also a prominent subject within general husbandry guides and bestiaries such as Conrad Heresbach's *Four Books of Husbandry* (1577) and Edward Topsell's *Historie of Serpents* (1608). And although the seventeenth century witnessed some advancements in apiary design and maintenance, what is evident in this large body of writing is the significant influence of ancient and classical beekeeping knowledge and apian metaphors.

In the Greek tradition, bees were respected as important to humans, frequently offering models of laudable conduct. Homer's *Iliad* employs bee similes to describe the ways in which the people follow Agamemnon and fortify Trojan resolve against the persistent Achaean warriors who, like bees, "do not leave their hollow home, but stay to fight off hunters on behalf of their children."[30] To Cristopher Hollingsworth, Homer's apian imagery "treats the crowd as *the* natural unit of human cooperation."[31] Plato similarly takes up the mantle of the bee paradigm in his *Republic*, though there is some disagreement within scholarship about how the apian metaphor registers within his work. To Andre Stipanovic, Plato advances "the notion of the 'harmonious beehive'" as a positive model for human interaction, an idea that is demonstrated in Book VII where the philosophers are deemed "rulers and kings of our hive."[32] For Rana Saadi Liebert, by contrast, the figure of Socrates in the text "exploits various traditions of bee-related metaphors," especially those of the drone and the sweetness of honey, "to strengthen his case against poetry."[33] What is most notable in Plato's use of the bee is the focus specifically on the laziness and deception of the drone. Indeed, Plato is responsible for popularizing the contempt for this single class of bee while still maintaining respect for the rest of the hive and its inner workings. Aristotle, in his own philosophical meditations, similarly advances the concept that bees and humans are both social species willing to submit themselves to a ruler under a shared set of natural laws.

The most significant and enduring classical contribution to the seventeenth-century apiary and to idealized notions of the beehive as a paradigm for human social structure, however, comes from Virgil. William Moeck suggests that the bee similes of the *Aeneid* provide foundational intertexts to both Shakespeare and Milton.[34] As Hollingsworth puts it, "Virgil 'sharply defined' the Hive, clarifying its structure and mapping its extremes" in relation to other animal and natural metaphors for human culture.[35] The text had been translated into English by Abraham Fleming in 1589 and dedicated to the Archbishop of Canterbury. John Dryden's influential folio *The Works of Virgil: Containing His Pastorals, Georgics, and Aeneis* (1697) emphasizes the significance of the beehive to Virgil's work with beautiful and detailed apian illustrations. In his commentary on Book IV of the *Georgics*, he says that Virgil "singles out the Bee, which may be reckon'd the most sagacious of 'em for his subject," indicating that one of the most significant aspects of the poem is the way that it reveals the hive's "prudent and politick Administration of Affairs."[36] The *Georgics* establishes a common ground upon which English and colonial beekeepers would reinforce their notions of social structure and government, and yet this perspective would also form the basis of seventeenth-century challenges to religious and political hierarchies.

Virgil represents bees as the ultimate community, imbued with an otherworldly and superior knowledge, indicating that they are "bestow'd by *Jove* for secret Services" and "That Bees have Portions of Etherial Thought" (*Georgics*, 4.221, 322). To Virgil, the nature of bee exceptionalism is witnessed in their commitment to a collective vision and set of laws:

> Of all the Race of Animals, alone
> The Bees have common Cities of their own:
> And common Sons, beneath one Law they live,
> And with one common Stock their Traffick drive.
> ....
> All is the States, the State provides from all.
> Mindful of coming Cold, they share the Pain:
> And hoard, for Winter's use, the Summer's gain.
>
> (224–31)

The secret to the congenial nature of the Virgilian hive lies in the way that each individual contributes labor and submits to the collective mission, so that the community rises or falls together. In early modern England, the Virgilian hive would also continue to maintain its currency for writers who hoped to enforce what they deemed as a natural view of hierarchies of class, religion, race, and gender, ideas they hoped to propagate in the New World. However, the first true contentions with this concept would emerge in England and on the continent during the Reformation, as Protestants attacked a Catholic tradition that upheld a divine apian-like hierarchy that could dictate one's status relative not only to church hierarchy but also, presumably, to God himself. Amid this changing cultural landscape for the bee metaphor in post-Reformation England emerges a new means of interpreting humans' relationship to nature and creaturely life.

The Reformation Hive and Bernardian Ecology

Opposition to the notion of the hive as a model for human society started most notably with Philips van Marnix van Saint Aldegonde's *The Beehive of the Romish Church* (1569, English translation 1579). A hint of the satire of this treatise can be glimpsed in its condemnation of a Catholic Easter vigil prayer that subordinates humankind to that of the bee: "mans invention and knowledge is not to be compared."[37] It is unsurprising that Philips van Marnix would centralize his attack on the Catholic beehive, which had been established—from Saint Ambrose in the fourth century to the medieval bestiary—to reinforce the notion of a divine hierarchy. This configuration was believed to offer a natural paradigm for the structure of the church, with the pope as sovereign bee, the archbishops and bishops as his privileged counselors, and the workers and drones as common parishioners. Even under Protestant attack, Catholics continued to double down on their apian iconography, as beehives featured prominently in seventeenth-century Jesuit emblem books.[38] Philips van Marnix mockingly dedicates his treatise to "The Right Worshipfull, holy, profound, and learned Doctor, and *Magister noster*, Master Franciscus Sonnius," a Catholic bishop who vehemently opposed Calvinist doctrine. In this bitingly ironic preface, he reveals his true intentions through the perversion of the ancient art of collection:

> I have named it *The Beehive of the Romish Church*, thereby to give to understand, that as the hony bee doth not gather her hony out of one flower alone, but of many and diverse: so doth not the church of Rome stand upon one scripture, Bible, councels, or books of De-crees, but doth catche and snatch out of each of them, that which best serveth her purpose.[39]

Immensely popular in its original Dutch and in English translation, *The Beehive of the Romish Church* would be only the first in a series of re-formist texts throughout the sixteenth and seventeenth centuries, which culminated in England in the work of John Milton, that would invert the hive hierarchy to take down Catholic doctrine and practice. In the process of doing so, however, Philips van Marnix also opened the door to a productive means of conceptualizing the relationship between humanity and nature.

Bees and their human keepers did not simply suffer a symbolic critique during the Reformation; there were economic and social consequences to shifting attitudes toward bees as well. According to Prete, even by the eighteenth century in England,

> beekeeping had not recovered from the sharp drop in the demand for beeswax from which altar candles were made (due to the Refor-mation); for mead [a wine made with honey] (due to the increased importation of foreign wine); and for honey (due to the increased use of sugar).[40]

Put differently, what starts as a religious contention over honeybee ico-nography extends out to encompass multiple concerns. A burgeoning global economic system encouraged trade across borders and shifted the energies placed in maintaining hives. Whereas beekeeping suffered in England, it thrived in the colonies.

The one exception seventeenth-century English Protestants made in deriding the Catholic hive was in promoting the meditations of Saint Bernard of Clairvaux, the patron saint of beekeeping. Philips van Marnix sought to reclaim the work of Bernard for the Protestant cause, arguing that the saint "did very stoutly strive against the Priestes and Prelates, calling them the servants of Antichrist."[41] Bernard, a twelfth-century French Cistercian abbot, was associated with the bee for his melliflu-ousness and his frequent allusions to bees, honey, and wax in describing Christ and Christian virtue. Translations of Bernard's work, which were overwhelmingly popular in Elizabethan and Jacobean England, sought to reclaim the writing of this Catholic saint for the Protestant cause. Because Bernard heatedly condemned the corruption of church fathers in his own period, Luther, Philip van Marnix, and other prominent Protestants sought to claim him as an *avant la lettre* reformist. Indeed, Bernard was presented as an important dissenting voice among Cath-olics, in that he questioned what might happen if vice marred the top of the human hierarchy. In other words, what if the sovereign could be wrong—if the pope, unlike the queen bee, was failing his parishioners and thereby God himself? In *Five Books on Consideration: Advice to a Pope* (c. 1150), Bernard writes,

> It is a monstrous thing for the highest office to be filled with a man of the lowest character, for the first place to be occupied by a man fit for the last, for the tongue to be eloquent but the hand to be idle, for the talk to abound but results to be lacking, for the face to be grave but behavior capricious, for great authority to be vested in a man of faltering stability. Bring a mirror and let a dirty face recognize itself.[42]

The views of this medieval Catholic saint resonate in the seventeenth century, not only on a theological basis but also on a political one, in that the hive hierarchy only works if those at the top act with virtue and in the best interest of their collective hive. What seventeenth-century translators and readers of Bernard's work recognized was that the elite could not persist in compelling sacrifice from so-called lowly workers and drones if they failed to live up to their responsibilities to care for their people and make their own sacrifices in kind.

In his extensive canon, Bernard advocates inner character and good works over social status and power, a concept that would also reflect an important strain of ecological thought in the seventeenth century. One of the most prominent subjects to emerge in this reinvigoration of Bernard's ideas and words is his unique perspective on nature and the responsibilities that human beings have for preserving nonhuman life.

I term this phenomenon Bernardian ecology, a biocentric view that centralizes God's creation of all forms of life as possessing intrinsic value regardless of that life's utility to humans. The origins of Bernardian ecology begin in his sermon on the Canticles, or Song of Songs.[43] In particular, his meditation on the fifth verse, "I have come into my garden … I have eaten my honeycomb with my honey," outlines the differences in spirits between animals, men, and angels. Bernard draws upon Romans 1:20 to discuss God's unknowable intentions even with dangerous animals that could harm humanity:

> For although they be not killed for food, nor apt to render service, yet verily they exercise the wit, agreeably to that benefit of the common discipline which presides over all methods of putting things in use, by which "the invisible things of God are clearly seen, being understood by the things that are made."[44]

Bernard's notion that nature is the best educator also influenced Browne, who wrote in *Religio Medici* (1643), "what reason may not goe to Schoole to the wisedome of Bees … what wise hand teacheth them to doe what reason cannot teach us?"[45] So prevalent are these ideas that playwrights and poets like Shakespeare and Pulter would adapt and integrate these concepts into their work. Each of the chapters in this book will address the ways in which authors embrace, reject, or theorize other ways of approaching an early modern biocentrism that grants the creature privileged status in creation, as it should for those of humankind.

Bernardian ecology, which transcends notions of animals' use-value to human diet and economy, lies in distinct contrast with the utilitarian view of nonhuman life that stretched back as far as the Bible. In Genesis, God endows Adam with the naming and care of all creatures:

> And God said, Let us make man in our image, after our likeness: and let them have dominion over the fish of the sea, and over the fowl of the air, and over the cattle, and over all the earth
> (King James Version, 1:26)

This passage, and the ideology that stems from it, has long been used by instrumentalists or shallow ecologists to legitimize human dominion and exploitation of animals and nature. The speciesism that drives animal oppression and suffering, as Cary Wolfe has argued, is used as further justification for the oppression of those humans deemed less worthy.[46] Bernardian ecology and other challenges to anthropocentrism, wielded by an ardent minority of early modern writers and storytellers, I argue, disrupt the utilitarianism of Renaissance humanism, offering a more holistic approach to the value of nonhuman life and the treatment that all living beings should be accorded.

Honeybee Colonization and Pollination

The hive is the name of the honeybee's home, but its family unit of queen, workers, and drones is called a colony. The mission of this colony is communal survival, and no honeybee can live without her hive. There is some overlap between honeybee and human models of colonization, and these similarities were not lost upon the early modern colonists and their governors. For instance, when bees swarm to produce new colonies, they do so in response to overcrowding. Enshrined in the Cambridge Platform (1648), which established the congregational polity of New England colonies, is the conviction that the settlers' mission was to swarm, like honeybees, to escape an overcrowded and resource-diminished England and to claim greater territory for God. Indeed, for colonists, the honeybee hive came to emblematize the process of English colonization itself, even though the distinctions between the bee's fastidious expansion and England's desire to conquer and dominate are vast.

Among bees, the swarm involves a contingent of workers and drones following the queen to a new home, and the English diverged in their colonial practice from this model. Whereas the English queen or king authorized particular subjects such as Sir Walter Ralegh to send settlers to establish colonies, the monarchs themselves remained in England, awaiting news of the colonists' success or failure. Nevertheless, other aspects of the English colonial mission did replicate the steps of the bee swarm. When a hive becomes overcrowded and cannot sustain its growth internally, scouting bees venture forth and form a consensus about the best location for their new hive. Over half of the hive, called the parent colony, follows their current queen to their new home while the remaining group, named the daughter colony, prepares to grow and provision their now-diminished population. In the process, neither hive seeks to supplant other bees or beings. Honeybees, with rare exception involving scarcity and hunger, reserve their aggression for defensive rather than offensive maneuvers. This quality in bees was recognized and praised as early as medieval England, where parishioners were asked to follow the peaceful example of the hive: "no bees lie in wait for other creatures, to take advantage of their toil; and none take a life by force."[47] In fact, Sir Thomas More's *Utopia* similarly figures the role of the honeybee within the colony to be one of abundance and benefit to all. Raphael Hythloday notes that the Utopians drink water boiled with honey "of which they have plenty" that they share their honey stores with other nations, mandating that one-seventh of it be distributed among the poor.[48]

The status of the honeybee in the early transatlantic offers an important perspective on the animal within the history of colonization. As Philip Armstrong notes of postcolonial animal studies, "several of the most potent and durable intellectual paradigms produced by European cultures at the height of their imperialist arrogance owe simultaneous debts to the colonial and animal worlds."[49] Similarly concerned with postcolonial theory, though from a posthumanist feminist perspective, Maneesha Deckha importantly emphasizes the significance of centralizing race and culture in an intersectional theory that allows critics "to navigate the postcoloniality of the animal question much better."[50] This posthumanist conception of race seeks to offer the animal as one of many axes upon which the exploitation of living beings turns during this period of conquest.

The role of the insect or the small creature also has much to contribute to posthumanism, and yet current scholarship has not fully mapped its significance. Bruno Latour's notion of "the social" is, in part, informed by De Candolle, for whom "corals, baboons, trees, bees, ants, and whales are also social."[51] Latour quips that Actor-Network Theory (A.N.T.) bears an insect-like association that decentralizes the human theorist: "An ant writing for other ants, this fits my project very well!"[52] Jane Bennett's discussion of the political ecology of actants begins with the similarly diminutive "'small agency' of the lowly worm [which] makes more of a difference than the grand agency of humans."[53] *Bees in Early Modern Transatlantic Literature* contributes to posthumanist animal and insect studies in centralizing the role of the honeybee as well as related species of bumblebees, yellowjackets, butterflies, spiders, serpents, snails, and larks in order to demonstrate the expansive representations of creatures and the burdens of labor and exploitation they share with human workers.

From an early modern perspective, the application of postcolonial theory has the potential to be read as ahistorical. According to Barbara Fuchs, "In order to address the history of expansion," it is essential to acknowledge

> the differenda of power within a society; the "othering," racialization, and exploitation of marginalized peoples; the resistance of those peoples to centralized power; the discursive strategies that serve to control and transform territory; [and] the cultural significance of borders and contact zones.[54]

In addition, from a contemporary Native American studies perspective, the idea of the "postcolonial" could similarly be understood as problematic for subordinating the concept of indigeneity—what came before and what continues to resist colonialism—to the invader's notion of supremacy. For instance, Jace Weaver, a Cherokee religious and legal scholar, has argued,

> As long ... as Western nation-states remain kleptocracies based upon the taking of native lands, as long as autochthones are denied

sovereignty and are pushed toward assimilation into the dominant culture, the postcolonial moment for indigenous peoples will not have arrived.[55]

Instead, many Native American and First Nation scholars favor a discussion of the ways in which decolonization, as a genuine effort to repatriate the land, resists a continuing settler colonialism.[56] In animal studies, Billy-Ray Belcourt, of the Driftpile Cree Nation, argues, "we cannot address animal oppression or talk about animal liberation without naming settler colonialism and white supremacy as political mechanisms that require simultaneous exploitation or destruction of animal and Indigenous bodies."[57] Native American nations were—and continue to be—not only denied political sovereignty but also subjected to colonists who used their imported beehives to suppress Indigenous agriculture and management of natural resources. Knowledge of bees and their keeping, I suggest, helped to instantiate the oppression that so many more-than-human beings continue to suffer in the name of expansion and dominion.

It is perhaps prescient that in the early seventeenth century English colonists would land upon the bee as its tool and metaphor for colonization given that statesmen had such an incomplete knowledge of the hive's full utility to them. While honey and wax remained valuable and life-sustaining commodities, used for foods, drinks, remedies, and candles, bees' most important role by far was in facilitating English propagation of seeds with their pollinating labor. Agriculturalists understood neither the mechanisms of plant reproduction nor bees' role within it. Nonetheless, the foundations of this knowledge would be established in England during the seventeenth century. Nehemiah Grew was the first researcher to compare plant and animal reproduction and to identify the parts of the plant involved. A well-respected member of the College of Physicians, Grew wrote *The Anatomy of Plants* (1682), the culmination of years of botanical study, as a collection of lectures delivered before the Royal Society. In 1676, after examining the parts of various flowers under a microscope, Grew identified an organ he named the seminiform (the stamen, or male portion of the flower). He identified this part as "a little Sheaf of *seed-like particles*; standing on so many *pedicills*," and noted that it was located near but distinct from "the Uterus or true seed-case."[58] And while Grew was aware that bees visited this portion of the flower in order to make honey, he did not perceive that the bee was responsible for transfer of the "seed-like particles" to the "uterus." Notably, however, Grew did connect his scientific discovery to a means for expanding England's store of knowledge. In dedicating *The Anatomy of Plants* to Charles II, Grew emphasizes the limitless possibilities of science: "In sum, Your Majesty will find, that we are come ashore into a new World, whereof we see no end."[59] And yet, Grew was also careful to distance his own botanical experiments from larger discoveries of lands and peoples. His epistle is carefully crafted:

> Your Majesty deeming it to be a more Noble Design, To enlarge the Territories of Knowledge, than those of Dominion: and the Highest Pitch of Human Glory, not to rule, in any sort, over many; but to be a Good Prince over Wise Men.[60]

In establishing for the king what he deems to be the scope of his work, Grew implies that knowledge is the main end, rather than the power for global expansion.

Botanists and apiculturists found an enthusiastic patron in Charles II. He consulted with a Royal Society charter member and author of *Elysium Britannicum* (c. 1650s) John Evelyn, who had himself adopted from Dr. John Wilkins at Wadham College a partially transparent hive that allowed for the safe extraction of honey.[61] As Evelyn wrote in his diary, Wilkins ornamented his hives to look like "Castles and Palaces," the center of human monarchical display of power.[62] In 1663, Charles II would make a special trip to Evelyn's famous gardens and apiary at Sayes Court in Deptford to visit the scholar's reproduction of Wilkin's majestic and practical hives: "his Majestie came on purpose to see and contemplate with much satisfaction."[63] For all the joy bee-saving hives brought Charles II, the technology and knowledge remained limited in scope. Even Evelyn himself had, at times, difficulty in implementing the proper technique to save his bees. He thus criticized those who failed to kill bees that were not properly provisioned for the winter:

> In forraine parts (where they spare the Apes emeritae for their good service) they *Vindemiate* [harvest] by Exsection ... about Autumn (without killing out right) but for many reasons this mercy proves to be a fruitlesse cruelty at last. And therefore our housewifes rather smother them then reduce them to these necessities

of freezing or starving to death.[64] Charles II remained interested in saving bees and thus diversified his opportunities to do so. In April 1675, he awarded Scottish beekeeper John Gedde a monopoly patent for a box hive that could save bees from being killed by their keepers. The proprietary nature of Gedde's design, however, seems to have prevented its widespread adoption, as the typical beekeeper (like Evelyn's housewives) could not afford to purchase such hives.[65]

The blurring of the boundaries between scientific and political exploration would ultimately lead to the discovery of honeybee pollination itself, a move that would be inextricably linked to the colonization of America. In 1750, Arthur Dobbs, a member of the Irish Parliament, sent a letter to the Royal Society connecting colonial power to the work of honeybees. Addressed to Charles Stanhope, Dobbs's letter laments the low prestige of maintaining a political position in a poor colony like Ireland, noting that his "view of doing good, by making discoveries of the great world has been disappointed, upon my retirement into this little corner of it."[66] Dobbs, as only one who is frustrated by career stagnation could do, observed his beehives with enough precision to ascertain that "Providence has appointed the Bee to be very instrumental in promoting the Increase of Vegetables," since the worker bees take "the Male Seed" of the plant, "entering the Pistillum or Matrix in the flower" in order to "impregnate[e] the Ovum, and mak[e] it prolific."[67] Dobbs's work on bees appears to have borne its own fruit, since, in less than four years, he would be appointed as a governor to North Carolina (at Newbern), a position he would occupy until his death at 82.

Beyond his momentous discovery of honeybee pollination—one that would revolutionize the practice of agriculture in Europe and the New World by affirming that farmers needed bees to pollinate many of their crops—Dobbs also popularized in his letter to the Royal Society a successful method for harvesting honey without killing bees. Dobbs instructs a larger audience (without claiming proprietary rights) in how to use their own box hives to harvest honey and wax without harming the insects. He indicates his respect for the French apiculturist René Réaumur who managed to extract honey without killing the hive. Réaumur advocated stupefying the bees with smoke and then cutting the honeycombs directly from the hive as the bees recovered. However, Dobbs proposed an alternative solution that would avoid stressing the bees or injuring the beekeeper:

> Now I think, that turning up the full Hive, and setting an empty Hive upon it, and driving the Bees into it, is preferable to smoking: For then a very few bees will remain in the full Hive; and those few may be stupefied, and the Bees in the empty Hive being put on a Table, the Combs may be taken out and selected at leisure, without Hazard; and afterwards the empty Hive may be turn'd up, and their old Hive set over them, so that they will go up without Scruple into their former Hive, and repair their Work.[68]

The method that Dobbs describes here, with few adjustments for newer technologies, such as moveable frames, remains one preferred even by modern beekeepers. From Dobbs's perspective, the great benefit of the system for both the bee colony and the beekeeper is that "the Society would not be lost."[69] For all of Dobbs's desire to minimize the needless death and suffering of his hives, however, this concern for life does not extend to those he deems as less-than-human obstructions to English colonization. Upon sailing to North Carolina to take up his political post, Dobbs "brought, as an acceptable oblation, several pieces of cannon and one thousand firelocks, a present from the king to the colony," in order to subdue the Native Americans of the region.[70]

Bees that were already exploited and killed by their human keepers in the seventeenth century were also weaponized in the process of colonization, being used to torture those deemed sub-human. Edward Topsell, for instance, explains that Spanish colonizers in the West Indies would regularly cover slaves with honey and place them in the sun:

> With which kind of punishment & torture, the Spanyards doe grievously vex the poore naked Ilanders of *America* at this day, (now called the West Indies) who are under their rule and government, not for justice sake, ... but for satisfaction and fulfilling of their barbarous wills, and beastly tyrannie, that they might seeme to be more cruell, then crueltie itself.[71]

Such actions undoubtedly account for the initial skepticism of Native populations of North America and the Caribbean about European honeybees. The colonized, then, had to contend not only with their colonizers but also with these stinging insects of which they had no knowledge. Despite the fact that seventeenth-century English beekeepers demonstrated a comparatively limited knowledge of pollination, they nevertheless benefited from thousands of years of European husbandry, knowledge that they denied to those whom they sought to conquer.

Honeybee Precariousness and Interspecies Coexistence

Unlike seventeenth-century beekeepers who could save the honeybee with some relatively simple adjustments to hive design, twenty-first-century entomologists and apiculturists cannot as easily counteract those human-driven forces that threaten the hive. We now have a much more comprehensive understanding of bees' significance to worldwide food systems. Approximately one third of all food derives from bee pollination, and this labor furthermore improves the quality or quantity of hundreds of crops.[72] Moreover, we know that the current pressing ecological crisis of bee decline is largely driven by human activity: pesticide use, industrial farming practice, pollution, habitat reduction, and Colony Collapse Disorder (CCD). I contend that the beehive offers to studies of the nonhuman an important model of precariousness, a term and a state of being that ultimately reveals the problematic nature of human colonization of lands, people, and animals. Critical animal studies scholar Richard Twine demonstrates how this concept shapes our understandings of inferiority and of labor:

> the moral significance of harming those deemed inferior has been denied by projecting a whole interconnected cluster of discursive

meanings onto "them," where, for example, the "animality" of "animals" is merely assumed, and the "animality" of various 'humans' is (also) culturally produced. Denial here is also applied to the material labour and active agency of the inferiorized.[73]

Like so many more-than-human beings, honeybees' lives, experiences, and deaths are subject to the whims of human economy, diet, and perhaps most significantly, their impulse toward expansion.

Precariousness—sometimes referred to as precarity—is characterized by a systemically unstable set of living and working conditions for animals or large groups of subordinated humans.[74] The term, which has been taken up within studies of the human and the animal, emphasizes the ways in which entire categories of animate beings are subject to larger systems and markets beyond their control. Judith Butler, in describing the effects of precariousness on humans, for instance, asserts that it boils down to social structures that dictate the conditions of life, noting that these "are pervasively social, establishing not the discrete ontology of the person, but rather the interdependency of persons, ... and relations to the environment and to non-human forms of life."[75] James Stanescu clarifies and extends the idea that precariousness is a social ontology that leads to an exploration of interdependence and "shared vulnerability" across types of life that are human and more-than-human.[76] In terms of how the culture of the human is built upon the suffering of the creature in the early modern period, Raber has argued,

> there is no such thing as a "human" without animals ... there is no such thing as human identity, history, *culture*, without the prior cooperation, collaboration, habitation, ideological appropriation, consumption of animals, without animals as the 'always already' of both materiality and culture itself.[77]

The beehive occupies a central role in the precariousness of various life forms in the seventeenth century.

When precariousness entered the lexicon of animal studies, it was already a mainstay of labor studies. For instance, Marcel Paret discusses how precarious politics have shaped the work of labor unions to address "the struggles of low-wage noncitizen workers" since the 1990s.[78] Given the overlap between animal and labor studies on the issues of a precarious life, it is useful to consider what socialist readings might lend to the discussion of bees in the seventeenth-century transatlantic. Nevertheless, it would be reductive to graft Marx's proletariat onto the concept of the worker bee. Perhaps the greatest potential of the hive to socialist critique, then, has to do with the notion of the web of life in relation to world ecology. Shifting views of sovereignty combined with the relentless oppression of the worker lends to the honeybee's prominent position within ever-changing ecological and social epochs. In relation to our current era, scholars of both the Anthropocene and what Jason W. Moore calls the Capitalocene (an acknowledgment of how "inequality, commodification, imperialism, patriarchy, [and] racial formations" factor into our contemporary age) tend toward a teleological narrative underpinned by a dominant ideology of exploitation and anthropocentrism that begins to emerge in nascent form during the agricultural revolution of the seventeenth century.[79] What the transatlantic authors and works studied here demonstrate, however, is that the notions of sovereignty and labor between and among forms of life were highly contested. Moreover, these debates would be shaped by a number of factors related not just to agricultural or scientific revolutions, but also to colonization, norms regarding the gendered division of labor, the Puritan work ethic, and, significantly, to the outcomes of the English Civil Wars (1642–51) and King Philip's War (1675–6).

Precariousness, as it is discussed by critics, is largely a posthumanist theoretical paradigm that undoubtedly bears relevance in discussing how humans and nonhumans both share in the contingencies of mortal life. Richie Nimmo, for instance, argues that a posthumanist reading of the relationship between bees and beekeepers as "interspecies practitioners" who respond reciprocally and collaboratively to one another demonstrates that "the task of a posthumanist critique is to relentlessly excavate and to foreground the cosmopolitics of 'living with' others that are incipient within apicultural practices."[80] In discussing the "hybrid multispecies assemblage" of contemporary beekeeping practice, Nimmo's work similarly aligns with that of posthumanist feminist scholars Carla Hustak and Natasha Myers who examine the "affectively charged, multisensory partnership" between orchids, bees, and human observers of their "co-evolution."[81] Interpreting the hive through the lens of posthumanist theory encourages an expansion toward considerations of relationality, aesthetics, curiosity, and the passage of time.

It was commonplace in the seventeenth century for apiculturists to sympathize with the members of the hive even as they exploited their labor. Within the early modern multispecies assemblage, there is both affection toward and exploitation of the hive by their keepers. John Worlidge suggests in his *Apiarium* and an expanded edition *The Complete Bee-Master* (1698) that beekeepers should take their cue from their bees' own inclinations, noting that the effective apiculturist (including the "poor and ignorant Country housewife") will

> remove all obstructions that stand in their way, that you might rather ingratiate your self into their favour, by pleasing them in every thing, than in the least to thwart or cross them, for which Love of yours to them, they will recompense you manifold.[82]

And yet, even Worlidge reveals a speciesist ideology that points to the well-loved hive's precariousness. Like Wilkins, Hartlib, Brown, and

Evelyn before him, Worlidge advocates the use of moveable bee boxes, but he dispenses with the notion that a beekeeper can avoid killing his hive:

> it is best to take them by the usual way of Smothering by the fume of Brimstone, admitted by some hole in the bottom of the Beehouse. ... For let not any one imagine, that their Honey can be taken from them and the Bees preserved.[83]

Worlidge's common sentiment, which was skeptical about mid-century efforts to save the bees, indicates that even those who love their bees feel that human convenience justifies hive precariousness. It is this shared experience of bee and human worker precariousness that drives the readings of early modern literary and oral traditions in this book.

The first three chapters focus especially upon how various writers grapple with the beehive's role in England's colonization of the New World. Chapter 1, "Bee Time: Shakespeare," shows how Shakespeare's drama intervenes in larger conceptions of work and time at the dawn of the English colonial enterprise. I explore the blurred margins between conceptions of time among human, animal, and magical beings in *The Tempest*, particularly as they relate to the energy expended serving others versus the time spent pursuing inclinations and preparing the community for the future. Chapter 2, "Hive Split: The New World Colonists," shifts its focus to space and cultural status as it explores how colonists turned to the beehive as a divinely ordained model that would justify their plans to settle in the colonies to spread God's word and to claim greater territory for England. Examining charter documents, sermons, Francis Daniel Pastorius's *The Beehive* (1696), and news articles about women's spinning bees, I show how the apian metaphor encapsulates English narratives of domination and communal work. Chapter 3: "Stingless and Stinging: Native American Kinship" discusses the oppositional nature of various Native American and Mesoamerican reactions toward native bees and European honeybees. Whereas Wyandotte, Wampanoag, and Pocasset responses to the bee emphasized the sting of this winged invader as a tool of the English colonizers, Hopi and Sioux traditions sought to integrate the honeybee into their cosmologies and lifeways. I argue that many Native American and Mesoamerican cultures established co-constitutive kinship bonds with bees regardless of their origin, and that these connections have made significant contributions to the work of decolonization.

The next two chapters pivot back to England as it reconceptualizes sovereignty and scientific discovery during the Civil War, Interregnum, and Restoration. Chapter 4, "Honey Production and Consumption: Milton," examines Milton's apian icon from his polemic to his epic, demonstrating the ways in which he consistently deploys the hive as a means of registering harsh critiques of earthly monarchy, feminine influence, and Catholic superstition. In particular, I explore the ways in which Milton derides the sovereign bee paradigm by focusing on what he views as royalists' perverse process for digesting propaganda about their executed king, drawing connections with Eve's labor and unauthorized consumption in Eden. Chapter 5, "Worker Bee Sacrifice: Pulter," charts the means by which Pulter's royalist poems reclaim apian and arachnid imagery to demonstrate a range of potential responses to living under an oppressive regime. I reveal how Pulter's ecological world view, one that engages with Bernardian ecology, critiques Baconian scientific theory while anticipating some of the key tenets of contemporary ecofeminism, particularly in light of women's maternal labor and ethics of care.

Each of these chapters explores how writers activate a specific facet of apian culture within their work to consider qualities of human-nonhuman relationships, including bees' conceptions of time, swarming practice, stinging capacity, honey production, and penchant for self-sacrifice for the collective hive. What emerge in these literary engagements with beehive social structure and practices is a larger set of ecological views that complicate the relationship between human and creaturely life. For instance, Native American interactions with the bee speak to lifeways that solidify kinship bonds with animate and inanimate lives. These Indigenous perspectives share similarities with the biocentrism of Bernardian ecology explored in both Shakespeare's *The Tempest* and Pulter's emblem and nature poems while ultimately developing independently from the English tradition. By contrast, the early English colonists in America adhered to a conventional humanist instrumentalism that relied upon the bee swarm metaphor to authorize their use of God's bounty in the "New World." Milton's *Paradise Lost* registers yet another perspective, offering the hive of Pandemonium and the female worker bee of Eden to reveal the tensions between the prelapsarian ideal in the human and the nonhuman, and the postlapsarian reality of creaturely subordination and suffering.

Each of the writers and storytellers in this book also engages substantively with emerging knowledge about an exemplary female workforce. From Miranda's reflections on hauling logs and remembering her serving women, to colonist women's spinning and sewing bees, to the centrality of Native American women and of Eve in both cultivation and food preparation, to the maternal labor that occupied many of Pulter's poems about caring for her 15 children, each chapter considers the marginalized work of human women in relation to the dominance of the apian queen and workers. Ultimately, this book treats a tumultuous period of early transatlantic interactions to uncover the dynamic and shifting relationships between those forms of life honored or subordinated by their race, class, gender, or species. The beehive stands as a potent metaphor and practical tool of human husbandry to explore what it means to be or to overtake a sovereign being.

Notes

1 Edmund Southerne, *A Treatise Concerning the Right Use and Ordering of Bees* (1593), sig. D2r.
2 William Shakespeare, *Henry IV, Part 2*, ed. James C. Bulman (London: Bloomsbury, 2016), 4.5.201–08.
3 All quotations from Virgil will be cited in text from *The Works of Virgil: Containing his Pastorals, Georgics, and Aeneis*, trans. John Dryden (London, 1697), *Georgics* IV.366–7.
4 Samuel Hartlib, *The Reformed Commonwealth of Bees* (London, 1655), 3.
5 Gervase Markham, "For Profit, Pleasure, Policy and Fame," in John Levett, *The Ordering of Bees: Or the True History of Managing Them* (London, 1634), sig. B3r.
6 John Levett, *The Ordering of Bees*, 68.
7 Giorgio Agamben, *Homo Sacer: Sovereign Power and Bare Life*, trans. Daniel Heller-Roazen (Palo Alto, CA: Stanford University Press, 1998), 15.
8 Agamben, *Homo Sacer*, 28.
9 For a discussion of post-Enlightenment sovereignty as a concept "reserved for those farthest from the 'animal,'" see Judith Grant and Vincent G. Jungkunz, ed., "Introduction," *The Importance of the Animal/Human Question for Political Theory* (Albany: SUNY Press, 2016), 4.
10 Peggy McCracken, *In the Skin of the Beast: Sovereignty and Animality in Medieval France* (Chicago, IL: Chicago University Press, 2017), 7.
11 Thomas Hobbes, *Leviathan: Or the Matter, Form, and Power of a Commonwealth Ecclesiastical and Civil* (London, 1651), 87.
12 Hobbes, *Leviathan*, 119.
13 There were stingless bees native to Mesoamerica and Caribbean islands, but the European honeybee was required to pollinate many of the seeds brought to the colonies.
14 Thomas Morton, *New English Cannan: Or New Canaan Containing an Abstract of New England* (n.p., 1632), 14.
15 William Shakespeare, *The Second Part of Henry VI*, ed. Michael Hattaway (Cambridge: Cambridge University Press, 1991), 4.2. 67–8.
16 Levett, *The Ordering of Bees*, sig. A4v.
17 See Erica Fudge, *Perceiving Animals: Humans and Beasts in Early Modern English Culture* (London: Palgrave, 2000) and *Brutal Reasoning: Animals, Rationality, and Humanity in Early Modern England* (Ithaca: Cornell University Press, 2007). See also Bruce Boehrer, *Animal Characters: Nonhuman Beings in Early Modern Literature* (Philadelphia: University of Pennsylvania Press, 2010) and *Shakespeare Among the Animals: Nature and Society in the Drama of Early Modern England* (New York: Palgrave/St. Martin's Press, 2002).
18 Karen Raber, *Animal Bodies, Renaissance Culture* (Philadelphia: University of Pennsylvania Press, 2013), 6.
19 See Laurie Shannon, *The Accommodated Animal: Cosmopolity in Shakespearean Locales* (Chicago, IL: University of Chicago Press, 2013). See also, Laurie Shannon "'Poore wretch, laid all naked upon the bare earth': Human Negative Exceptionalism Among the Humanists," in *Shakespearean International Yearbook 15: Shakespeare and the Human*, ed. Tiffany Werth (Burlington: Ashgate, 2015), 205–10.
20 Eric C. Brown, "Introduction," *Insect Poetics* (Minneapolis: University of Minnesota Press, 2006), x–xi.
21 Qtd. in Joyce Lee Malcolm, ed. *The Struggle for Sovereignty: Seventeenth-Century English Political Tracts*, vol. I (Indianapolis, IN: Liberty Fund, 1999), xxxiv.

22 Joseph Campana, "The Bee and the Sovereign (II): Segments, Swarms, and the Shakespearean Multitude," in *The Return of Theory in Early Modern English Studies*, vol. II, ed. Paul Cefalu, Gary Kuchar, and Bryan Reynolds (New York: Palgrave Macmillan, 2014), 76. See also Joseph Campana, "The Bee and the Sovereign? Political Entomology and the Problems of Scale," *Shakespeare Studies* 41 (2013): 94–113.

23 Frederick R. Prete, "Can Females Rule the Hive? The Controversy over Honey Bee Gender Roles in British Beekeeping Texts of the Sixteenth—Eighteenth Centuries," *Journal of the History of Biology* 24, no. 1 (1991): 118.

24 See Thomas Seeley, *Honeybee Democracy* (Princeton, NJ: Princeton University Press, 2010).

25 Charles Butler, *The Feminine Monarchie, or a Treatise Concerning Bees and the Due Ordering of Them* (Oxford, 1609), 3v.

26 In the Bible, bees arose out of rotting carrion as in the book of Samuel when David discovered a hive in the carcass of the lion he had killed. Virgil similarly speculated that they self-generated while gathering nectar from flowers.

27 Aristotle, *History of Animals*, trans. Richard Cresswell (George Bell: London, 1897), 267.

28 Southerne, *A Treatise*, sig. B4v.

29 Levett (the younger), *The Ordering of Bees*, sig. A2v.

30 Homer, *The Iliad*, trans. Barry B. Powell (New York: Oxford University Press, 2014), 12. 146–7.

31 Cristopher Hollingsworth, *Poetics of the Hive* (Iowa City: University of Iowa Press, 2001), 41.

32 Andre Stipanovic, "Bees and Ants: Perceptions of Imperialism in Vergil's Aeneid and Georgics," in *Insect Poetics*, ed. Eric C. Brown (Minneapolis: University of Minneapolis Press, 2006), 14.

33 Rana Saadi Liebert, "Apian Imagery and the Critique of Poetic Sweetness in Plato's Republic," *Transactions of the American Philological Society* 140, no. 1 (2010): 99.

34 William Moeck, "Bees in My Bonnet: Milton's Epic Simile and Intertextuality," *Milton Quarterly* 32, no. 4 (1998): 122–35.

35 Hollingsworth, *Poetics of the Hive*, 77.

36 Virgil, *Georgics*, 122.

37 Philips van Marnix van Saint Aldegonde, *The Beehive of the Romish Church*, trans. George Gilpin (London, 1579), 349v.

38 See Richard Dimmler, "The Bee-Topos in the Jesuit Emblem Book: Themes and Contrast." *Symbola ed emblemata* 3 (1992): 229–46.

39 Philips van Marnix, *The Beehive*, 3.

40 Prete, "Can Females Rule the Hive?," 134.

41 Philips, *The Beehive*, 20.

42 Bernard of Clairvaux, *Five Books on Consideration: Advice to a Pope*, vol. 13, trans. John D. Anderson and Elizabeth T. Kennan (Kalamazoo, MI: Cistercian Publications, 1976), 64.

43 For a discussion of the prevalence and significance of Bernard's sermons on the Canticles, see Elizabeth Clarke, *Politics, Religion, and the Song of Songs in Seventeenth-Century England* (London: Palgrave Macmillan, 2011). See also Noam Flinker, *The Song of Songs in English Renaissance Literature* (Cambridge: D.S. Brewer, 2000).

44 Qtd. in James Cotter Morison, *The Life and Times of Saint Bernard, Abbot of Clairvaux* (New York: Macmillan, 1863), 202. Early modern pastors and translators regularly referenced Bernard's sermons on the Song of Songs; see *Certaine Sermons of Saint Augustine* (London, 1557), 244–5.

For a discussion of Montaigne's reading of Romans 1:20, see Shannon, *The Accommodated Animal*, 46.

45 Thomas Browne, *A True and Full Copy of that which was Surreptitiously Printed before under the Name of Religio Medici* (London, 1643), 30–1.

46 See Cary Wolfe, *Animal Rites: American Culture, the Discourse of Species, and Posthumanist Theory* (Chicago: University of Chicago Press, 2003).

47 *The Aberdeen Bestiary*, Special Collections, University of Aberdeen, 64r. https://www.abdn.ac.uk/bestiary/.

48 Sir Thomas More, *Utopia*, trans. Clarence H. Miller (New Haven, CT: Yale University Press, 2001), 55.

49 Philip Armstrong, "The Postcolonial Animal," *Society and Animals* 10, no. 4 (2002): 414.

50 Maneesha Deckha, "Toward a Postcolonial, Posthumanist Feminist Theory: Centralizing Race and Culture in Feminist Work on Nonhuman Animals," *Hypatia* 22 (2012): 541.

51 Bruno Latour, *Reassembling the Social: An Introduction to Actor-Network-Theory* (Oxford: Oxford University Press, 2005), 6.

52 Latour, *Reassembling the Social*, 9.

53 Jane Bennett, *Vibrant Matter: A Political Ecology of Things* (Durham, NC: Duke University Press, 2010), 98.

54 Barbara Fuchs, "Imperium Studies: Theorizing Early Modern Expansion," in *Postcolonial Moves: Medieval through Modern*, ed. Patricia Clare Ingham and Michelle R. Warren (London: Palgrave Macmillan, 2003), 74.

55 Jace Weaver, "Indigenousness and Indigeneity," in *A Companion to Postcolonial Studies*, ed. Henry Schwarz and Sangeeta Ray (New York: Wiley, 2000), 233.

56 Eve Tuck and K. Wayne Yang, "Decolonization is Not a Metaphor," *Decolonization: Indigeneity, Education and Society* 1 (2012): 1–40.

57 Billy-Ray Belcourt, "Animal Bodies, Colonial Subjects: (Re)Locating Animality in Decolonial Thought," *Societies* 5 (2015): 3.

58 Nehemiah Grew, *The Anatomy of Plants* (London, 1682), 167.

59 Grew, *The Anatomy of Plants*, ii.

60 Grew, *The Anatomy of Plants*, ii.

61 Wilkins' hive was modeled on one designed by Sir Christopher Wren when he was a fellow at All Soul's College in the 1650s.

62 D. A. Smith, ed., *John Evelyn's Manuscript on Bees from Elysium Britannicum* (Bristol: Bee Research Association, 1966), 11.

63 Smith, *John Evelyn's Manuscript*, 11.

64 John Evelyn, *Elysium Britannicum: or the Royal Gardens*, ed. John E. Ingram (Philadelphia: University of Pennsylvania Press, 2001), 285.

65 See D. J. Bryden, "John Gedde's Bee-House and the Royal Society," *Notes and Records of the Royal Society of London* 48, no. 2 (1994): 193–213.

66 Arthur Dobbs, "A Letter from Arthur Dobbs, Esq. to Charles Stanhope, Esq. Concerning Bees and Their Methods of Gathering Wax and Honey," *Proceedings of the Royal Society of London* (November 8, 1750): 536.

67 Dobbs, "A Letter," 539.

68 Dobbs, "A Letter," 548–9.

69 Dobbs, "A Letter," 549.

70 John Hill Wheeler, *Historical Sketches of North Carolina from 1584 to 1851* (Baltimore: Genealogical Publishing, 1993), 46.

71 Edward Topsell, *Historie of Serpents* (London, 1608), 75–6.

72 Marcelo A. Aizen, Lucas A. Garibaldi, Saul A. Cunningham, and Alexandra M. Klein, "How Much Does Agriculture Depend on Pollinators? Lessons

from Long-Term Trends in Crop Production." *Annals of Botany* 103, no. 9 (2009): 1579.

73 Richard Twine, "Revealing the 'Animal-Industrial Complex'—A Concept and Method for Critical Animals Studies?" *Journal for Critical Animals Studies* 10, no. 1 (2012): 22–3.

74 A range of terms from precarity to precarization (a process that drives precarity), to the precariat (a class of human workers beholden to an insecure position in society and the economy) has been proposed. See Donatella della Porta, Sakari Hänninen, Martti Siisiäinen, and Tiina Silvastri, *The New Social Division: Making and Unmaking Precariousness* (London: Palgrave Macmillan, 2015), 1.

75 Judith Butler, *Frames of War: When is Life Grievable?* (London: Verso, 2009), 19.

76 James Stanescu, "Species Trouble: Judith Butler, Mourning, and the Precarious Lives of Animals," *Hypatia* 27, no. 3 (2012): 575.

77 Raber, *Animal Bodies*, 28.

78 Marcel Paret, "Precarious Labor Politics: Unions and the Struggles of the Insecure Working Class in the United States and South Africa," *Critical Sociology* 41 (2013): 758.

79 Jason W. Moore, *Capitalism in the Web of Life: Ecology and the Accumulation of Capital* (New York: Verso, 2015), 170.

80 Richie Nimmo, "Apiculture in the Anthropocene: Between Posthumanism and Critical Animal Studies," in *Animals in the Anthropocene: Critical Perspectives on Non-Human Futures*, ed. Human Animal Research Network Editorial Collective (Sydney: Sydney University Press, 2015), 193.

81 Nimmo, "Apiculture in the Anthropocene," 193. Carla Hustak and Natasha Myers, "Involutionary Momentum: Affective Ecologies and the Sciences of Plant/Insect Encounters," *differences: A Journal of Feminist Cultural Studies* 23 (2012): 78.

82 John Worlidge, *The Complete Bee-Master* (London, 1698), sig. A3r-v.

83 John Worlidge, *Apiarium: Or a Discourse of Bees* (London, 1676), 21.

1 Bee Time
Shakespeare

Bees keep time. It is not necessarily in the human measures of seconds, hours, and years, but their timekeeping goes far beyond instincts of diurnal activity and nocturnal rest. From the hive's perspective, bee time is both cyclical and generational, a concept that applies across many animal and insect species (including humans). Bees' lives and labor are organized by a concept called temporal polyethism, where an individual worker's labor designations shift with her age, as she graduates from feeding pupae the day she hatches to gathering nectar by one month old. Even the bee's navigation is time-dependent, in that circadian rhythms constantly adjust her orientation of direction relative to the ever-changing position of the sun. Overall, the beehive structures its architecture, its labor, and its consumption and use of energy on the future. Bees are also keenly attuned to the seasons: spring and summer are times of collection and building food stores; fall brings the expulsion of male drones that would drain the hive's resources; all so that in winter, the female workers and queen can make use of the shelter and sustenance their past labor has afforded them. One essential aspect of bee temporality relies upon communication, as the hive consults on time-sensitive issues like when to raise a new queen. Timing is one critical component of what biologist Thomas D. Seeley calls "honeybee democracy."[1] Indeed, modern entomological research tells us that beehives engage in complex negotiations, demonstrating collective intelligence over decisions such as where to swarm. The ultimate goal of this communication is communal survival. And yet, a tension exists between the temporality of the individual worker bee and that of the collective hive.

I would contend that measures of nonhuman time, such as bee time, offer an important consideration in the study of animal and human cultures and how they interact across centuries and circumstances. Some modern critics have denied that insects or animals, more generally, experience time—at least in any way that is recognizable to humans—investing instead in a form of anthropomorphic romanticization of the nonhuman being that lives simply "in the moment." Nietzsche, for one, views livestock as inextricably linked, for better or for worse, to the present, noting that cows "do not know what is meant by yesterday or today ... fettered to the moment and its pleasure or displeasure."[2] He thus generalizes all creatures' relationship to time: "the animal lives un-historically: for it is contained in the present."[3] On the topic of bees, Michael Pollan similarly muses, "presumably insects can look at a blos-som without entertaining thoughts of the past and the future."[4] How-ever, animals' experiences undoubtedly shift across histories, cultures, and technologies of domestication, or policies of eradication. I would suggest that consideration of animal time need not be subsumed by ar-guments about consciousness and its relationship to human timepieces or calendars. Indeed, animal time holds the potential to open up larger considerations of the interdependence between animals and humans, the effects of human displacement of animals (like those shipped to the New World colonies), and animal architecture and aesthetics (where and how they structure their lives). From an early modern perspective, bees and other animals share a complex set of temporalities that factor in not only their labor and suffering, but also their drives, inclinations, and pleasures. Though animal time has broad implications, this chapter will focus specifically on the ways in which Shakespeare's exploration of bee time reveals the toll of exploitation and servitude on living beings. In *The Tempest*, particularly in the figures of Ariel and Caliban, Shake-speare ultimately reflects upon what it means to look to a future beyond service and struggle.

Sixteenth- and seventeenth-century beekeepers observed with admira-tion the hive's seemingly inscrutable and precise communication about timekeeping. They perceived the enigmatic yet crucial interface between the temporality of the individual worker bee and that of her collective swarm. For instance, Edward Topsell's *Historie of Serpents* (1608) takes from Aristotle the notion that an individual bee is responsible for hive waking and sleeping schedules:

> When night approacheth, the signe and token being given by his Honny-pipe, or Cornet, (if you will so call it) a generall proclama-tion is made through the whole Hive, that every one shall betake himselfe to rest, so the watch beeing appointed, and all things set in order, they all make themselves ready and go to bed.[5]

Topsell's observation of the striking nature of the timed "signe and to-ken" is also echoed in John Milton's famous bee simile in Book I of *Paradise Lost*. Milton's epic, which I discuss in Chapter 4, describes the inhabitants of Pandemonium "[a]s Bees / In spring time, when the Sun with Taurus rides" and notes the amazement of the demon hive's simultaneous transformation: "Till the signal given, / Behold a wonder!"[6] This signal is responsible for synchronizing the sudden shrinking of Satan's minions to minute size in preparation for "the great consult."[7] Milton's use of the signal is indicative of the knowledge that the bee communicates orders to the hive instantaneously. Yet the passive construction of "the signal given" begs the question: who gave the signal? And how did the rest of the hive receive it? Another notable timekeeping bee appears in Andrew Marvell's "The Garden," where God as "the skillful gard'ner" guides nature through both hourly and monthly time: "And, as it works, th' industrious bee / Computes its time as well as we."[8] Although we now understand a great deal more about the role of pheromones, dance, vibration, touch, and smell, the early moderns could neither conceptualize nor replicate this means of instant communication and compliance among their own human laborers.

The hive is an excellent subject for exploring connections in the early modern period between time, labor, and the animal. Karen Raber has observed that critics "do not credit animals ... with generating a consciously weighted cultural act. They find instead in animal labor a 'natural' sculpting of bodily material that sidesteps issues of a stratified and exploitative labor system."[9] Current research accepts that honeybees are eusocial, or live in a complex social structure, with discrete individuals forgoing personal reproduction and instead performing the various functions and tasks of a larger superorganism.[10] Moreover, within this framework, the individual bee is capable of displaying emotional responses, such as pessimism.[11] However, in the early modern period, understandings of bee culture ultimately served human metaphors and perceptions of apian work and socialization. Indeed, beekeepers justified their reliance on essential bee labor by interpreting human expectations of yield as less exacting than the hive's own. In particular, they highlighted a conviction that among bees any individual drive is necessarily subsumed by that of the collective. Charles Butler, for instance, speaks to the work ethic of elder bees in *The Feminine Monarchie* (1609): "they wil[l] never give over, while their wings can bear them: & then when they cease to worke, they will cease also to eate: such enemies are they to idleness[s]."[12] According to this logic, to the worker bee, her past labor is irrelevant to present service. What is so exemplary to Butler—the lesson to be gleaned for human consumption—is the bee's sacrifice. Although a worker bee born in spring will not survive until the winter, she nevertheless prepares for a future in which she will never share.

The natural and moral positionality of the bee also offers a unique contribution to our understanding of what animal studies critics have termed human exceptionalism or negative human exceptionalism, where the human constitutes a distinct category among living beings, for better or for worse.[13] The challenge to this paradigm posed by the status of the bee stems from the fact that it is regarded as at once superior and inferior to the human. In metaphorical terms, the beehive was promoted as an exemplum for human society: All members of a kingdom should be as obedient, self-sacrificing, and industrious as the bee. And yet in actuality, the hive was placed in service of human husbandry and economy, as its honey and wax were viewed as commodities for the benefit of humankind. These competing ideas of the hive speak to the larger representations of nonhuman life in the period. For instance, Ayesha Ramachandran and Melissa E. Sanchez have demonstrated the ways in which the human as a category stands as "productively ambiguous and malleable," considering that "animals ... ghosts, angels, subjects of conquest and colonization, and corporations could be both distinguished from and assimilated into the category of the human for polemical, economic, or experimental purposes."[14] Nonetheless, even within this framework of creaturely ambiguity, it is difficult to escape the specter of human dominance within animal studies. Indeed, as Joseph Campana has importantly argued, "to focus on capacity and capabilities" in nonhuman animals "even when invoking shared capacities, shared environments, or shared corporealities—may not be to dislodge the human from a position of centrality and privilege."[15] In Shakespeare's apian metaphor, the dominant status of the human is inescapable, as his worker bee also reflects the struggles of the individual laborer in society.[16] As Richard Grinnell observes, Shakespeare's works frequently invoke bee imagery as "political placeholders for humans themselves."[17] In *The Tempest*, Shakespeare reveals a conflict between, on the one hand, human valorization of the hive's work ethic, and on the other, the worker's desire to follow her own inclinations.

In what follows, I will first trace the beeline forged through theorizations of the animal from Saint Bernard of Clairvaux to Protestant cleric Edward Topsell to contemporary ecocritics in order to examine the competing scales of servitude and authority in Shakespeare's work. Second, I will examine the ways in which those designated by the Europeans of the play as creatures—especially Ariel, Caliban, and the bee—claim solidarity with suffering human laborers. In doing so, I explore the acoustics and musicality of Ariel's song, "Where the Bee Sucks," which has been ascribed to Blackfriars' composer Robert Johnson especially for Shakespeare's *The Tempest*. Third, I will discuss Miranda's unique perspective on labor, which operates outside of typical European understandings of time and the individual. What is at stake in Shakespeare's interventions into popular conceptions of the hive is the matter of whether the worker's value is instrumental—contingent upon one's usefulness to the human social structure—or intrinsic—based on one's own merit within nature. In this chapter, I argue that Shakespeare, in concert with Johnson's song, explores the boundaries between time and labor in the human and the animal in order to question what is lost and who gains when the collective is compelled to spend its time in the service of the few.

Bernardian Ecology and Animal Salvation

Shifts in the human metaphor of the hive in response to emergent political and theological debates speak to larger understandings of what it means to live in a hierarchical society. Traditionally, popes and monarchs deployed the apian metaphor to enforce subservience among the disempowered masses. Following the Reformation, however, Protestants and resistance theorists sought to dismantle the notion of the Catholic and monarchical hive—a top-down hierarchy, where power and influence flow from one centralized source. As animal studies scholar Paul Waldau indicates, "the dominant views of nonhuman animals changed again and again—ancient views were supplanted in Western Europe during the medieval period by heavily symbolic approaches, which in turn gave way to modern views that were much more representational."[18] In the case of bees, in particular, ongoing questions about the use and value of God's creatures set the conditions for their exceptional and yet shifting status among humans, animals, and insects. In this instance, changes in the perception of the hive are part of a conscious divergence from the Catholic faith and the reverence for bees in Catholic writing and iconography that stretched back over four centuries.

A honeybee cannot survive independently without a hive, and the Catholic Church encouraged the faithful to adopt an apian posture of communal responsibility. Evidence of this agenda can be found in medieval texts like the *Aberdeen Bestiary* of the twelfth century, which describes bees as an industrious society of workers that shared in the task of promoting the common good without inflicting harm on others:

> see how the bees all compete with each other in carrying out their duties: some keeping watch over those who are seeking food; some keeping a careful guard on the fort, that is the hive; ... you can see too, however, that no bees lie in wait for other creatures, to take advantage of their toil; and none take a life by force.[19]

Also in the twelfth century, St. Anthony of Padua takes the comparison between bees and parishioners even further by saying, "the small bees are penitents, who are little in their own eyes, and are always employed about some work, lest the devil should come and find their house empty and idle."[20]

The most influential and resounding connection between Catholicism and bees is forged in the writings and iconography of Saint Bernard. This twelfth-century French Cistercian abbot is still popularly depicted with a beehive since he was known as the "mellifluous doctor." In his writings, Bernard frequently used references to bees and honey as symbols of consolation and God's grace. For instance, in a translation of his work by Cambridge fellow W.P., *His Meditations, or Sighes, Sobbes, and Tears Upon Our Saviors Passion* (1611), Bernard speaks to Christ's death and passion with a honey comparison: "Oh let the Meditation" on *consummatum est* "be more sweet unto mee, then the honie which Sampson found in the carkasse of the Lyon," referring to the moment in Judges when Samson discovers the heaven-sent honey that stands as a symbol of God's approbation of his mission to undercut the Philistines' rule over Israel.[21]

To Bernard, honey is also a potent symbol of Christianity and Christ himself. In *The Sentences*, he demonstrates the significance of honey to the resurrected Christ: "Honey still in the wax ... represents charity in one's observances of the New Testament. Lest anyone think that these should be ignored, after his resurrection Christ is said to have eaten honey with wax, that is the honeycomb."[22] Christians should read Christ's consumption of the honey and its comb as a metaphor for pursuing a more charitable life, not in surface-level deeds, but rather through a desire issued from the conscience:

> Honey is separated from the wax in order to bring it to the peak of its strength and sweetness. So too charity is set apart from the observances of the law in the precious and pure vessel of the conscience, in order to be offered to the Lord to taste. Freed from the rote observances as the honey is from the wax, charity naturally develops into a more precious thing of spiritual brilliance. It becomes the candle which, when placed on the lampstand which is Christ, shines equally on all who are in the house of God.[23]

The honey and wax of bees here are not merely the stuff of physical or spiritual sustenance. Rather, they represent one of the foundations of faith itself: conscience. Bernard also compares the soldiers who crucified Christ to a swarm of bees, and the wax reminds him of his own sinful nature: "let some spectacle of their barbarous crueltie bee presented unto mee, that mine eyes may waxe dimmeth with weeping, ... for my guiltie conscience doth tell mee that my sinnes were as fewell, to kindle their rage."[24]

Bernard's frequent use of the apian metaphor aligns with his reverence for the natural world and nonhuman beings. He was quoted as having said to a pupil,

> You will find something far greater in the woods than you will in books. Stones and trees will teach you that which you will never learn from masters. Think you not you can suck honey from the rock? ... Do not the mountains drop sweetness? the hills run with milk and honey, and the valleys stand thick with corn?[25]

Beyond this view of the value of nature's instructional bounty, Bernard also believes that animals possess a similarly intrinsic worth. Indeed, he addresses critiques that some animals are dangerous or seemingly do not have a use to human society by making a contention about their divine significance:

> Although they be hurtful, although they be pernicious to human safety in this world, still [animals'] bodies do not lack that which

worketh together for good to those who, according to the purpose are called saints. For although they be not killed for food, nor apt to render service, yet verily they exercise the wit, agreeably to that benefit of the common discipline which presides over all methods of putting things in use, by which "the invisible things of God are clearly seen, being understood by the things that are made."[26]

This passage provides one illustrative example of Bernardian ecology, an assertion of the inherent and God-given worth of all creatures regardless of whether or not they display an immediate utility to humankind. To Bernard, the faithful are compelled to show an appreciation for the "invisible" divine intentions that created life and nature in the first place. Implicitly, the unknowable intentionality of God's design also serves a future-oriented agenda: To preserve God's plan on earth, whatever that may be, humankind must protect the divine creation in the present. Bernardian ecology provides a foundational idea that, with some revision, would centuries later be promoted by ecocritics.[27]

Bernardian ecology has continued to maintain greater currency than has been acknowledged, particularly in its opposition to the notion of instrumentalism that has dominated so much of humanist discourse. Even in the modern world, Pope Francis's encyclical, *On Care for Our Common Home* (2015), is framed by Bernard's ecological perspective, as it laments the mass extinction of nonhuman life on earth due to human activity: "Because of us, thousands of species will no longer give glory to God by their very existence, nor convey their message to us. We have no such right."[28] Looking back to the early modern period, Robert N. Watson's analysis of the impact of the Reformation on views of the natural world suggests that such values arise largely from a distinction between the Catholic focus on the sensual experience of the body versus the Protestant emphasis on the word of Christ.[29] Despite some of the doctrinal differences in views on the environment, evidence in early modern religious discourse also reveals Bernard's role in larger understandings of creaturely life. Martin Luther himself referenced Bernard's work over 500 times in his own writing.[30] In England, John Panke claimed that Bernard was an ahead-of-his-time Protestant while Antonie Batt, a Benedictine monk living in exile, insisted on reclaiming the saint for Catholicism.[31] More than merely a debate over religion, however, Bernard's legacy confronted the notion of creaturely worth. Although Bernard did not grant that animals had rational souls, he did assert that they had lives and bodies worthy of pursuing pleasures and taking rest. Just as significant, he also believed that it was a matter of conscience for humans to protect God's creatures. Bernardian ecology runs counter to the view of the ruling class, in which the worker bee offers the ideal metaphor for the toiling masses because she rejects the laziness of the male drone and spends all of her waking hours at her occupation.[32]

In *The Tempest*, however, Ariel's song, "Where the Bee Sucks," imagines a different life for the laboring bee, one in which she laments her current servitude and longs for future freedom. Ariel, as a flying being (albeit a magical rather than an organic one), addresses the question of intrinsic worth from the perspective of the unceasing laborer herself. The song frees the insect from her use-value to humans by considering a potential space and time for her leisure. More significantly, as I will demonstrate, Shakespeare's depiction of nonhuman beings in the play also reflects upon the concept of futurity, or the anticipation of the future and the notion of an existence after mortal struggle.

The context of "Where the Bee Sucks," which has received considerably less scholarly attention than Johnson's other song for *The Tempest*, "Full Fathoms Five," can best be understood alongside the seventeenth-century discourses of ecology and value. One of the greatest adherents of Bernardian ecology in the time of Shakespeare also happens to be one of the most influential writers for scholars of early modern animal studies. Topsell is most often cited for his *Historie of Four-Footed Beasts* and *Historie of Serpents*, and yet, as Erica Fudge notes, even in these works, Topsell sought to "draw out the animal's multiple meanings" to make "the work of God ... more visible and thus more meaningful."[33] In his own time, he was most well known as a respected Protestant cleric who also published his own and others' sermons and meditations. Most notably, his *Times Lamentation: Or an Exposition on the Prophet Joel* (1599) frequently references Bernard, even containing an epigraph from *The Sentences* on the title page. The guiding principle of Topsell's meditation is that "Time is the measure of all things" because it quantifies the period before the individual reaches heaven and collective humanity faces its final judgment.[34] Unsurprisingly given his larger body of work, Topsell's reflections on scripture invoke the role of the animal, particularly the insect. He warns against neglecting the smallest and least powerful members of a society, speaking of the biblical famines wrought by palmer worms, grasshoppers, and tiny insects:

> small creatures com[e] with great force to invade this countrey ... [so] that a flocke of little wormes should overthrow a whole nation: and these beasts should come successively the one after the other, that whosoever escape the first, should be taken by the last.[35]

Topsell also notes that the suffering of animals is caused by human iniquity because creatures are incapable of the "faultie or sinfull" behavior that would incur God's wrath:

> the beastes are punished for mans cause which is the doctrine of this verse ... even for our sakes are they pined, and fatted, beaten and bru[i]sed, because of the sinnes which we have committed: All the

men in the world could not beare their own plague; but the innocent and harmlesse beastes must helpe out with the matter.[36]

His sympathetic portrayal of animals' suffering demonstrates their intrinsic worth even as their utility to humans makes them subject to anguish. In Topsell's religious prose, creatures serve as a reminder of the injustice wrought by humans' sin and greed, particularly that of the wealthiest and most powerful.

Indeed, it is unmerited creaturely suffering at the mercy of human-kind that drives Topsell, in collaboration with fellow preacher Henry Holland, to extend the bounds of Bernardian ecology in his model of conservationism. In *The Historie of Adam, or the Foure-fold State of Man* (1606), Topsell revises and edits the rough papers of the late Holland as a tribute to his friend. In the prefatory matter, Topsell indicates that the papers were so disorganized and difficult to interpret that it required serious prayer to God to "contrive it and bring it into such fashion as might be plaine and intelligible to the English Reader."[37] In the text, Topsell and Holland provide a glimpse of the world after the final judgment:

> Wherefore those words being understood of the Elect after the res-urrection, like as is afterward, the new city, her foure gates, her pavement with the twelve precious stones, her water, her fruites, her trees, her leaves, her garments all allegoricall. I conclude, that the first division which God made of waters shall stand, both above and beneath the firmament, and that the sea shall not worke nor bee tossed with windes, nor destroy any of the creatures renewed upon the face of the earth, but unto the Saints, they shall no more looke upon sea or land.[38]

In other words, at the end of days, the entirety of redeemed humanity will retreat to heaven (and the damned to hell) while the animals remain free to roam the earth without the interference of humanity or the at-tendant suffering they faced for the sins of mankind. In this passage, Topsell and Holland imagine redemption—a heaven on earth—for ani-mals that need no longer serve humans with their labor. During a period when many sought to justify humans' superiority over animals either through biblical justification or Cartesian logic, Topsell, throughout his sermons, landed firmly on the side of the suffering creature.

Although Topsell outdoes Bernard in his view of the intrinsic worth and future peace of animals, he also simultaneously promotes a util-itarian perspective on creatures in their capacity to promote human reform. For Topsell, creatures in the present provide a future-oriented labor model that can act as a guide for human action. Accordingly, these nonhuman beings must continue to serve their function until human redemption eventually leads to freedom for all beings. In fact, in *The Historie of Serpents*, Topsell insists that God crafted the beehive as an exemplum for human culture:

> Whereas the Almightie hath created all things for the use and service of man, so especialy among the rest hath he made the Bees, not onely that they should be unto us patternes and presidents of politicall and oeconomicall vertues ... but even Teacher and Schoolmaisters instructing us in certaine divine knowledge, and like extraordinary prophets, promonstrating the successe & events of things to come.[39]

What is unique about Topsell's perspective is the notion that the example of the beehive, if heeded, could herald the salvation of humanity. More significantly, Topsell in *The Reward of Religion Delivered in Sundrie Lectures Upon the Booke of Ruth* (1596) links the bee to God's elect, "the poore Saintes of God," who "are the bees for whose sake you enjoy the hony for your delight, and the hony combe for the pleasure of your meat."[40] He continues by emphasizing how interconnected human beings are, so that the wealthiest and most powerful people all rely upon the virtue of the faithful:

> there is not a usurer, but he hath his money for their sake; there is not a Gentleman, but hee hath his lands for their sake; there is not a Prince but hee hath his Crowne for their sake ... there shoulde bee no peace, prosperitie or plenty, if it were not for them, for the Angelles are their servants, the earth is their mayntenaunce, and heaven is their inheritance.[41]

To Topsell, the faithful, then, are God's worker bees, promoting the common good without inflicting harm on others. By the logic in Topsell's larger ecological theology, when the human faithful reap their heavenly inheritance, the bees will remain on earth to live without the interference of humans who killed them to take their honey and comb. Though the prophetic hive of the faithful suffers mortal trials, they do so in order to earn their promised spiritual deliverance, a reward by which other nonhuman creatures will also benefit.

Apian Music, Time, and Labor

As in Topsell's meditations, futurity is the organizing principle of Ariel's song in *The Tempest*. In it, Ariel also demonstrates that the concept of salvation is not exclusive to human beings. Scholars have noted the centrality of this play to Shakespeare's boundaries between the human and the animal, and yet these insights could also benefit by considering the role of temporality in relation to the nonhuman in the play. Tiffany Jo

Werth, for instance, points to Prospero's unique position as "sometimes more than, sometimes less than, human. He slips into, out of, below, and above a human register."[42] Steven Mentz makes a case for Ariel as the instrument for restoring human order in the play, noting, "Ariel captures an alien ambivalence at the heart of the human relationship to our nonhuman environment."[43] A crucial distinction between Prospero as master and Ariel as servant lies in Prospero's status as a mortal and thus temporally bound being. When Ariel tells Prospero of Lord Gonzalo's tears and the repentance of Alonso, Antonio, and Sebastian, Prospero asks if his affections belie some tenderness toward their suffering. The magical sprite responds, "Mine would, sir, were I human," (5.1.19) causing Prospero to chastise himself for not feeling mercy toward "one of [his] kind" (5.1.23).[44] Ariel steps in as the reminder of Prospero's conscience and his responsibility to those under his care. Like Topsell's bee, however, as Ariel leads the path to human redemption, he continues to suffer his master's threats and commands.

Ariel's song, which he sings to Prospero while helping to dress him in preparation for his final revelation of truth, showcases the simultaneous disappointment and hope of the nonhuman laborer awaiting a future reward. Directly following one of Prospero's frequent promises to free Ariel (one of seven such assurances), the winged being reflects upon the location and function of the single worker bee:

> Where the bee sucks, there suck I,
> In a cowslip's bell I lie;
> There I couch, when owls do cry.
> On the bat's back I do fly
> After summer merrily.
> Merrily, merrily, shall I live now,
> Under the blossom that hangs on the bough.
>
> (5.1.88–94)

Ariel likens himself in his work for Prospero to the laboring bee collecting nectar. Like the bee, Ariel goes about his work in a way that preserves the integrity of nature, not harming the flower upon which he "couch[es]." Cowslip (*Primula veris*) blooms in spring, a busy time for bees, and yet the song anticipates future rest, "after summer merrily. / Merrily, merrily, shall I live," a time after his service has ended. Ariel toys with the notion of a defiance of duty; if he hides "under the blossom" at night "when owls do cry," he is neither where he is supposed to be, nor engaging in any work. In Ariel's imagination, he steals time away from his expected duties to Prospero by catching a surreptitious ride on the back of a bat. Ariel eagerly awaits his imagined life after instrumentality; one in which he has the time to pursue his own pleasures. It is not just the lyrics, however, that drive the relevance of Ariel's song.

As Michael Neill notes of the audience of *The Tempest*, the play "reasserts the primacy of their ears."[45]

Unlike *The Tempest* itself, which observes the unities of time and space, Ariel's song offers a clash of temporalities in both its lyrics and its musicality. In addition to the lyrics, which transition within four lines from spring to autumn, the music also shifts as the season changes.[46] According to Jennifer Linhart Wood, starting with "after summer merrily," there is "an audible metrical shift between duple and triple time," hastening the meter of these last lines of the song.[47] Jacquelyn Fox-Good suggests that the musicality of the song reflects the desire for liberty demonstrated in its lyrics. Discussing the second part of the song, she notes, "Johnson now takes the harmony more swiftly from one key to the next, beginning again in G, modulating to D, briefly suggesting D minor, then returning to G. These successive and now more rapid movements between tonic and dominant" create a "sensation—of energies breaking out—[which] helps realize Ariel's longing for release."[48]

The sonic resonance of "Where the Bee Sucks" also represents the best knowledge seventeenth-century beekeepers had about bees' songs in nature. For instance, Butler describes the sounds made by the hive prior to a swarm, particularly in spring. As a virgin queen (which Butler calls a princess) emerges, she "beginneth the musick in a begging tune, as if she did pray her queen-mother to let them go."[49] As the swarming preparations intensify, the princess and departing bees "sing both in triple time," so that the sounds of the collective hive "agree in a perfect third," just as the last half of Ariel's bee song.[50] Although the bees swarm to another hive in order to fulfill another generation's obligation to communal labor, they also, in the process, free themselves of their original hive and its maintenance, offering new possibilities for the shape of their labor in their collectively chosen new home.

The potential collaborative efforts in the composition of "Where the Bee Sucks" also serve to highlight the focus on the status of the worker. The song's lyrics were initially recorded in the First Folio, but its sheet music first appeared in Bodleian MS Don.c.57 (1625–50), which incorrectly designated Dr. John Wilson, who was a child when *The Tempest* was written and performed, as the composer.[51] However, in Wilson's own *Cheerfull Ayres* (1660), he attributes the music to Robert Johnson, who was by the account of Ross W. Duffin, an indentured servant to the Lord Chamberlain George Carey.[52] Like his father before him, George Carey, Baron Hunsdon, was patron to the Lord Chamberlain's men. Johnson continued to live in Blackfriars after Carey's death in 1603. According to John P. Cutts, Johnson was from 1607 to 1617 "writing incidental music continuously for the Blackfriars productions of the King's Men Company of Players, and for this company only," including pieces for the plays of Shakespeare, Middleton, Beaumont and Fletcher, Webster, and Jonson.[53] Indeed, Johnson had composed several songs for Shakespeare's late plays, including music for *Cymbeline* and *The Winter's Tale*, and possibly for a revised production of *Macbeth*.[54] In addition to the musical arrangement, the lyrics of "Where the Bee Sucks" are very much consistent with Ariel's other songs and speeches about servitude and freedom throughout the play, lending credence to the possibility of collaborative effort in integrating the play script and songs for performance at Blackfriars and at court.

Ariel's song reveals important distinctions between the worker bee on a human-dominated earth and the magical being on an island controlled by Prospero. In reality, the worker bee returns to the hive to sleep under the watch of the sentinel bee. Ariel, by contrast, forgoes his nightly shelter in order to practice for his future, a time when he might be free of Prospero's demands. Ariel embraces an apian model of efficiency. On his next errand, he far exceeds Prospero's orders by restoring the ship to working order while performing the designated minor task of fetching the boatswain. Prospero applauds Ariel's ingenuity and forward thinking, "my tricksy spirit!" (5.1.226). Nevertheless, Ariel anticipates Prospero's future needs and accomplishes the tasks ahead of schedule in order to hasten his own liberation. Ariel's immortality would offer him a unique relationship to time. Prospero's human life is finite, and thus Ariel's obligations would die with him. Yet Ariel endures his present labor by looking forward to the pleasures of following his own inclinations, of living on his island home after the humans who hold him in durance have left. Ariel's circumstances as a magical being freed from service to humanity, in other words, bear striking similarities to Topsell and Holland's conception of the animal-occupied world after the Last Judgment.

The time and labor of human and nonhuman beings help to frame their mutual suffering as well as their relationship to futurity. Topsell, for instance, connects the subordination of animals with that of human servants. He again refers to Bernard in criticizing those who compel service on the Sabbath:

> As if there were none that had any soule but those that are called the rulers of families. We may say of them as *Bernard* saide of the church committed to careles[s] clergie men, ... O miserable soules lead by such bridegromes which keepe them for to serve the lustes of their owne bellies, ... [imploring masters to] search ... in the harts of your servants, that you may bring soules into the kingdom of heaven.[55]

In emphasizing the responsibility of the patriarch to attend to the souls of his inferiors, Topsell also provides a means of justification for servitude. When applied to the paradigm of apian labor, those in power squeeze greater productivity out of their workers with the promise of the immortality of the soul. As Marx puts it when he criticizes how the Christian reward of heaven incentivizes relentless service,

> Do you not claim your reasonable right in this world, do you not complain at the smallest increase in taxes, are you not beside yourself at the slightest infringement of your personal liberty? But you have been told that present suffering is nothing compared with future glory, that suffering in patience and bliss in hope are the cardinal virtues.[56]

When Ariel steals away leisure time, it is an act of resistance against the expectations of the patriarch. Yet leisure time is not a practice that would be encouraged for human laborers. With the exception of festival, rest and recreation were largely considered luxuries reserved for the elite.[57] Prospero calls the sprite's song of transgression "dainty," presumably because the stolen time is at night when the master does not demand productivity from his worker. Ariel's magical exceptionalism signals his privileged status in the economy of beings. When Prospero finally frees Ariel in his last words before the epilogue—"Be free and fare thou well!"—he offers a way out that neither the bee nor those precarious non-magical beings (Caliban, the boatswain, Stephano, or Trinculo) would be granted (5.1.319).

The valorization of the ever-working bee as an example for human workers may serve the interests of the elite, but, from a modern perspective, it is based upon an incomplete understanding of the individual worker bee and her relationship to labor. Current entomological research involving color-coded and labeled bees in observation hives indicates that under ordinary hive conditions, it is a mischaracterization to suggest that the worker engages in relentless labor. According to entomologist Mark L. Winston, author of *Bee Time*, each worker spends up to two-thirds of her life "doing nothing," leading him to quip, "based on how they spend their time, 'resters' rather than 'workers' would be more accurate nomenclature for worker bees."[58] Researchers' theorization of bees' rest state is largely evolutionary. There are several circumstances, including predators, weather, or beekeeping practice, in which the hive may lose a significant portion of its workforce at once. In these instances, the remaining bees accelerate along their progression of temporal polyethism—guarding or foraging earlier than they otherwise would have done in order to make up for the hive's losses. In doing so, these prematurely aged bees, who are responsible for the survival of the collective, significantly reduce their own lifespans. Without individuals taking rest under optimal conditions, the hive would never survive the onslaught of any number of crises it could face. Early modern beekeepers and political theorists who promoted the apian model of industry in human society had no knowledge of the individual workers' need for rest, and thus only focused on the collective productivity of the beehive. From the seventeenth-century perspective, if a bee could work relentlessly, then a human, particularly a low-status human, should also do the same.

What if there is no future reward, but only the option—like that of the bee—to work until death? When Caliban curses Prospero and Miranda, Prospero threatens him with apian pain: "thou shalt be pinched / As thick as honeycomb, each pinch more stinging / Than bees that made 'em" (1.2.329–31). One act later, Caliban is still contemplating this threat, reflecting on the ways that Prospero's magical spirits are beholden to his will, "they'll nor pinch me ... unless he bid 'em" (2.2.4–7). One of the common uses of the term "pinch" during this period, according to the *Oxford English Dictionary* (and also recognized in Topsell's *History of Foure-Footed Beasts*), had not to do with catching flesh between fingers, but rather "to torment, torture; to inflict bodily pain." Despite the pain these spirits induce in Caliban, he recognizes some kinship with them, including Ariel, telling Stephano, "They all do hate [Prospero] as rootedly as I" (3.2.94–5). Unlike these spirits, however, Caliban has no true hope of leisure, and thus no distinct promise of futurity. He often reverts instead to memories about the island before Prospero's arrival: "This island's mine ... which thou tak'st from me" (1.2.332–3). His role in the play provides an interesting case in relation to the boundary between the human and the nonhuman. As Werth suggests, Caliban's status defies stable categorization: "Prospero's language grudgingly acknowledges ... Caliban to be of 'human shape.' Yet his word choice retracts that human honor even as it concedes it: calling Caliban a 'whelp' from a 'litter' animalizes him."[59] Raber also notes that Caliban, as "afish-human hybrid ... discovers that the promise of full enlistment in humanity was a fraud in part because 'humanity' requires others like himself against which it can be defined."[60] Prospero, like the master in Topsell's sermon, seemingly fails to acknowledge Caliban as one possessing a soul worthy of redemption.

Undoubtedly, Caliban's ambiguous racial identity would, for the early modern audience, complicate its understanding of his soul and relationship to futurity. As Kim F. Hall has argued of the varied perspectives on his race, "Caliban has been read alternatively as African, Afro-Caribbean, and Native American; however, in all these permutations, he embodies and resists ideologies of dark and light even as he is continually read as dark other."[61] Caliban's mother Sycorax, a "blue-eyed hag," was left on the island after being exiled from Algiers (1.2.269). Caliban's descent from an Algerian witch, marks him not merely as a colonized islander, but also as one who, by English accounts, may have been cursed through his maternal line. Several sources in the period, based on a fabricated lineage from Genesis, traced Africans as the descendants of Ham. As David Mark Whitford argues, this false genealogy "became one of the most persistent ideological and theological defenses for African slavery and segregation" in the early modern period.[62] Indeed, Prospero's account of Caliban's paternity is no less threatening, as he says that he is "got by the devil himself / upon thy wicked dam" (1.2.320–1). Prospero and Miranda teach Caliban language for ease of communicating their commands, and yet there is no reference in the play to converting him to Christianity. In addition to the African/demon roots that mark Caliban in the text as racial and religious other, the ambiguity about the island of his birth and its potential American, Caribbean, Irish, and/or Mediterranean contexts all demonstrate the ways in which England is, as Barbara Fuchs has put it, "closely bound up, temporally, materially, and rhetorically, with its burgeoning experience of empire building."[63] Moreover, this colonial enterprise is driven by the dual impulses of genocide and enslavement. As I will demonstrate in Chapter 2, even in one location, such as New England, the English held several conflicting theories about the humanity, soul, and race of the colonized. What is clear in *The Tempest* is that if Prospero fully accepted Caliban's humanity, regardless of his spiritual status, it would be more difficult to ignore his prior claim to the island. As Hulme comments on Prospero and Miranda's reliance on their slave: "Prospero has taken control of Caliban, … [but] Caliban is indispensable to Prospero, the usurper depends upon the usurped."[64] Caliban, as the once-sovereign islander turned tortured slave, embodies the doctrine of instrumentality without the potential release of salvation in the corporeal or celestial realms.

Caliban is undoubtedly treated as an inferior by Prospero, Miranda, Stephano, and Trinculo, and yet there is some evidence to suggest that Ariel may recognize Caliban's perpetual suffering. Caliban is soothed by the sounds of the island—the only home he has ever known—but some of this auditory intake has also been shaped and crafted by Ariel. Scholarly commentary on Caliban's speech about the island's noises has been varied. Terry Comito focuses not on Caliban's feelings and perception of the music of the island but rather on our own: "In our role as audience, we are encouraged to share Caliban's sense that the island is full of stirring possibilities."[65] And yet the possibilities that many critics have derived seem to speak to Caliban's inferiority. Catherine M. Dunn's Civil Rights-era essay on music in *The Tempest* frames Caliban's speech through her perception of his primitivism, "it is perfectly natural for even a 'brutish monster' like Caliban to feel the music's force," even if she does not grant him the capacity for understanding the music's true engagement with "the Neoplatonic doctrine of the divine order of the universe."[66] Tom MacFaul suggests that Caliban's speech reflects his innocence and plays upon the oft-invoked early modern trope that sites of colonial conquest were viewed as prelapsarian: "His ability to *hear* is crucial, and may suggest an unfallen aspect of his character, for it was thought that the ability to hear the music of the spheres was something lost in the Fall of man."[67] Alternatively, Rebecca Laroche and Jennifer Munroe's ecofeminist approach considers Caliban's own perceptions and feelings:

> the postcolonial identification with Caliban is not simply about the subjected character, but also about his intimacy with the world around him: his lack of fear in hearing the "sounds, and sweet airs, that give delight and hurt not" of the island as well as his deep sense of loss felt in waking to a world of enslavement.[68]

In other words, the consolation Caliban derives from the sounds of the island and the dream of reward helps him to cope with his waking hours of labor and torture.

And yet, the text does not conclusively determine that the music Caliban hears is, in fact, only to be interpreted as *musica mundana*. Could he also hear a combination of the comforting sounds of home as well as music orchestrated by spirit magic? Caliban reassures Stephano and Trinculo:

> Be not afeard. The isle is full of noises,
> Sounds and sweet airs that give delight and hurt not.
> Sometimes a thousand twangling instruments
> Will hum about my ears; and sometimes voices,
> That if I then had waked after long sleep,
> Will make me sleep again, and then in dreaming,
> The clouds, methought, would open, and show riches
> Ready to drop upon me, that when I waked
> I cried to dream again.
>
> (3.2.135–43)

We know that Ariel is capable of inducing sleep in those on the island at Prospero's request. As Garrett Sullivan has observed, this magical influence on sleep reflects not only the boundaries of the Aristotelian tripartite soul, but also encompasses larger concerns about genre: "the charmed sleeps induced by Prospero and Ariel are integral to the unfolding of *The Tempest*'s romance conclusion."[69] I would add that Ariel demonstrates a precise mastery of whom he puts to sleep, in what state of rest, and how he releases them from their enchanted slumber, as, for instance, he puts Alonso and Gonzalo to sleep while leaving Antonio and Sebastian awake to observe their private intentions against the king. When in Act 1 Prospero wants to speak privately to Ariel, he offers soporific directions to Miranda: "Thou art inclined to sleep; 'tis a good dullness, / And give it way: I know thou canst not choose" (1.2185–6). In other words, Prospero wants his daughter to experience a peaceful sleep while he strategizes with Ariel, suggesting his awareness that magic may not merely induce sleep, but also affect its quality. Caliban relishes in his dream state because it offers him imagined riches that could help him to escape his servitude. The only other "sweet airs" on the island are songs performed by Ariel and his spirits. Whereas Ariel, as a relatively privileged servant, is able to envision a time to avoid sleep in order to feel the freedom of catching a ride on a bat, Caliban has never been given hope of future liberation. Before the tempest, Caliban can only imagine riches and leisure in his blissful dream state.

In Act 2, Caliban sings his own composition, the "'Ban, 'ban, Ca-caliban" song, in order to distract from the burden of his labor. To Bruce Smith, this song is central to the soundscape of the play: "Within the broad acoustic horizons of *The Tempest*, between noise and music, Caliban stands dead center."[70] Smith further notes that the song's "rhythmic irregularities are extreme," suggesting at once an anti-masque, an inverted ballad, and "a distinctively African sense of rhythm."[71] Caliban's song may defy the European expectations of an air, and yet, its function is consistent with Ariel's song, in that it offers solace to the laboring being. In comparing Ariel's "Where the Bee Sucks" with Caliban's song, Fox-Good argues, "Ariel's freedom song recalls Caliban's but has moved beyond protest for freedom to what such protest has led to: an unsubjugated living within one's native place ... and native sounds."[72] That being said, the distinct difference in status between Ariel and Caliban also helps to account for the divergence in their approaches to songs of freedom. Caliban, with no hope of immediate liberty, opens his song with a lament, "a plague upon the tyrant that I serve" (2.2.159). Caliban imagines a life not dictated by fetching fish and firewood for Prospero and Miranda and cleaning their dishes: "'Ban, 'ban, Ca-caliban / Has a new master, get a new man. / Freedom, high-day; high-day, freedom; freedom, high-day, freedom" (2.2.179–81). In this song, Caliban significantly does not imagine unqualified liberty from service, as even his "freedom, high-day" is circumscribed by "a new master" he must ultimately serve.

Caliban, Miranda, and Futurity

The Tempest's winged beings—both magical and apian—reflect on the service of humans. In the distinct hierarchy of the island, royal characters vie for supremacy of Naples and Milan while enslaved and lower-status characters like Caliban and the boatswain serve greater physical utility in doing all of the practical work. The one figure in the play who has the least knowledge of the function of time and labor within human society is Miranda. In her unique position being raised on the island with only her father and Caliban, she lacks complete understanding of European systems of class and hierarchy. Her sole memory of life in Milan in early childhood, however, is filtered through a connection to women servants: "Had I not / Four of five women once that tended me?" (1.2.46–7). Prospero is amazed at his daughter's memory of those who served her, "But how is it / That this lives in thy mind?" (1.2.48–9). Miranda's isolated memory of life in Milan does not betray to her the lineage that would dictate her rank within Europe because she has no context for understanding that the number of servants a household employs reflects its status in society. Miranda's relationship to work is mediated by her perceptions of what she experiences on the island. In observing her father's interactions with his "slave," Miranda perceives that Caliban's inferiority justifies his servitude and thus his uncertain connection to futurity.

Miranda's understanding of Caliban's slave status is shaped by the past threat he posed to her. In recalling his thwarted attempt at her virtue, she calls Caliban "Abhorred slave, / ... capable of all ill" (1.2.351–3), noting that she had previously shown kindness to Caliban in teaching him the language that would "endo[w] thy purpose" (1.2.358). In other words, Miranda views her voluntary labor in instructing Caliban to communicate with her as a beneficial act that renders his thoughts and expressions not just as legible, but also potentially as civilized. Miranda thus feels betrayed that her pupil should revert to "thy vile race" in order to harm her (1.2.359). From Miranda's perspective, Caliban is "deservedly confined into this rock" (1.2.362). Caliban, by contrast, denies and reframes Miranda's account of his ingratitude and enslavement: "You taught me language, and my profit on't / Is I know how to curse" (1.2.364–5). A European tongue, for Caliban, has more direct drawbacks than benefits to him, as it becomes the means for conveying his required tasks and obligations. It is small comfort to him that he may use that medium to air his grievances about the arduous duties he is compelled to perform under the constant threat of pain and violence. Even as Caliban acknowledges his attempt at Miranda's honor, his grammar starts cautiously: "O ho, O ho! Would't had been done; / Thou didst prevent me, I had peopled else / This isle with Calibans" (1.2.350–2). This statement represents a rare moment in Caliban's speech, which starts in passive voice, using the past unreal conditional in "Would't had been done." And yet Prospero's intervention precludes this potential future in which Caliban imagines an island of his own progeny. Caliban believes his only hope of a shift in circumstance comes in the potential for choosing a new master in Stephano, which involves the bleak prospect of being exploited as a curiosity to the consumers of England: "When they will not give a doit to relieve a lame beggar, they will lay out ten to see a dead Indian" (2.2.31–2). However, Caliban is not the only character whose value could increase in Europe over the island.

Temporal polyethism is a concept that is observed among eusocial insect species, and it helps to account for why these creatures take on increasingly skill-oriented tasks that widen not only their physical interactions with the broader world, but also their social bonds among their kin. Evaluating Miranda's status in relation to this apian concept allows us to note how her value to Prospero increases as she reaches marriage-able age. Miranda remains unaware of the significance of her role, and yet, Prospero's aspirations to regain his dukedom and solidify his bonds with Naples rely upon his daughter's marriage to Ferdinand. The fact that Miranda's inclinations align with her father's designs has to do with the generic expectations of romance; nonetheless, she is still expected to fulfill the role of wife, which she could scarcely have imagined prior to the shipwreck. The only physical task performed by a royal person in the play is when Ferdinand begrudgingly moves logs for Prospero—a task usually reserved for Caliban. Miranda's response is to offer to conduct the work for him: "If you'll sit down, / I'll bear your logs the while" (3.1.23–4). In her naiveté, she is unaware that the offer would activate the conventions of chivalry in the prince: "No, precious creature, / I had rather crack my sinews, break my back, / Than you should such dishon-our undergo / While I sit lazy by" (3.1.25–8). Whereas Ferdinand has not yet determined Miranda and Prospero's status within the hierar-chy off of the island, he errs on the side of treating Miranda as a lady rather than as a lower-class woman, who would be expected to engage in such physical labor. Miranda, lacking knowledge about the class-based stratification of gendered labor in European culture, responds with her willingness to share the work in order to ease Ferdinand's burdens: "It would become me / As well as it does you, and I should do it / With much more ease, for my good will is to it, / And yours it is against" (3.1.28–31). Miranda does not perceive shame in being compelled to work. Indeed, she even factors labor into the courtship ritual:

> I am your wife, if you will marry me;
> If not, I'll die your maid. To be your fellow
> You may deny me, but I'll be your servant,
> Whether you will or no.
>
> (3.1.83–6)

Miranda here frames servitude not as a compulsory state dictated by birth or social status, but rather as a voluntary service determined by the laborer regardless of the will of her master. Neither Ariel nor Caliban has the ability to conceive of labor in these terms, as they are each com-pelled to serve Prospero with or without guarantees of future liberty.

Notably, Miranda is not the only European to imagine a labor system that differs from the hierarchy of a dukedom or kingdom. Indeed, Gon-zalo's speech about the potential for creating a commonwealth on the is-land, which was inspired by John Florio's 1603 translation of Michel de Montaigne's "Of Cannibals," envisions a place with "no occupation, all men idle, all: / And women too, but innocent and pure; / No sovereignty" (2.1.155–7).[73] From Edward McLean Test's perspective, "Gonzalo

imbues his utopia with a communal and idealized Native American culture."[74] And yet, George Hoffman notes that the source text in Montaigne's work "serve[s] as the target of irony" in *The Tempest* even as "it
runs directly counter to the rest of the essay, in which Montaigne takes
great pains to demonstrate that the natives have evolved a highly complex civilization."[75] The irony is not merely a function of Sebastian and
Antonio's mockery of the speech: "the latter end of his commonwealth
forgets the beginning" (2.1.159). Rather, Gonzalo's earlier interactions
with the mariners reveal his elitism and reinforcement of sovereignty
and servitude. During the tempest when Gonzalo chides the boatswain
for insubordination, the mariner reveals his frustration with the worldly
hierarchy that subordinates him to officials who lack the skills required
to save them from the storm, directly accusing Gonzalo, "You mar our
labor," and complaining of the councilor's interference, "A plague upon
this howling. They are louder than the weather or our office" (1.1.13 and
1.1.35–6). Within this moment of peril, Gonzalo stands upon ceremony
and status, "remember whom thou hast aboard" (1.1.19). The boatswain's retort serves as a reminder of his own intrinsic human worth,
"None that I love more than myself" (1.1.20). Gonzalo, near the top of
the human hierarchy, possesses the status to envision a commonwealth
grounded in natural pleasures rather than exploitation and work, and
yet his treatment and attitude toward his inferiors suggests otherwise.
To implement such a system would necessitate freeing all humans not
only from labor, but also from threats of violence. Nevertheless, even
in Gonzalo's imagined commonwealth, Caliban and Ariel, who cannot
lay claim to the categories of "men" or "women," would not be freed of
their servitude to their human master.

Caliban's words offer some insight into his experience as a slave de-
prived of potential worldly salvation. His only speech about pursuing
pleasure comes when Stephano promises to kill Prospero: "I am full of
pleasure / Let us be jocund. Will you troll the catch / You taught me?"
(3.2.116–8). Caliban turns to a song taught to him by his new Neapol-
itan master as an escape from his current servitude and suffering under
Prospero. Perhaps part of his relish in the ballad is in the liberating
theme of the lyrics, "Flout 'em and scout 'em. / ... / Thought is free"
(3.2.121–3). Nevertheless, Caliban soon awaits punishment for the plot
against Prospero's life, recalling his master's threat of an apian-induced
suffering, "I shall be pinched to death" (5.1.276). Certainly, Caliban's
ultimate fate following the play is much more ambiguous than Ariel's,
as Prospero admits, "this thing of darkness I / acknowledge mine" without offering a final judgment upon him (5.1.275–6).[76] Prospero points
to his own mortality, "every third thought shall be my grave," but also
in the epilogue gestures toward the immortality of his soul being "re-
lieved by prayer" (5.1.311; epilogue 16). No such declarations are made
about Caliban's life and death, or even his life after this moment. Bee

time for the less-than-human Caliban does not signal a Topsellian immortal salvation; rather, bees themselves and the pinch of their stings remain an ever-present threat of physical suffering at the hands of his human master. His thoughts are not free to imagine futurity so long as his body is subject to physical violence. Shakespeare and Johnson's songs of time and labor, sung in Ariel's otherworldly voice, underscore the intrinsic worth of animate life while foreclosing the possibility of human and privileged status for workers. It is not enough to serve a utility, for the promised time for leisure and pursuing pleasures may never come.

Notes

1 See Thomas D. Seeley, *Honeybee Democracy* (Princeton, NJ: Princeton University Press, 2010).

2 Friedrich Nietzsche, *Untimely Meditations*, ed. Daniel Breazeale, trans. R. J. Hollingdale (Cambridge: Cambridge University Press, 1997), 60.

3 Nietzsche, *Untimely Meditations*, 61.

4 Michael Pollan, *The Botany of Desire: A Plant's-Eye View of the World* (New York: Random House, 2001), 69.

5 Edward Topsell, *Historie of Serpents* (London, 1608), 67.

6 John Milton, *Complete Poems and Major Prose*, ed. Merritt Y. Hughes (New York: Prentice Hall, Inc, 1957; Indianapolis, IN: Hackett Publishing, 2003), 768–9, 776–7.

7 Milton, *Complete Poems*, 798.

8 Andrew Marvell, *The Poems of Andrew Marvell*, ed. Nigel Smith (New York: Longman, 2003), 154.

9 Karen Raber, *Animal Bodies, Renaissance Culture* (Philadelphia: University Pennsylvania Press, 2013), 131. See also See Margo DeMello, *Animals and Society: An Introduction to Human-Animal Studies* (New York: Columbia University Press, 2012), esp. 256–80.

10 See Thomas D. Seeley, "The Honeybee Colony as a Superorganism." *American Scientist* 77, no. 6 (November 1989): 546–53.

11 See Melissa Bateson, Suzanne Desire, Sarah E. Gartside, and Geraldine A. Wright. "Agitated Honeybees Exhibit Pessimistic Cognitive Biases," *Current Biology* 21, no. 12 (June 2011): 1070–3.

12 Charles Butler, *The Feminine Monarchie: Or a Treatise Concerning Bees and the Due Ordering of Them* (Oxford: Ioseph Barnes, 1609), B6v.

13 See Laurie Shannon, *The Accommodated Animal: Cosmopolity in Shakespearean Locales* (Chicago, IL: University of Chicago Press, 2013). See also Shannon, "'Poore wretch, laid all naked upon the bare earth': Human Negative Exceptionalism Among the Humanists," in *Shakespearean International Yearbook 15: Shakespeare and the Human*, ed. Tiffany Jo Werth (Farnham: Ashgate Publishing, 2015), 205–10.

14 Ayesha Ramachandran and Melissa E. Sanchez, "Spenser and 'the Human': An Introduction," *Spenser Studies: A Renaissance Poetry Annual*, 30 (2015): ix.

15 Joseph Campana, "Humans: Exceptional Humans, Human Exceptionalism, and the Shape of Things to Come," in *Shakespearean International Yearbook 15: Shakespeare and the Human*, ed. Tiffany Jo Werth (Farnham: Ashgate Publishing, 2015), 50.

16 For a discussion of bees and honey in Shakespeare's drama and poetry, see Nicole A. Jacobs, "Bees: The Shakespearean Hive and the Virtues of Honey," in *Shakespearean International Yearbook 15: Shakespeare and the Human*, ed. Tiffany Jo Werth (Farnham: Ashgate Publishing, 2015), 101–21.

17 Richard Grinnell, "Shakespeare's Keeping of Bees," *Interdisciplinary Studies in Literature and the Environment* 23, no. 4 (2016): 835.

18 Paul Waldau, *Animal Studies: An Introduction* (Oxford: Oxford University Press, 2013), 214.

19 *The Aberdeen Bestiary*, Special Collections, 64r, University of Aberdeen. https://www.abdn.ac.uk/bestiary/.

20 Anthony, *Medieval Preachers and Medieval Preaching*, ed. and trans. J. M. Neale (London: J & C Mozley, 1856), 244.

21 Bernard, *Saint Bernard, His Meditations, Or Sighes, Sobbes, and Teares Upon Our Saviors Passion*, trans. W. P. (London, 1611), 386.

22 Bernard, *The Sentences*, trans. Francis R Swietek (Kalamazoo, MI: Cistercian Publications, 2000), 209–10.

23 Bernard, *The Sentences*, 210.

24 Bernard, *His Meditations*, 162–3.

25 James Cotter Morison, *The Life and Times of Saint Bernard, Abbot of Clairvaux* (New York: Macmillan, 1863), 22–3.

26 Qtd. in Morison, *The Life and Times*, 202.

27 See Carolyn Merchant *Radical Ecology: The Search for a Livable World* (New York: Routledge, 1992). According to Merchant, "radical ecology" emphasizes "a new consciousness of our responsibilities to the rest of nature and to other humans" (1).

28 Francis, *Laudato Si': On Care for Our Common Home* (Huntington, IN: Our Sunday Visitor, 2015), 22.

29 Robert N. Watson, *The Green and the Real in the Late Renaissance* (Philadelphia: University Pennsylvania Press, 2006), 36.

30 See Franz Posset, "Bernard of Clairvaux as Luther's Source," *Concordia Theological Quarterly* 54, no. 4 (October 1990): 281–304.

31 See John Panke, *Collectanea, Out of St. Gregory the Great, and St Bernard the Devout Against the Papists* (Oxford, 1618). See also Antonie Batt, *A Hive of Sacred Honiecombes Containing Most Sweet and Heavenly Counsel* (Oxford, 1631).

32 Although we now understand the male drone is responsible for mating with the queen and thus ensuring the future survival of the hive, early modern theorists tended to view him as a lazy degenerate who sought to exploit the labor of others.

33 Erica Fudge, *Quick Cattle and Dying Wishes: People and Their Animals in Early Modern England* (Ithaca, NY: Cornell University Press, 2018), 127.

34 Edward Topsell, *Times Lamentation: Or an Exposition on the Prophet Joel* (London, 1599), A2.

35 Topsell, *Times Lamentation*, 66.

36 Topsell, *Times Lamentation*, 194.

37 Henry Holland and Edward Topsell, *The Historie of Adam, or the Fourefold State of Man* (London: Thomas East, 1606), sig. iir.

38 Holland and Topsell, *The Historie of Adam*, 167v.

39 Topsell, *Historie of Serpents*, 73.

40 Edward Topsell, *The Reward of Religion Delivered in Sundrie Lectures Upon the Booke of Ruth* (London,1596), 298.

41 Topsell, *The Reward of Religion*, 298–9.

42 Tiffany Jo Werth, ed. "Introduction: Shakespeare and the Human," in *Shakespearean International Yearbook 15: Shakespeare and the Human* (Farnham: Ashgate Publishing, 2015), 2.

43 Steven Mentz, "Airy Spirits: Winds, Bodies, and Ecological Force in Early Modern England," in *Shakespearean International Yearbook 15: Shakespeare and the Human*, ed. Tiffany Jo Werth (Farnham: Ashgate Publishing, 2015), 34.

44 Quotations from *The Tempest* will be cited in-text from William Shakespeare, *The Tempest*, ed. Virginia Mason Vaughan and Alden T. Vaughan (London: Arden, 1999).

45 Michael Neill, "'Noises, / Sounds, and sweet airs': The Burden of Shakespeare's Tempest," *Shakespeare Quarterly* 59, no. 1 (Spring 2008): 37.

46 The music for this song can be found in Folger MS V.a.411 11v.

47 Jennifer Linhart Wood, personal communication, July 27, 2018. For a discussion of some other songs and sounds in *The Tempest*, see Jennifer Linhart Wood's "Sounding Spaces: *The Tempest's* Uncanny Near-East Echoes," *Shakespeare Studies* 44 (2016): 173–9.

48 Jacquelyn Fox-Good, "Other Voices: The Sweet, Dangerous Air(s) of Shakespeare's Tempest," *Shakespeare Studies* 24 (1996): 265.

49 Butler, *The Feminine Monarchie,* Sig. E8v.

50 Butler, *The Feminine Monarchie*, Sig. F1r.

51 Ross W. Duffin, *Shakespeare's Songbook* (New York: Norton, 2004), 455.

52 Duffin, *Shakespeare's Songbook*, 455–6.

53 John P. Cutts, "Robert Johnson: King's Musician in His Majesty's Public Entertainment," *Music & Letters* 36, no. 2 (1955): 110.

54 Cutts, "Robert Johnson," 110.

55 Topsell, *Times Lamentation*, 38.

56 Karl Marx, "Religion, Free Press, and Philosophy," *Writings of the Young Karl Marx on Philosophy and Society*, trans. Loyd D. Easton and Kurt H. Guddat (New York: Doubleday, 1967), 126.

57 See William James Booth, "Economies of Time: On the Idea of Time in Marx's Political Economy," *Political Theory* 19 (1991): 7–7. As Booth notes, "Free time was the precondition of friendship, of citizenship in the better polities, and of the pursuit of the good life, and it was one of the philosophical boundary lines separating the free from the unfree" (7–8).

58 Mark L. Winston, *Bee Time* (Cambridge, MA: Harvard University Press, 2014), 174–5.

59 Werth, "Introduction," 2.

60 Karen Raber, *Shakespeare and Posthumanist Theory* (New York: Bloomsbury, 2018), 97.

61 Kim F. Hall, *Things of Darkness: Economies of Race and Gender in Early Modern England* (Ithaca, NY: Cornell University Press, 1995), 142.

62 David Mark Whitford, *The Curse of Ham in the Early Modern Era: The Bible and the Justifications for Slavery* (Burlington, VT: Ashgate, 2009), 3–4.

63 Barbara Fuchs, "Conquering Islands: Contextualizing *The Tempest*," *Shakespeare Quarterly* 48 (1997): 62.

64 Peter Hulme, *Colonial Encounters: Europe and the Native Caribbean, 1492–1797* (London: Methuen, 1986), 127.

65 Terry Comito, "Caliban's Dream: The Topography of Some Shakespeare Gardens," *Shakespeare Studies* 14 (1981): 48.

66 Catherine M. Dunn, "The Function of Music in Shakespeare's Romances," *Shakespeare Quarterly* (1969): 404, 405.

67 Tom MacFaul, *Shakespeare and the Natural World* (Cambridge: Cambridge University Press, 2015), 184.

68 Rebecca Laroche and Jennifer Munroe, *Shakespeare and Ecofeminist Theory* (London: Bloomsbury, 2017), 133.

69 Garrett Sullivan, *Sleep, Romance and Human Embodiment: Vitality from Spenser to Milton* (Cambridge: Cambridge University Press, 2012), 19.

70 Bruce R. Smith, *The Acoustic World of Early Modern England: Attending to the O Factor* (Chicago, IL: University of Chicago Press, 1999), 337. Neill examines this song as indicative of Caliban's burden of slavery, "Noises, / Sounds," 40.

71 Smith, *The Acoustic World*, 338.

72 Fox-Good, "Other Voices," 265.

73 For a discussion of the use of source texts for Gonzalo's speech, see Kenji Go, "Montaigne's 'Cannibals' and *The Tempest* Revisited," *Studies in Philology* 109, no. 4 (Summer 2012): 455–73.

74 Edward McLean Test, *Sacred Seeds: New World Plants in Early Modern English Literature* (Lincoln: University of Nebraska Press, 2019), 94.

75 George Hoffman, "Anatomy of the Mass: Montaigne's 'Cannibals,'" *PMLA* 117, no. 2 (2002): 208.

76 See Ania Loomba, *Shakespeare, Race, and Colonialism* (Oxford: Oxford University Press, 2002).

2 Hive Split
The New World Colonists

In the beehive, the act of raising up a new queen presages the demise of the current queen, with one notable exception. When a hive has grown too populous to sustain itself, it will prepare its current space for a new generation of workers, drones, and queen, so that an adventurous contingent can join its reigning sovereign in striking off to seek a new home. The new hive with its old queen, called the daughter colony, leaves the new queen and its parent colony behind in simultaneous acts of survival and expansion. In nature, this process is called swarming. However, in bee husbandry, the intentional separation and creation of a new hive is known as hiving off or splitting, and it runs the chances of both high risk and high reward. Apiculturists routinely initiate hiving off, but in doing so they gamble overall production, in that failed splits can compromise that year's harvest of honey and wax and potentially lead to the failure of the colonies. However, when hiving off succeeds, the apiary stands to prosper greatly in the long term, with more colonies encompassing greater territory.

In seventeenth-century England, both the dangers and the potential of uprooting to the New World terrified and thrilled would-be investors and settlers who chose the colony of bees as its founding metaphor for the English colonial enterprise in America. This metaphor would not only focus on communal survival of the colonists and their beliefs, but also on the domination of Native Americans and their culture. The various and competing perspectives on the hive—colonial and Indigenous—have a great deal to teach us about the precarious alliances and divisions in the first century of contact. While the next chapter will focus on Native American reactions to the swarm, this chapter will outline the various ways in which the honeybee hive served colonists' self-image from establishing their right to the land to shaping the early American intellectual tradition to authorizing women's labor and participation in public life in the colonial era.

Although the Mayas had great success in harvesting honey from stingless bees in Mesoamerica, the first hive of European honeybees on the east coast of America was shipped by English settlers to Virginia in December 1621, as the bees kept to their hive in diapause—a period of decreased metabolic activity—for the winter.[1] This beehive would have made landfall early in 1622, more than a year after the founding of the Plymouth settlement in Massachusetts.[2] According to apiculturist and bee historian Eva Crane, historical and anthropological records indicate that the highest concentration of hive beekeeping in early seventeenth-century America was in the Massachusetts Bay Colony.[3] From Plymouth to Danvers to Newbury, individuals and communities kept apiaries to generate a reliable supply of honey and wax. Due to the scarcity of provisions in the early days of the settlements, these commodities were especially useful in producing food, drink, remedies, and candles. For instance, a guide enticing settlers to Maryland suggested that each English family bring "a gallon of honey" for personal household use along with additional stores for commodity exchange.[4] However, there was a much more significant effect of beekeeping in the Massachusetts Bay Colony: settlements with hives thrived. And while there are many contributing factors to this success, including learning from the early mistakes in Roanoke, Jamestown, and other colonies, the presence of hives served a vital function.[5]

With the introduction of these highly effective pollinators, English plants could finally survive, offering both human and livestock transplants the greatest chance to increase and multiply. And while the colonists lacked the important discovery of pollination, they did recognize that sites of thriving bee colonies lent themselves to productive human colonies as well. Early New England colonist Thomas Morton would go so far as to say that bees' survival in New England offered evidence that the region was *zona temperata*, and thus hospitable to the English colonists.[6] To transform America into what settlers would view idealistically as "a new Canaan, a land of milk and honey," as Tammy Horn observes, the English would have to engage in European husbandry of cows and bees.[7] These two essential agricultural animals formed the basis of many important English colonial commodities. Early in the days of colonization, Narragansetts would target and kill English cows to hamper their settlement, but they did not have the knowledge or means to overcome honeybee hives.[8]

In the European tradition, bees were respected as sovereign beings of a sovereign colony. These tiny winged insects assumed greater significance than mere conduits of physical or cultural pollination for the English. Dating back to the fifteenth century, papal orders and decrees had declared a "doctrine of discovery" that adjudicated how to divide up the land of the New World, a process that allowed Catholic kings to claim any land that was not already subject to the rule of another Christian sovereign. Indeed, the command of Pope Innocent VIII in a papal bull of 1486 was that Europeans' "commission from heaven is the propagation of the orthodox faith … the salvation of barbarous nations, and the repression of the infidels and their conversion to the faith."[9]

And yet in the post-Reformation context of the English settlement, when international law supplanted the authority of the Vatican, the doctrine of discovery was replaced by the right of conquest. This no less invasive dictate was used as a tool to seize American land and resources by claiming dominion over what Europeans viewed as *terra nullius*, or empty lands.[10] Applying European legal and philosophical paradigms to usurp the sovereignty of Native nations, the English settlers of the northeast turned to the apian metaphor to advance their own fiction of sovereignty that sought to invalidate established Indigenous culture and agriculture.

What is clear about this early conflict is that English colonists specifically deployed the beehive to assert an image of hierarchy and power that had not in actuality been achieved, in part to convince themselves and in part to assure shareholders and naysayers in England that their mission was both just and righteous. Under the guise of a "natural" order, the English justified their conquest of the northeast and its resources, altering in the process the land they claimed as theirs. At the same time, Indigenous societies sought to retain cultural traditions and governing structures—that, relative to English standards, were less hierarchical and gendered—while recruiting partners in trade and warfare against neighboring nations. These disparate social structures helped to fuel conflicts over resources. As William Cronon observes, for instance, "the way Indians had chosen to inhabit that world posed a paradox ... for Europeans ... [who were] struck by what seemed to them the poverty of Indians who lived in the midst of a landscape endowed so astonishingly with abundance."[11] As the fiction of the sovereign hive slowly came into being—with the English expansion of settlements—colonists would continue to cultivate the apian metaphor, thereby helping to shape the larger patterns of culture and labor in colonial America.

This chapter demonstrates how colonists used bees as a means of physical and symbolic domination, an attempt to justify their violence against sovereign Indigenous nations through a culturally ingrained European metaphor of the natural world. First, I draw upon the work of seventeenth-century clerics and historians to show how the symbolism of the hive organized colonists' understanding of their divinely ordained mission. Second, I turn to the work of Germantown founder and beekeeper Francis Daniel Pastorius, examining both the physical and cultural roles of the hive as well as his encouragement of Quaker women's writing within the early American intellectual tradition. Third, I explore the continued relevance of the apian icon as it relates to the women's spinning bee, which illustrates the expectations of women's labor and virtue in colonial America. In so doing, I examine the repercussions of the hive on the ecosystem and labor systems of the colonies. Among settler inhabitants of the northeast, I argue, the beehive represents their approach to the natural world and its resources, one that relies upon a familiar English trope to reimagine the social fabric of their new world.

The Colonial Swarm

From the inception of the English exploration of North America, tiny insects played a significant role in the colonists' conceptualization of difference and similitude in the land and cultures they encountered. John White accompanied the first expedition sponsored by Sir Walter Ralegh to found Roanoke in 1584, returning in subsequent missions over the next few years to Virginia and Chesapeake Bay as governor. His grand-daughter, Virginia Dare, was the first English subject born in America, but she would be lost with the other members of the Roanoke colony. A noted illustrator, White drew several watercolors of local flora, fauna, and people, as well as maps for future settlers. One image, in particular, elucidates the simultaneous wonder and fear that New World insects could instill in English explorers. On the top of the image are three different views of fireflies, which were not native to England and thus unfamiliar.[12] The caption for these drawings is "A flye which in the night semeth a flame or fyre."[13] At the bottom of the page is a watercolor of another insect with a prominently striped abdomen—identified by modern curators as a gadfly—with the inscription, "a dangerous byting fly." Gadflies (otherwise known as horse flies) were native to England, so why might White choose to illustrate this common insect? The answer most likely lies in the difference in variety and aggression the colonists witnessed in these flies. The French colonist, Louis Armand, Baron of Lahontan, who was Lord Lieutenant of Placentia (Newfoundland) before it transferred to English control, wrote a book *New Voyages to North America* (1703), which was immediately translated into English. In it, he describes the insects popularly known as "Gad-bees," which "are a sort of Flies about twice as big as Bees; ... They sting only between Noon, and three a Clock in the Afternoon; but then they do it so violently, that they fetch Blood."[14] The colloquialism gad-bees, despite the identification as a type of fly, speaks to the view that these insects are distinct from European varieties. The gad-bees' aggression posed a challenge that colonists would have to learn to cope with in settling the land. Framed within White's images of New World humans and insects is an early glimpse at the lands and peoples the English sought to conquer. Both would simultaneously inspire awe and amazement but could also signal a potential threat of danger to the colonists. The introduction of the European honeybee early in the colonial endeavor enacted a cultural shibboleth. On the one hand, hundreds of years of English knowledge of bee husbandry facilitated their use and exploitation of the bee, and on the other, Indigenous societies' lack of prior experience with managing the hive placed them at a distinct disadvantage.

The sovereign hive came to symbolize the English world view regarding nature and the beings within it. Unlike Topsell and Shakespeare, the colonists took a more conventional, non-Bernardian perspective on bees and those beings viewed as non-human. Indeed, to the English settlers, much of the natural world—animals, peoples, plant life, and land—were viewed largely as tools or divine gifts to further their aims. In fact, one anonymous 1643 text, *New Englands First Fruits,* actually interprets the ease of colonization as a sign of God's approbation, "in sweeping away great multitudes of the Natives by the small Pox, a little before we went thither, that he might make room for us [and] in giving us such merveilous safe Passage from first to the last."[15] By this commonplace account, God approved of the utilitarian understanding of nature and thus authorized colonists' self-promotion to the exclusion of those who already inhabited the coastal northeast for millennia. The English colonizers, more so than the French, the Spanish, or the Dutch relied upon the metaphor and utility of the hive to serve their particular vision of supremacy and industry.[16] The English deemed Native Americans—in a specifically racialized, gendered, and religiously motivated exclusionism—as ripe for conversion, domination, or outright genocide. Moreover, the distinction between the English's top-down monarchy and many Indigenous nations' more egalitarian social structures served as further justification to the English of their own "civilized" action in contrast to the so-called "barbarity" and disorder of their rivals for land and resources. Early in the period of colonial expansion two distinct dichotomies between colonizer and colonized included the human/nonhuman and the Christian/heathen.

The racialized representations of colonists as human and Native Americans as nonhuman would not yet be fully codified in colonial America as they would later come to be after the Revolution. Nevertheless, this early distinction in the order and chain of being was clearly used to justify European suppression of the various nations they encountered in the coastal northeast. According to Luca Codignola, "The extent of the humanness of the American Indians and their rank within human society was the subject of a long debate among Europeans."[17] Bruce R. Dain traces the emerging categories of race to the sixteenth century, "when animal breeding terminology seems to have fused with ancient ideas about aristocratic familial legacy and 'blood.'"[18] Within this human and nonhuman paradigm, the Indigenous people are cast as descending from inferior breeding and blood, potentially, as many early modern theorists contended, as a lost tribe of Israel. This early colonial dichotomy would serve as a precursor to the complicated fiction of "Indian blood," which not only provided, in a settler mindset, a pretense for violence and genocide, but more importantly, as Kim Tallbear argues, continues to shape the political sovereignty and legal standing of Native Americans in contemporary society.[19] Drawing from critical race theory, postcolonial theory, and feminist theory, Mary Hawkesworth and Lisa Disch add that the processes of racialization and gendering both "create and sustain divisions, stratifications, and modes of domination within and across intellectual and national borders," remarking upon the irony with which "biology was used to create an allegedly empirical justification for racial and sexual hierarchies at the very moment when the language of political equality was deployed against the feudal order."[20] Apian society, as a tended female-dominated social structure that to their minds required English husbandry and served English needs, figures at the center of this racialized and gendered discourse in the early process of colonization.

Like the human/nonhuman paradigm, the English relied upon the Christian/heathen hierarchy for additional justification for the cultural suppression and physical genocide of Native American societies. Indeed, the Christian and savage dichotomy is repeated throughout seventeenth-century sermons and essays used to bolster the missionary zeal of the northeastern settlers. More specifically, the time-tested apian metaphor helped to advance several religious and political aims for the English: (1) settlers viewed it as their civic duty to settle in America to increase English yields of power and reputation; (2) the colonists emigrated to the New World to seek new grounds for their religious autonomy; (3) clerics believed they were ordained by God to spread His Word and ecclesiastical governing powers abroad; and (4) they interpreted the beehive and its honey as a powerful symbol for disseminating English cultural knowledge and political thought.

The swarming hive is essential to the propagation of Puritan thought in early colonial America. It is most notably featured in *A Platform of Church Discipline* (1649), known historically as the Cambridge Platform, a guide produced by the synod of Cambridge to direct church congregational polity in the Massachusetts Bay Colony. This founding ecclesiastical dictate notably describes the intended growth of the faith through the apian metaphor:

> As Bees, when the hive is too full, issue forth by Swarms, and are gathered into other Hives, so the Churches of Christ may do the same upon like necessity, and therein hold forth to them the right hand of fellowship, both in their gathering into a Church, and in the Ordination of their Officers.[21]

The Cambridge Platform's hive image thus serves to assure congregants that the new churches that crop up will hold true to the original mission; in other words, they will not dilute the message in the swarming process of expansion. This structure gave congregations a great deal of autonomy, but it also granted pastors significant power over those they chose to minister to since, under the synod's design, individual churches, like hives themselves, were not specifically accountable to a larger and centralized governing structure.[22]

However, the Cambridge Platform was not the first Puritan use of the hive splitting metaphor for the English colonies. Reverend John Cotton, an English preacher, would after his emigration to New England become the pastor of the First Church of Boston. In his sermon, *God's Promise to His Plantation*, which was delivered upon the departure of the Winthrop fleet in England in spring 1630, he discusses the providence of the colonial mission:

> To plant a Colony, that is, a company that agree together to remove out of their owne Country, and settle a Citty or Common-wealth elsewhere. Of such a Colony wee reade in Acts 16.12 which God blessed and prospered exceedingly, and made it a glorious Church. Nature teacheth Bees to doe so, when as the hive is too full, they seeke abroad for new dwellings: So when the hive of the Commonwealth is so full, that Tradesmen cannot live one by another, but eate up one another, in this case it is lawfull to remove.[23]

Cotton unifies his biblical reference to the Philippi colony to that of the bee colony to justify the seizing of lands by God's chosen people. Moreover, he suggests that there is both virtue and economic reward in settling a new colony to stave off financial hardship in the motherland. In representing colonization as an apian formulation, Cotton casts resources and finances as God-given and thereby authorizes the pursuit of prosperity without the sin of greed.

This early establishing bee metaphor survives the initial struggles of the colony, as Cotton's grandson Cotton Mather revives and expands the imagery in the wake of war between the colonists and Indigenous nations. In *Magnalia Christi Americana: or Ecclesiastical History of New England from Its First Planting in the Year 1620* (1702), Mather reflects on the expansionist impulse of the early colonists:

> It was not long before the Massachuset[ts] Colony was become like an hive, overstocked with bees; and many of the new inhabitants entertained thoughts of swarming into plantations extended further into the country. The colony might fetch its own description from the dispensations of the great God ... and say *O God of Hosts, thou hast brought a vine out of England; thou hast cast out the heathen and planted it; thou preparedst room before it, and didst cause it to take deep root, and it filled the land.*[24]

In the 70 years between Cotton and Mather's analyses, the Massachusetts Bay Colony had gone from a fledgling attempt to a vast and flourishing set of settlements. What remains consistent in this time is the prominence of the related bee and agricultural images: the Puritans have, from their perspective, successfully planted themselves in inhospitable soil. In doing so, they have confirmed the symbolic and physical primacy of bee husbandry to the colonial endeavor. Indeed, the title page of Cotton's 1630 sermon includes 2 Samuel 7:10: "Moreover, I will appoint a place for my people Israel, and I will plant them, that they may dwell in a place of their own, and move no more." Cotton and Mather's interpretations similarly align with that of Martha's Vineyard pastor, Thomas Mayhew, who in 1650 described his conversion of Wampanoags to Christianity as "God's husbandry," which "may be a fruitful glorious spreading vine."[25] What Mayhew did not mention in his agricultural metaphor is the practice he used to effect these religious conversions. According to Wampanoag elder, Helen Vanderloop Manning, in 1645 when Martha's Vineyard was beset by plague, the English used medicine to convince dying Wampanoags that "their God is more benevolent and powerful than the Wampanoag Creator."[26]

Within the agricultural imagery evoked so frequently in seventeenth-century literature, the designation of colonies as plantations is significant. The *Oxford English Dictionary* defines plantation as a noun, "settlement in a conquered or dominant country," but also includes a verb, "the action of planting seeds or plants in the ground." The dedication to William Hubbard's *A Narrative of the Troubles with the Indians in New England* (1677) reads,

> What God hath planted, shall not by man, or any of Satan's instruments be plucked up. It is with young Colonies, as it is with Trees newly planted, which those winds, as one saith, that are not so boisterous as to blow down, doe so far advantage as to shake them to a greater fastness at the root.[27]

Hubbard goes on to discuss the early plantations and colonies as "so filled with Inhabitants, that like Swarms of Bees they were ready to swarm."[28] Despite Cotton and other colonists' interpretations of the early church settlement as being responsible for either casting out or purifying the "heathens," the rootedness of the plantation emblem belies the unstable realities of the English colonies at their inception, as these settlements would shift over conflicts and land disputes. The ever-swarming apiary thus offers the English colonists a symbolic means for their aspirations of establishing themselves in a multiplying cascade of localized plots.

King Philip's War, also known as Metacomet's Rebellion (1675–6), was fought between colonists and various Indigenous nations of the northeast, including the Wampanoags, Pocassets, and Narragansetts. The war, which continued even after the execution of Metacomet and the enslavement of many of the fighters, had generational roots. The powerful Wampanoag sachem (a cultural and political consensus builder) Massasoit had forged strong bonds with particular English colonists, like Edward Winslow and Roger Williams. Indeed, upon their advice, he capitulated to the Narragansetts' land demands, eventually feeling enough shame over the decision to restyle himself as Ousamequin, or "Yellow

Feather."[29] According to Wampanoag elder Chester P. Soliz, Massasoit's close links to the colonists inspired him to request that his sons Wamsutta and Metacomet be given Christian names, Alexander and Philip, respectively, and that they be granted admission to Harvard.[30] When after Massasoit's death Wamsutta/Alexander was imprisoned by the English and died in jail, his brother Metacomet/Philip, as a newly minted sachem, lacked faith in the English and their promises. He allied himself with his former sister-in-law, the Pocasset sachem Weetamoo, who secured the aide of the Naragansetts. Subsequent arrests and executions escalated into a war between the English and many of the Algonquian societies of the northeast that would result in the deaths of approximately 5,000 Native Americans and 2,500 English settlers.[31]

The organization of peoples of the coastal northeast in sachemships differed significantly from English monarchy and absolutist conceptions of the human hive. Within Indigenous political configurations, a sachem acted as a spokesperson who made political decisions and determinations about the use of resources, and he or she tended to organize power through kinship relationships, most of which were solidly rooted in reciprocity. As James V. Fenelon and Thomas D. Hall observe, the notion of a "chief" is an imprecise and ahistorical imposition of the Western scholarly tradition, as "nearly all American Indian societies" seek consensus as dictated by a representative rather than endowing a leader with absolute power.[32] Particularly in times of war, the sachem was expected to consult with, as Wayne E. Lee puts it, "a council of elders" and sometimes "a more or less formal council of women" to seek a communally beneficial and agreed upon resolution.[33] Unlike the European system—promoted by the apian icon—of the divinely ordained and absolutist monarch, whose right and display of power must remain unquestioned, the sachem worked toward securing and maintaining his or her position by redistributing valuable resources and handling negotiations with other nations and colonial governments. David J. Silverman writes,

> a sachem had to cultivate support among leading families with strategic marriages and council appointments, and among the broader public with generosity and high oratory, for there was always a risk of his followers leaving for another jurisdiction or shifting their allegiance to one of his political rivals.[34]

Among Wampanoags on Martha's Vineyard, for instance, women held sachemships prior to and in the first century of English contact. According to Laura Arnold Leibman, "Seventeenth-century and eighteenth-century documents regarding conflicts between colonists and [Martha's Vineyard] island *squa-sachems* show that these women had broad bases of power and were supported by their communities."[35]

The colonists' enlisted the bee metaphor in their efforts to maintain physical territory through military force. Hubbard's *A Narrative of the Troubles with the Indians in New England,* for instance, claims that the primary means of establishing permanent dominance is through apian industry and self-reliance. In describing a battle during King Philip's War between English colonists and Narragansetts in December 1675 near Pettiquamscott, Hubbard writes,

> There might one have seen the whole Body of that little Regimental Army, as busie as Bees in a Hive, some bravely fighting with the Enemy, others ha[u]ling off, and carrying away the Dead and Wounded Men (which I rather note) that none may want the due testimony of their valour and faithfulness.[36]

Hubbard's account is a very conventional representation of hive industry and solidarity that specifically praises the colonial military effort against Native American fighters. Along with Cotton, his work demonstrates the significance of hive symbolism to the colonists during this violent conflict.

Beyond the call to war, the standards of industry expected in the Massachusetts Bay Colony similarly employ the apian metaphor. Of those early settlers who fail to thrive in the New World and then criticize it in England as a hostile landscape, New England colonist William Wood argues that they demonstrate a "droanish disposition, that would live of the sweate of another mans browes" and "hope to live in plenty and idleness, both at a time," thereby failing to realize that a settlement and its land cannot thrive without "the husbandrie of man."[37] This comparison of failed colonists to drones makes sense, in that drone bees were regarded with very little sentimentality, as they were believed to be a non-contributing drain on communal resources. If, then, the drone mentality gained traction among settlers, the concern was that the colonial enterprise would fail. So, while dronish settlers were cast out of the colony and criticized for their laziness, all those who intended to stay were expected to possess the industry and efficiency of the worker bee or the dominance of the queen.

In addition, drone-like behavior also speaks to the racial and religious divide between colonizer and colonized. In Mayhew's work to convert Wampanoags to Christianity, he addresses their unreceptive brethren as "these poor Heathans who seeme to be the dregs and refuse of Adam[']s lost posterity."[38] So while Mayhew's image, on the one hand, acknowledges Native Americans' descent from Adam and consequently their humanity, he also, on the other, disparages them through a similarly drone-like or specifically racial inferiority. To the pastor, the apian metaphor serves as justification for English dominance over the so-called heathens. But how would the English respond to those Indigenous peoples who they could not represent as drone-like?

One exception to the human/nonhuman dichotomy established by European hegemony is that of the converted Native American Christian. Pastor Henry Whitfield frames Christian Native Americans as martyr-like in their faith, saying that they are "industrious and pursue the things of their salvation, rest they cannot, have it they must, what ever it cost them, bearing up strongly against all opposition."[39] Whitfield thus calls upon the commonplace anthropomorphic descriptions of bees' qualities of industry, perseverance, and self-sacrifice to address the challenges faced by those who commit to the Christian faith even in the face of resistance by fellow Native Americans and elitist Europeans alike. John Eliot would publish the first bible in America in 1663, which was written in the Natick dialect, in order to encourage Christian conversion and literacy. Abraham Peirson, a pastor at Branford, published *Some Helps for the Indians: Shewing Them How to Improve Their Natural Reason to Know the True God and the Christian Religion* (1658) with embedded translations of the Lord's Prayer as well as religious doctrine in English and a form of Algonquian dialect. The text emphasizes the shared humanity between the English and their Indigenous brethren: "God made of one blood all nations of men / God keztaunkq' wutche pasakun nepuk wame arkiz renawauk."[40] Granted, these cases relative to the general American Indian populations were quite small. Daniel Gookin includes a census taken of Native American Christian converts by 1674, indicating, for instance, that one of the nations with the highest number of converts was the Naticks with 145 men, women, and children. Nevertheless, of the hundreds of thousands of Indigenous peoples in North America, Gookin only found evidence of 1,100 Christian converts.[41]

But colonists are not the only ones to highlight the exceptionalism of converted Native American Christians. William Apess was a nineteenth-century pastor from the Pequot people of Connecticut. He founded a church for the Mashpee Wampanoags who were fed up with the opportunism and exploitation of their white pastor Phineas Fish, who was selling off their timber and refusing to minister to non-whites. In a sermon at the Odeon in Boston in 1836, Apess spoke movingly of Native American ethics and resistance, the text of which was published as *Eulogy on King Philip*. In it, Apess writes, "My image is of God, I am not a beast. But all men are governed by animal passions who are void of the true principles of God, whether cultivated or uncultivated."[42] While Apess focuses on a requisite faith in the Christian God regardless of race, he promotes the intrinsic value of all those who resisted colonial stereotypes of the uncultivated and nonhuman Native American. He similarly goes on to praise Wampanoag political resistance to their so-called Christian invaders in Plymouth:

[The pilgrims] without asking liberty from any one, they possessed themselves of a portion of the country, and built themselves houses, and then made a treaty, and commanded them to accede it. This, if now done, would be called an insult, and every white man would be called to go out and act the part of a patriot, to defend their country's rights; and if every intruder were butchered, it would be sung upon every hill-top in the Union, that victory and patriotism was the order of the day.[43]

In Apess's counter-narrative, the English colonists break their faith through domination and coercion. He comments upon the irony that invaders should be considered patriots, given the lack of virtue in their actions. The hero of Apess's sermon is Metacomet, the "all-accomplished son of the forest, that died a martyr to his cause, though unsuccessful, yet as glorious as the *American* Revolution."[44] In Apess's view, Metacomet's commitment to resisting colonial authority and saving his people shows him to be a model of virtue and patriotism against the deceitful English. Apess advocated for resistance within the governing structures available; in 1833, he drafted a Declaration of Independence for his parishioners, which was signed by 102 Mashpee Wampanoags. In Apess's view, it was not race, but rather virtue that earned human status. His message, however, was not widely accepted by white colonists. According to historian Charles Hamilton, "soon after making his speech on King Philip, ... Apess disappeared mysteriously. Where or how he died is not known."[45]

The historical record demonstrates that the English, despite some outward signs of diplomacy, were largely concerned with the physical cultivation of the land and the production of property titles that would allow them to retain it indefinitely. Their tolerant attitude toward Christian Native individuals was premised upon their level of control of the converts. By the time of King Philip's war, the English extended peaceful negotiations primarily in those circumstances in which they could flex their technologies of conquest. One of these mechanisms, the New World swarm, transformed from an image of English subjects' expansion and autonomy to a more actively aggressive symbol of authorized English dominance. According to Soliz, King Philip's War

> turned out to be the single most cataclysmic event of 17th-century colonial New England. An ecological revolution took place, which disrupted the Indian gathering, hunting, and agricultural production with the introduction of new plants and animals, fenced-in lands, as well as fur and timber removal.[46]

The English hive facilitated not only the change in the land and its people but also attitudes toward its use. Some of the same colonial beekeepers who killed their hives to seize their honey viewed their Native American allies as similarly disposable. This utilitarian perspective would shape the early figuration of the bee swarm in America. And yet this metaphor would also encompass additional layers of meaning in the late seventeenth and early eighteenth centuries.

Francis Daniel Pastorius's *The Beehive* and the Early American Intellectual Tradition

Like the natural swarming of honeybees that would in a matter of decades colonize most of the northeast, colonial efforts quickly extended between the Massachusetts and Chesapeake Bays to encompass additional settlements, including Pennsylvania. During this early period of colonization, Francis Daniel Pastorius, who founded Germantown in 1683, produced a large commonplace book called *The Beehive* (1696) and a precursor collection of notes *Alvearialia*, meaning "things related to beehives."[47] He collected thousands of excerpts and observations about the various books he read, reflections about being a beekeeper, original poetry, and copies of letters, speeches, and tributes he wrote to his friends and colleagues. To organize both a colony and an intellectual movement under the banner of the hive is to celebrate and recreate in America an elitist European-inspired hierarchy.

Pastorius was guided in his principles and sense of justice by his devout faith. He came to America from Germany as a Pietist, a member of a sect of Lutheranism that emphasizes "the inward response of the individual to God."[48] He would eventually join the Quaker meeting in Philadelphia and, along with Garret Hendericks and Derick up de Graeff, pen the *Quaker Protest Against Slavery* (1688), the first abolitionist petition in America.[49] Pastorius's representation of Native Americans praised their temperance and familial bonds, but as Patrick M. Erben observes, Pastorius's idealized vision of the Lenape (who were soon to be driven from the land by William Penn) failed to acknowledge "the true effects of European immigration on Native American peoples."[50] Pastorius engaged the European apian tradition in his writing with all of the weight of hierarchy and elitism that would entail. The time he spent traveling in England and especially in Cambridge made a significant impact on his approach to colonization in Pennsylvania, evidence of which can be seen in the large proportion of English literature and theory in *The Beehive*. Although his book includes work in German, Latin, and other languages, he also notes that his primary objective is to "collec[t] the Best out of England."[51] Pastorius's collection of poems, prose tracts, essays, and other materials in the commonplace book, which was taken from his own library and borrowed books from friends and associates, focuses especially on classical learning, contemporary theory (with many titles ranging from 1660 to the early 1700s), and Quakerism.[52]

In naming this sizeable volume *The Beehive*, Pastorius places himself— and by extension, his contribution to early American literary knowledge production—in conversation with the florilegium, a well-established genre in moral philosophy and classical learning in which authors collect particular types of knowledge, proverbs, or biblical and theological passages for intellectual and spiritual edification. These collections, like Pastorius's itself, require painstaking reading and intertextual reference. The compiler of such wisdom—as the honeybee with blossoms—was relied upon to select and bring forth the most fruitful and relevant choices from the raw material available. As Michael P. Brown notes in his examination of transatlantic book culture, the bee trope "was used as a storehouse of art and information," one that was especially "power[ful] for devout settlers."[53] Such was the value of this knowledge and labor that Pastorius insists that his sons John Samuel and Henry keep this volume and his other writings

> to themselves & their heirs forever, and not to part with them for anything in this World, but rather to add thereunto some of their own etc Because the price of Wisdom is above Rubies, and cannot be valued with the precious Onyx or Sapphire: and to get understanding is rather to be chosen than Silver and Gold.
>
> (1)

Clearly his heirs took up his call, given that Pastorius's death is recorded by one of his kin in one of the three volumes. Pastorius is not alone among colonists placing value in such a repository of knowledge; indeed, Whitfield requested funds to furnish Thomas Mayhew, Jr., son of the Martha's Vineyard missionary, with books, "for young S[c]holars in *New England* are very poor in books, as he is in extreme want."[54]

For Pastorius the bee is an emblem of the exceptionalism of settlers versed in the European intellectual and Christian traditions. According to Erben, Pastorius "privately preserved the elitist notions of the European intelligentsia in the erudite aphorisms of his commonplace books, while publicly advancing the civic and educational life of the fledgling German-American settlement."[55] Appointed by William Penn (and soon reelected by his constituents) as the first mayor of Germantown, Pastorius was an authority figure and cultural icon, positioned as Margo M. Lambert notes, as "the legal bridge between the newly autonomous Germantown and the larger Anglo society."[56] The structure of the volume suggests that Pastorius did not necessarily envision the ultimate scope of his text from the outset, as there are several title pages and indexes as his collection expands. Initially, his goal was to promote learning with apian-like industry: "Let us spend more of our Time in Study than Idleness; and slip not one hour, wherein we should neglect or lose any Opportunity to lay up something in store for the future" (7). As that future manifests, however, Pastorius reinforces the original vision, taking stock of the first hundred pages: "Francis Daniel Pastorius' Hive or his Bee-stock, containing above two thousand little Honey-combs, begun in the year 1696 and continued for his children" (105). In the process, the goal remains to share productive work in his gathering and writing: "But as Bees do not extract the Venom of herbs, do not ye wring out the dregs" of his book (51).

In addition to his meticulous collection of excerpts, Pastorius on multiple occasions throughout the volume comments upon his own experience as a beekeeper, an effort that brings him a great deal of joy and some pain. Poem 126 emphasizes the fact that beekeeping constitutes recreation for Pastorius: "A little time of leisure Full of the greatest Pleasure / A mouth full of fresh air among my Bees, the sweetest of all Birds, man ever sees" (155). Whereas Shakespeare's Ariel imagines life as a bee seeking leisure, Pastorius demonstrates that human beekeepers may view their interactions with the hive as restorative and enjoyable. Indeed, his marginalia to the poem eschews beekeeping for profit, reading "honey before Money" (155). Part of the pleasure in keeping an apiary derives from the fact that Pastorius views bees as kindred spirits in their appreciation of virtue: "Brave harmless Creatures, which do always sing zum, zum! Never bite but sometimes sting / Unchaste & wanton ones and Drunkards too" (155). For Pastorius, the pain of beekeeping is not physical, but rather emotional and based upon the bond he has with his hives. In Poem 132, he laments losing three of his four hives to "Frost's violence" over the winter, recalling the horror of seeing his "poor innocents ... slain ... each in her own crany. Oh! What misery! That you so soon must dye" (156). It is not lost to Pastorius that he founded Germantown on the feast day of the patron saint of beekeepers Bernard of Clairvaux. In a speech to the settlement on August 20, 1715, the 32nd anniversary of Germantown's founding, Pastorius noted that the day was special because it is "Dedicated by the Papists to their St. Bernhard, and being the Anniversary Feast of our happy arrival in this province" (190).

Like Wood before him, Pastorius also uses the symbol of the drone to criticize those colonists who fail in their contribution to society; indeed, for Pastorius, the figure of the drone is meant to spur others into action in pursuing their faith. In his poem, "An Alarum to the Wise and Foolish Virgins," Pastorius urges young Quakers to prepare for the coming judgment: "Rise from your Bed, / Heave up your head, / Redemption's very near" (135). He also, however, has a warning for those who fail to act:

> But foolish ones,
> As idle Drones,
> Spend theirs in Slothfulness;

Yet dare presume,
That they will come
To Heaven neretheless.

(135)

When Pastorius calls out the drone-like individuals among the youth, he indicates that they do not get a pass on industrious good works and the pursuit of virtue merely due to their age. He uses this bee image to emphasize the importance of communal responsibility among all settlers.

Pastorius's *The Beehive* also reveals his penchant for emblem poems, especially those that use natural imagery to convey a moral. He defines the emblem in the following way: "metaphorically (or in figurative manner of Speech) Emblems signify Mottos or Devices, which point at a mystical or hidden sense of pictures. Emblems are Speaking Pictures, containing general Documents, Instructions, and Morals" (75). In particular, he frequently references Francis Quarles's *Emblems* (1635) in his volume. So prominent is the genre to his commonplace book that Pastorius opens with this guiding image, writing, "I am a Bee, (no Drone) tho' without Sting, / Here you may see, what Honey-combs I bring" (4). The original poem that follows takes its inspiration from English verse emblems like Quarles's:

To painful Bees some do prefer (I spie)
The idle Drone, the Wasp & Butterflie;
Alas! To these they give more leave to thrive
Than Honey-Birds, who labour for the Hive:
And when perhaps once gotten into Grace,
By Gnats again are beaten out of Place
So Men of good Desert
Must often stand apart.

(4)

Pastorius views himself in his extensive reading and gathering as superior to the type of dronish settlers he critiques, and he thus sees himself as responsible for civilizing his settlement. His bee emblem promotes the apian work ethic while criticizing the social norms that allow less industrious members of a colony to thrive with political or cultural favor.

Along with the literary definition of the form, Pastorius also connects the emblem to needlework, noting "for whatsoever is laid in, embroidered, checkered or engraved of many pieces of diverse colours may properly be called an Emblem" (75). It is not the only time he connects verse and cloth work. In an apology for a miscellany of 40 poems, he explains to the reader, "I would not have him think, that I made them with a purpose to be accounted a Poet, ... but only to try whether Versifying and Turning of the Spooling-wheel were things compatible at the same time" (133). Appreciated as a polymath with an extensive knowledge of the law, Pastorius demonstrates his abilities in this statement about simultaneous poetry writing and spooling. Even while engaged in domestic labor, he also occupied himself with intellectual pursuits. Challenging himself to unify his hands and mind would speak to the colonial ideal. As Stephen Innes has indicated, social norms in the colonies involved "an ethic that enjoined men and women to labor incessantly with their hands as well as their wits" and encouraged them "to eschew the temptations of worldliness," which, in the process, "made psychological demands of a wholly new order."[57]

Pastorius similarly encouraged the young Quaker Elizabeth Hill of Philadelphia to join the tasks of writing and needlework in order to serve God. Hill's 11-year old sister Hannah had suffered an untimely death, and the account of her faith in her final reflections had been published in *A Legacy for Children, Being Some of the Last Expressions and Sayings of Hannah Hill* (1717). Hannah's final recorded words to Elizabeth were, "Dear Sister! my desires are, that thou mayest Fear God; be Dutifull to thy Parents, Love Truth; Keep to Meetings, and be an Example of Plainness."[58] Elizabeth had sent a copy of the published book to Pastorius, who wrote that he "read it over thrice a day," but sent it back to her having written two poems in the volume for her comfort, both of which he transcribes in *The Beehive*. One of the poems assures Elizabeth of the state of Hannah's soul: "Hereafter wearing that bright Crown, / In Heaven for all faithfull-ones, / Laid up" (198). As a contrast to Hannah's state, he reiterates his oft-employed drone image to signify the damnation of those who failed to live up to Hannah's example: "whenas both Wasps and Drones / Lake-ward are going, when they die" (198). In the second poem, Pastorius instructs Elizabeth to take up her sister's writing:

> Dear Betty! Then succeed in Sister Hannah's stead,
> The holy Scriptures oft, with other good books read:
> Delight in Needlework, Delight likewise to write,
> And Letters full of Sense (as she did,) do indite.
>
> (198)

In one line, Pastorius unifies the purpose of needlework and writing, in that both allow the embroiderer/writer to "reap great Profit to our minds" (198). Pastorius indicates that if Elizabeth can avoid the fate of the drone and embrace the dual purposes of sewing and writing, then she would be "the most Accomplished Maid in Philadelphia" (198).

Pastorius's bolstering of Elizabeth Hill as a burgeoning writer is not an exceptional moment in *The Beehive*, but rather part of a larger pattern where he encourages young women to read and write poetry for spiritual and intellectual edification. Jane Fenn (later Hoskens) was servant to Chief Justice David Lloyd. By Fenn's own account, after speaking in her first meeting with the Society of Friends in Chester, David Lloyd and his wife approached her and said, "this young woman is or will be a preacher, they were both tendered, and it was fixed in their minds, that they were to take me under their care, and nurse me for the Lord's service."[59] When in 1718 Fenn sent Pastorius some of her poetry, he was overwhelmingly supportive. In the copied transcription of Pastorius's response to Fenn's writing, he says that even though one of her lines "wants some feet," lacking consistent meter, he emphasizes the fact of "the Matter being Sound" (199). He calls her a Poetess who has the potential to be "as *famous* Sappho was" (199). Fenn, who was English, had defied her family because she felt called by God to go settle in the colonies. Rescued from debtor's prison by Quakers once she arrived in Pennsylvania, Fenn would go on to become a respected member of the Society of Friends and a traveling preacher who would eventually write *The Life and Spiritual Sufferings of That Faithful Servant of Christ, Jane Hoskens, a Public Preacher among the People Called Quakers* (1771). Pastorius remained one of the early supporters of her work. Not only did he refer in his letter to biblical precedents of virtuous women, such as the Virgin Mary and Deborah, but he also nurtured her aspirations by heralding a strong tradition of women writers who hailed from the British Isles. Specifically, he referred to Jane Grey, Anne Askew, Mary Wroth, Katherine Philips, Margaret Cavendish, Mary Sidney Herbert, Elizabeth Carew, Mary Morpeth, and Mary Mollineux as "these Nine Muses of Great Britain" to whom he would "add the Tenth, sprung up in New England, viz. Anne Bradstreet" (199).[60] Pastorius not only references the name of Bradstreet's published volume of poetry but also seemingly takes up the challenge in her poem "The Four Seasons of the Yeare," where she writes, "Now swarmes the busie buzzing hony Bee. / Whose praise deserves a page, from more then me."[61] While Fenn Hoskens would not go on to become a poet, she did come to be an important writer and preacher; her *The Life and Spiritual Sufferings* was the first autobiography of a Quaker woman in America.

What is clear from Fenn Hoskens's text is that her service to God involved a community of woman working for a common cause. In her account, she travels with a woman companion on each of her preaching missions—Elizabeth Lewis, Abigail Bowles, Rebecca Minshall, and Susannah Brown—to various locations on the Atlantic coast from New York to Nantucket, to North Carolina, as well as to Barbados. Her life's work was part of a larger Quaker social organization that J. Hector St. John Crèvecoeur would describe as similar to the early settlers' hive-like swarming:

> Sometimes they have emigrated like bees, in regular and connected swarms. Some of the Friends (by which word I always mean the

people called Quakers) fond of a contemplative life, yearly visit the several congregations which this society has formed throughout the continent.... They are generally good preachers, friendly censors, checking vice wherever they find it predominating ... by thus travelling they unavoidably gather the most necessary observations concerning the various situations of particular districts, their soils, their produce, their navigable rivers, the price of land, &c.[62]

Prominently respected as a farmer and beekeeper who took as much joy in his hives as Pastorius did (though with greater knowledge of bee husbandry), Crèvecoeur views the Society of Friends as earnest in their commitment to their faith. That being said, he also appreciates the pragmatism of their "regular and connected swarms," which provide them with valuable knowledge on where to buy excellent farming land to found new settlements, such as *New Garden* in North Carolina, which had been purchased by a group of Nantucket Quakers in 1766.

At first glance, Pastorius's imagery in *The Beehive* might appear to reiterate the early colonial uses of the swarm. That being said, Pastorius also extends his apian metaphor in significant ways. While he relies upon the European tradition of the florilegium, he also distinguishes his *Beehive* by using it to demonstrate the cultural ethics and mores particular to colonial society. Central to Pastorius's vision is a valorization of relentless labor even among those of high status. In the commonplace book, Pastorius chronicles his balance of intellectual, political, legal, and domestic responsibilities. And yet, his aim in this instructive manual for his children and heirs does not focus on self-promotion. On the contrary, Pastorius seeks to demonstrate that his unceasing labor is consistent with that of many colonists, both German and English alike. Pastorius, like David and Grace Lloyd, understands that women are essential contributors to the work of the colonial hive. As the next section demonstrates, by the late eighteenth century, women in the colonies would be expected to embody the perpetual labor and personal sacrifice of the worker bee. Like Jane Fenn, they would engage in a hive-like model of collective work in the name of God and their colonies. Nonetheless, there would also be a strict hierarchy that would recognize only the work of women of status and fail to acknowledge the forced and coerced labor of slaves and Native Americans.

The Spinning Bee: Women's Labor and Virtue in New England before the Revolution

The October 16, 1769 edition of Benjamin Edes and John Gill's *Boston Gazette* (at that time titled *The Boston Gazette and Country Journal*) compiled letters from four rural New England communities regarding a practice that was growing in popularity: the spinning bee. This event typically involved the gathering of women to engage in communal domestic labor for the benefit of their ministers, congregations, or those in need within their towns. Especially in rural settlements, events that harnessed the work of several community members would often take on the title of a bee—such as a barn-raising bee, a corn-shucking bee, and, later, a quilting bee—due to the hive-like and harmonious nature of the labor conducted. The notion that colonists, like the beehive, would work together for the common good was, by the eighteenth century, a well-entrenched value in colonial culture. One of the chief aims of the spinning bee was to embrace collective industry, such that participants often competed with one another or with other communities to provide the greatest quantity of spun cotton, wool, flax, or linen. On a practical level, this material was necessary for the weaving of cloth on a loom to produce clothing, bedding, and table linens. However, the spinning bee also offers insight into the economic and social standing of young white women in New England, linking their labor and virtue to the long-standing perceptions of the beehive's industry and exemplary moral character.

The first of the letters, from Taunton, Massachusetts, speaks to the dedicated and hard-working nature of the 20 "young blooming virgins … beauties of sixteen" present at the bee.[63] According to the letter, the girls assembled at the Liscome household in Taunton "for a Spinning Match: (or what is call'd in the Country a Bee)" for a period of 12 hours, by the end of which they had each spun approximately 3 to 4 yards of cotton or linen yarn. This contributor does not simply praise the young women for their charity, but also for the virtues that distinguished the New Englanders from those of the European tradition. A poem on the spinning bee reflects on how the girls' upstanding conduct bodes well for the colonies:

> In ancient Times, a sacred Writer said,
> The Man who finds a virtuous Maid,
> That Rubies one with her could not Compare;
> Such was the Value of the virtuous Fair.
> Rouse then, ye fair, your Fingers to employ,
> 'Twas Hellen wrought the Fate of ancient Troy:
> New England's Daughters their Frugality,
> In Spite of all, will make us Blest and Free.

(713)

To the writer, these "beauties of sixteen" do not lack the physical allurements of Helen of Troy, but they exceed her in their virtue, which is far more valuable. In rousing their fingers at spinning for a common cause, the young women demonstrate a quality that speaks to the moral fiber of New England. Like Pastorius, who asserted that "the price of wisdom is above Rubies," the Taunton contributor uses rubies' value as a metric by which to measure women's virtue. Both of these colonial reflections on the bee promote character over material gain. Also implicit in the poem is the hope inspired by a generation that "will make us Blest and Free"—raised in the colonies to respect collective labor for the benefit of their community.

Yet just because the women at a spinning bee work tirelessly for others' benefit does not mean that the praise showered upon them for the act cannot be quantified. As Laurel Thatcher Ulrich notes, it is common among newspaper stories of the era to list the precise quantities produced at spinning bees, and she speculates that the practice was driven by both "Puritan inheritance" and "a larger consumption-driven and politically reinforced shift toward rationalized production," which was also witnessed in women's diaries as well: "these diarists measured their days, not in coffee spoons, but in knots and skeins."[64] Just as Pastorius had encouraged less than a century earlier, women colonists were uniting the practices of needlework and writing in their diaries. According to the same issue of *The Boston Gazette*, in Northborough, Massachusetts, 44 women organized an unconventional spinning bee in which they conducted the work in their respective homes, but gathered at Reverend Peter Whitney's house at a planned date and time to present

> the Fruit of their Labor and Industry, upon computing it was found that they had brought 70 Fourteen Knotted Skeins of Linnen, 94 Seven Knotted Skeins of Tow [a heavy weight linen], and 83 Seven Knotted Skeins and 4 Knots of Cotton amounting to 2,223 Knots.
>
> (713)

In addition to spinning yarn, the women also contributed finished woven material, including a linen sheet and two towels. Whereas weaving had previously been a male occupation for generations, young women of this generation had gained the training and skills to make it a widespread domestic task where they shared equipment and resources among their neighbors. As Ulrich notes, "of the 19,276,043 yards of cloth made in New England in 1810 and recorded in the federal census of that year, only 4% was produced in 'manufactories,'" meaning that the other 96% was woven in homes, primarily by women.[65] Calculating the sums of spinning bee contributions allows the communities to claim bragging rights for the work of their women. In Northborough, the contributor writes,

> it is presum'd that this Act of Generosity, much exceeds what any other People have done for their Minister, in this Way, that we have heard of: especially will it be thought so, when the *smallness* of the place, the *fewness* of its Numbers; that this was Spun at their *own Houses*, and out of their own *Materials*, are considered.
>
> (713)

That such praise of industry is commonplace in newspapers seems to offer a challenge to inspire women in other communities to try to best the neighboring towns in what they contribute.

Growing, raising, or purchasing the raw material required to spin yarn to make cloth had become increasingly important but also more challenging and politically vexed given the state of British legislation imposed on the colonies. Moreover, these political circumstances help to account for why there is such an emphasis in the *Boston Gazette* on women's choice of refreshment at these events. The Townshend Acts of 1767 "consisted of a series of taxes on goods imported into the American colonies, [and] a reorganized Board of Customs Commissioners stationed in Boston to collect the taxes and enforce other revenue measures."[66] According to T.H. Breen, 1769, the year of the *Boston Gazette* edition on spinning bees, was a watershed moment in colonial and British relations, in that "an imperial dispute triggered by parliamentary taxes on imported goods encouraged middling sorts of people who generally had little impact on the shape of the political culture to participate in the affairs of the day."[67] Indeed, directly under the banner head of the same edition of *The Boston Gazette* was a report of merchants deemed traitors to the colonies in "A List of the Names of those who have Audaciously counteracted the UNITED SENTIMENTS of the Body of Merchants throughout North America by importing British Goods contrary to the agreement" (713). The Townshend Acts had placed the taxes on tea that would in four years erupt in the Boston Tea Party, an event that would also be prominently covered in the same publication. Nevertheless, by 1769, especially in New England, drinking tea was viewed by many as a capitulation to unreasonable British demands. The Taunton writer notes, "It is to be observed that the whole of the young Ladies refused the repast of the pernicious Plant Bohea" (713). Indeed, Bohea tea, which was imported by the East India Company and popular in England and the colonies, would be the variety of tea plunged into Boston Harbor as an act of resistance to the British policy of "taxation without representation." Another spinning bee letter similarly speaks not only to the alternatives to tea drinking but also to the values demonstrated in making that choice. In Berwick, Maine, the participants: "as true Daughters of Liberty ... made their breakfast upon Rye Coffee." Within these entries, the spinning bee demonstrates the centrality of women's labor to colonial politics and hopes for independence. The Lexington writer, anticipating critique, warns,

> If any should be inclin'd to treat such Assemblies [spinning bees] or the Publication of them, with a Contemptuous Sneer ... Such Persons would do well first to consider what would become of one of our (so much boasted) Manufactures, on which we pretend the Welfare of our Country is so much depending, if those of the fair Sex should refuse to lay their 'hands to the Spindle,' or be unwilling to 'hold the Distaff.'
> (713)

In this formulation, women's collective labor, like that of the worker bees, is essential not only to survival but also to separation from the parent colony: England. Whereas at the inception of the colonial project Mather believed the profit of the worker bee was a righteous and divinely ordained reward, the writers on the spinning bee emphasize commitment to the collective political vision of the colonial hive over that of personal gain.

Also significant in the praise of the Northborough ladies' labor is not only the hours of work but also the personal sacrifice of resource commodities required to make these contributions. In the case of young women at spinning bees, the raw material they used to spin did not just represent their family's generosity, but often the bee-participant's own financial stability. By the 1760s, many families sought to translate their daughters' spinning knowledge into more advanced and equipment-heavy weaving technique on the loom so that they might weave much of their own trousseaus, thereby sparing the family of the cost of purchasing cloth. For instance, after Samuel Lane, a tanner in New Hampshire, spent 42% of his eldest daughter's £1,298 portion on textiles, he offered his subsequent daughters education in how to weave.[68] "In some households," argues Ulrich, "daughters achieved almost total control of their own earnings in the years before marriage."[69] The expectation is that young women will engage in relentless labor not only for the benefit of the colonies, but also to secure their future domestic lives. As a result, social norms regarding the work of women of middling and upper classes diverges in the colonies from those in England. The women of the New England spinning bee proudly represent their labor as distinct from the idleness of English gentlewomen. That being said, the colonial spinner will not work herself to death as the bee does. Unlike Shakespeare's Caliban, these women are afforded leisure and reward for their efforts; indeed, their current labor assures their future success.

Given the financial independence that spinning and weaving could offer to young women, it might seem surprising that they would compete with one another in gifting significant shares of their marital portion. That being said, the spinning bee also provided an opportunity for young women to demonstrate their marriageability publicly. In Taunton, following the bee, the young ladies were "properly regaled" and "waited upon by a Number of young Gentlemen, and spent the Evening in Mirth and Innocent Amusement" (713). Similarly, in Berwick, "the young Gentlemen the Sons of Liberty, waited upon the young Ladies and treated them with Cake and other Necessaries" as refreshment for their labor (713). And thus, the young women's generosity is also inscribed within a cultural imperative to demonstrate their skill, commitment to the colonies, and fitness to lead a household. The bee also provided an opportunity for the young women of the town to come into their own in demonstrating their gratitude and support of their local ministers. Within eight years of the Berwick spinning bee, Reverend Foster and his family would need to relocate because the town was not capable of paying his salary.[70]

The spinning bee was not merely orchestrated to meet the Foster's clothing needs before winter but also to offer a public gesture of support of the reverend's ministry.

As with the earliest colonial uses of the apian metaphor, there were also unacknowledged racial dynamics in the colonists' practice of the working bee. For instance, Taunton, the southeastern Massachusetts town that promoted the gentility of its "young blooming virgins" at the spinning bee, is also the same community that during King Philip's War had prominently displayed the severed head of Pocasset sachem Weetamoo on a pole "within sight of a prisoner-of-war camp" in order to drive her people to lament and despair.[71] Weetamoo was a powerful military leader who left her English-sympathizing second husband to form an alliance with the Naragansetts and ally with Wampanoags to fight the colonists.

In addition to suppressing local Indigenous populations, colonists also began to rely on the labor of black slaves. While there does not appear to be evidence of slave labor contributing to the specific spinning bees referenced in *The Boston Gazette*—in Massachusetts during the late eighteenth century "rural slavery was rare"—it would become an integral yet unrecognized aspect of later bees.[72] By the mid-nineteenth century, the spinning bee had all but disappeared due to changing market and political conditions. But with the decline of the spinning bee, came the rise of the quilting bee, an event that retained the value of white women's communal labor, but refocused its energies on solidifying social connections and demonstrating the material wealth of the gentry in showpiece quilts and petticoats. Quilting bees required a great deal of preparation of rooms and refreshment, equipment, and maintenance of other household duties for the host and her quilting guests. Marla R. Miller observes that among the elite "such labor was supplied by enslaved and hired laborers," noting that one such quilting bee attended by Elizabeth Porter Phelps in Hadley, Massachusetts could not have happened without the labor of her slaves Peg, Phillis, and Roseanna, along with the slaves of each of the other five attendees of the bee.[73] The legacy of the sewing bee then, while reliant on the work and sacrifice of slave and Indigenous women, neither attends to their needs nor acknowledges their own alternative acts and metaphors of collectivity or resistance to their captors and colonists.

Eventually, the language of "the bee" would extend far beyond the original colonists' uses to be coopted by white supremacists and members of the Ku Klux Klan. In the late nineteenth and early twentieth centuries, perpetrators of mob violence adopted the label "the lynching bee" in order to give the appearance of propriety to their unlawful acts of racialized terror.[74] As historian Randy Finley argues, "the use of the word *bee* almost suggest[s] that the brutal realities of lynching had been incorporated comfortably into scenes of domesticity."[75] Reaching its

frenzied height in the 1890s but extending well into the twentieth century, the lynching bee became a ritualized performance of torture, including beatings, castration, mutilation, lynching, and burning of black
community members for the gratification of a primarily white public.[76]
Far from the virtuous and organized nature of the earlier hive split or
spinning bee metaphors, the lynching bee represented a macabre inver-
sion of the communal industry of the hive. The lynching bee produces
neither honey nor provisions; it only produces terror and injustice.

The trajectory of the hive metaphor in America thus often demonstrates a will to dominate, of an impulse to identify only white and privileged people as those who could claim likeness with this sovereign colony.
Moreover, the so-called bee participants acted with an impunity witnessed from the inception of racial tensions in America with Hubbard's
praise of the colonial army "as busie as Bees in a Hive" when fighting the
Naragansetts during King Philip's War. According to Mitchell G. Hall's
letter to the U.S. Attorney General written in Cordele, Georgia in 1921,
the same "man who it was said tied the victim to the buggy and drove
it out to the lynching bee was appointed a Superior Court Judge."[77]
These accounts—over two centuries apart—demonstrate the potential
outcome of apian unification, regardless of whether or not that collective
labor is directed toward virtuous action.

Shakespeare's representation of race, servitude, and torture in *The
Tempest* interestingly extended to later racist iterations in the lynching
bee. William Ellery Leonard's poem "The Lynching Bee" (1920) narrates
a tale of a black man murdered by "twelve true men" in "ghostly cones"
(Klan hoods), "(The sort who pay their bills, and cast their votes, / Or
file to jury boxes on hot afternoons)."[78] This victim, however, has not
been offered due process or a jury of his peers. Leonard describes the
man's comportment on the way to an execution that will include geld-
ing, lynching, and burning: "Like Caliban he shuffles, only bigger."[79]
The same Shakespearean character threatened with the "pinch more
stinging / Than the bees that made" the honeycomb becomes an emblem
for the subject of the lynching bee.[80] Neither Caliban nor the tortured
man accede to their white tormentors, but both live under the constant
threat of their bees' sting. From the New World swarm to Pastorius's
Beehive to the Revolutionary spinning bee to the Jim Crow-era lynching bee, the apian metaphor sustains its centrality in American myth-
making even as the exclusion of racialized others continues to unfurl in
violence and torture.

Notes

1 Modern scientific designation of the western honeybee is *Apis mellifera*, and
  of the stingless honeybee of Mesoamerica is *Melipona beecheii*, but in order
  to remain consistent with seventeenth-century knowledge and nomenclature, I will refer to them as the honeybee and the stingless bee, respectively.

2 Eva Crane, *The World History of Beekeeping and Honey Hunting* (New York: Routledge, 1999). According to Crane, on December 5, 1621, the Council of the Virginia Company wrote a letter to the Governor of Virginia indicating that he had included beehives in the shipment of the *Bona Nova, Hopewell, Darling,* and *Discovery,* which would have reached the Virginia coast in early 1622 (358–9).

3 Crane, *World History,* 303.

4 *A Relation of Maryland* (London, 1635), 58–9.

5 Karen Ordahl Kupperman, "The Beehive as a Model for Colonial Design," in *America in European Consciousness, 1493–1750,* ed. Karen Ordahl Kupperman (Chapel Hill: University of North Carolina Press, 1995), 272–94.

6 Thomas Morton, *New English Canaan: Or New Canaan Containing an Abstract of New England* (n. p., 1632), 14.

7 Tammy Horn, *Bees in America: How the Honey Bee Shaped a Nation* (Lexington, KY: University Press Kentucky, 2005), 5.

8 Elisha R. Potter, Jr. *The Early History of the Narragansett: With an Appendix of Original Documents* (Providence, RI: Marshall, Brown, and Co., 1835), 158.

9 Luca Codignola, "The Holy See and the Conversion of the Indians in French and British North America, 1486–1750," in *America in European Consciousness, 1493–1750,* 195.

10 See Elizabeth Cook-Lynn, *A Separate Country: Postcoloniality and American Indian Nations* (Lubbock, TX: Texas Tech University Press, 2012), 8–9.

11 William Cronon, *Changes in the Land: Indians, Colonists, and the Ecology of New England* (New York: Hill and Wang, 1983), 33.

12 See R.H. Cherry, "Insects in the Mythology of Native Americans," *American Entomologist* 39 (1993): 16–22.

13 John White, *Fireflies and Gadfly,* 1585–93, painting, British Museum, London, Museum Number: 1906,0509.1.67.

14 Louis Armand, *New Voyages to North-America.* Vol. 1 (London, 1703), 242.

15 *New Englands First Fruits: In Respect, First of the Conversion of some, Conviction of Divers, Preparation of Sundry of the Indians* (London, 1643), 20.

16 See Neal Salisbury, "Native People and European Settlers in Eastern North America, 1600–1783," in *The Cambridge History of the Native Peoples of the Americas,* vol. I, part I, ed. Bruce G. Trigger and Wilcomb E. Washburn (New York: Cambridge University Press, 1996), 399–460. See also Karen L. Marrero, "Women at a Crossroads: Trade, Mobility, and Power in Early French America and Detroit," in *Women in Early America,* ed. Thomas A. Foster (New York: New York University Press, 2015), 159–85.

17 Codignola, "The Holy See," 196–7.

18 Bruce R. Dain, *A Hideous Monster of the Mind: American Race Theory in the Early Republic* (Cambridge, MA: Harvard University Press, 2002), 7.

19 See Kim Tallbear, *Native American DNA: Tribal Belonging and the False Promise of Genetic Science* (Minneapolis: University of Minnesota Press, 2013), esp. 31–66.

20 Mary Hawkesworth and Lisa Disch, "Feminist Theory: Transforming the Known World," in *The Oxford Handbook of Feminist Theory* (Oxford: Oxford University Press, 2016), 4.

21 *A Platform of Church Discipline* (Cambridge: 1649), 26.

22 For a discussion of the synod, see William Kellaway, *The New England Company, 1649–1776: Missionary Society to the American Indians* (Longmans: London, 1961), 6.

23 John Cotton, *God's Promise to His Plantation*, ed. Reiner Smolinski. *Electronic Texts in American Studies* 22 (1988): 9.

24 Cotton Mather, *Magnalia Christi Americana: Or, the Ecclesiastical History of New England, from its First Planting in the Year 1620*, vol. 1 (1702; repr., Hartford, CT: Silus Andrus & Son, 1820), 74.

25 Qtd. In Henry Whitfield, *The Light Appearing More and More Towards the Perfect Day* (London, 1651), 13.

26 Helen Vanderloop Manning, *Moshup's Footsteps: The Wampanoag Nation / The People of First Light* (Aquinnah, MA: Blue Cloud Across the Moon, 2001), 50.

27 William Hubbard, *A Narrative of the Troubles with the Indians in New England* (Boston, 1677), ii.

28 Hubbard, *A Narrative of the Troubles*, 4.

29 Chester P. Soliz, *The Historical Footprints of the Mashpee Wampanoag* (Sarasota, FL: Bardolph and Company, 2011), 36.

30 Soliz, *Historical Footprints*, 43.

31 Soliz, *Historical Footprints*, 56.

32 James V. Fenelon and Thomas D. Hall, "Revitalization and Indigenous Resistance to Globalization and Neoliberalism," *American Behavioral Scientist* 51, no. 2 (2008): 1882.

33 Wayne E. Lee, *Barbarians and Brothers: Anglo-American Warfare, 1500–1865* (Oxford: Oxford University Press, 2011), 132.

34 David J. Silverman, *Faith and Boundaries: Colonists, Christianity, and Community among the Wampanoag Indians of Martha's Vineyard, 1600–1871* (Cambridge: Cambridge University Press, 2005), 124.

35 Laura Arnold Leibman, ed., *Experience Mayhew's Indian Converts: A Cultural Edition* (Amherst: University of Massachusetts Press, 2008), 58.

36 Hubbard, *A Narrative of the Troubles*, 53.

37 William Wood, *New England's Prospect: A True, Lively, and Experimental Description of That Part of America* (London, 1634), 48, 47.

38 Qtd. Whitfield, *The Light Appearing*, sig. B2r.

39 Whitfield, *The Light Appearing*, 45.

40 Abraham Peirson, *Some Helps for the Indians: Shewing The How to Improve Their Natural Reason to Know the True God and the Christian Religion* (Cambridge, 1658), 37.

41 Daniel Gookin, *Historical Collections of the Indians in New England* (Boston: Massachusetts Historical Society, 1792), 195.

42 William Apess, *Eulogy on King Philip*, 2nd ed. (Boston, 1837), 7.

43 Apess, *Eulogy*, 10–1.

44 Apess, *Eulogy*, 6.

45 Charles Hamilton, ed. *Cry of the Thunderbird: The American Indian's Own Story* (Norman: University of Oklahoma Press, 1972), 129.

46 Soliz, *Historical Footprints*, 56.

47 Patrick M. Erben, ed., *The Francis Daniel Pastorius Reader: Writings by an Early American Polymath* (University Park, PA: Penn State University Press, 2019), 113.

48 Lyman W. Riley, "Books from the 'Beehive' Manuscript of Francis Daniel Pastorius," *Quaker History* 83, no. 2 (1994): 119.

49 See Garret Hendericks, Derick up de Graeff, and Francis Daniel Pastorius, *Quaker Protest Against Slavery*, 1688, Special Collections, MS 99 B-R, Bryn Mawr Library. http://triptych.brynmawr.edu.

50 Erben, *The Francis Daniel Pastorius Reader*, 17.

51 Francis Daniel Pastorius, *The Beehive*, 1696, Specials Collections, MS Codex 726, University of Pennsylvania Library. Fol. viii. http://dla.library.

upenn.edu. All quotations from this volume, unless otherwise indicated, will be cited in text from this edition.

52 For discussions of Pastorius' humor and his impact on colonial writing, see Anthony Grafton, "The Republic of Letters in the American Colonies: Francis Daniel Pastorius Makes a Notebook," *The American Historical Review* 117, no. 1 (2012): 1–39.

53 Michael P. Brown, *The Pilgrim and the Bee: Reading Rituals and Book Culture in Early New England* (Philadelphia: University of Pennsylvania Press, 2007), 33.

54 Whitfield, *The Light Appearing*, 29.

55 Patrick M. Erben, "'Honey-Combs' and 'Paper-Hives': Positioning Francis Daniel Pastorius's Manuscript Writings in Early Pennsylvania," *Early American Literture* 37, no. 2 (2012): 160.

56 Margo M. Lambert, "Mediation, Assimilation, and German Foundations in North America: Francis Daniel Pastorius as Cultural Broker," *Pennsylvania History: A Journal of Mid-Atlantic Studies* 84 (2017): 152.

57 Stephen Innes, *Creating the Commonwealth: The Economic Culture of Puritan New England* (New York: Norton, 1995), 125.

58 Hannah Hill, *A Legacy for Children, Being Some of the Last Expressions and Sayings of Hannah Hill* (Philadelphia, 1717), 19.

59 Jane Fenn Hoskens, *The Life and Spiritual Sufferings of that Faithful Servant of Christ Jane Hoskens, a Public Preacher among the People Called Quakers*, ed. Paul Royster, *Electronic Texts in American Studies* 24 (2007): 17.

60 In 1718, Pastorius gifted to the family's wet nurse Anne Martle a primer in which he had transcribed some English verse, saying of his gratitude to her: "not ignorant to feed newborn babes that cry; moreover to apply all useful things to those rest-wanting women" (200).

61 Anne Bradstreet, *The Tenth Muse Lately Sprung up in America* (London, 1650), 58.

62 J. Hector St. John Crèvecoeur, *Letters from an American Farmer*, ed. Ludwig Lewisohn (1782; repr., New York: Fox, Duffield and Co., 1904), 185.

63 C.B., "Oblige Your Constant Reader." *The Boston Gazette and Country Journal*, October 16, 1769. 713. https://www.masshist.org/dorr/volume/2/sequence/755. All references to C.B.'s column, which includes letters and contributions from Taunton, Northborough, and Lexington, Massachusetts, and Berwick, Maine will be cited in text.

64 Laurel Thatcher Ulrich, "Wheels, Looms, and the Gender Division of Labor in Eighteenth-Century New England," *The William and Mary Quarterly*, 55, no. 1 (January 1998): 19

65 Ulrich, "Wheels, Looms," 22.

66 Robert J. Chaffin, "The Townshend Acts Crisis, 1767–1770," in *A Companion to the American Revolution*, ed. Jack P. Greene and J.R. Pole (Malden, MA: Blackwell, 2000), 134.

67 T.H. Breen, *The Marketplace of Revolution: How Consumer Politics Shaped American Independence* (Oxford: Oxford University Press, 2004), 248.

68 Ulrich, "Wheels, Looms," 16.

69 Ulrich, "Wheels, Looms," 16. See also Carole Shammas, "How Self-Sufficient Was Early America?" *The Journal of Interdisciplinary History* 13 (1982): esp. 247–50.

70 Wendy Pirsig, "Rev. John Tompson (1740–1828) and the First Parish Parsonage," Old Berwick Historical Society, updated 2007, http://oldberwick.org/oldberwick/index.php?option=com_content&view=article&id=128&Itemid=129

71 Gina M. Martino-Truror, "'As Potent a Prince as Any Round About Her': Rethinking Weetamoo of the Pocasset and Native Female Leadership in Early America," *Journal of Women's History* 27, no. 3 (Fall 2015): 37.

72 Christopher Clark, *The Roots of Rural Capitalism: Western Massachusetts, 1780–1860* (Ithaca, NY: Cornell University Press, 1990), 38.

73 Marla R. Miller, *The Needle's Eye: Women and Work in the Age of Revolution* (Amherst: University of Massachusetts Press, 2006), 107.

74 The lynching bee could also be directed at white victims, as in the thwarted lynching bee of Colonel Sherburn in Mark Twain's *The Adventures of Huckleberry Finn* (1884), but the majority of victims were African American.

75 Randy Finley, "A Lynching State: Arkansas in the 1890s," in *Bullets and Fire: Lynching and Authority in Arkansas, 1850–1950,* ed. Guy Lancaster (Fayetteville: University of Arkansas Press, 2018), 69.

76 For a discussion of the lynching bee as tourist attraction, see Jessica Adams, *Wounds of Returning: Race, Memory, and Property on the Postslavery Plantation* (Chapel Hill: University of North Carolina Press, 2012), 87.

77 Mitchell G. Hall, "To the U.S. Attorney General," in *Lynching in America: A History in Documents*, ed. Christopher Waldrep (New York: New York University Press, 2006), 203.

78 William Ellery Leonard, *The Lynching Bee and Other Poems* (New York: B.W. Huebsch, 1920), 13.

79 Leonard, 13.

80 William Shakespeare, *The Tempest*, ed. Virginia Mason Vaughan and Alden T. Vaughan (London: Arden, 1999), 1.2.330-1.>

3 Stingless and Stinging
Native American Kinship

Despite the fact that the honeybee hive's ubiquity in America was initiated by the transportation and husbandry of the English, Native American and Mesoamerican societies were already intimately acquainted with bees of various sorts. The 4,000 species of bees native to North America are responsible for pollinating various plants and include varieties of bumble bees, squash bees, blueberry bees, carpenter bees, sweat bees, leafcutter bees, and the *Perdita* genus (the smallest of bee species, only found in North and Central America). Most indigenous bees are solitary or semi-social, meaning that they do not live in hives, do not have workers who give up their reproductive capacity in favor of a queen, and do not produce honey. Given these various social organizations, North American bees were unlikely to inspire exemplary comparisons for the English who wished to reinforce a "natural" hierarchy that placed themselves at the top. Native American societies, by contrast, would appreciate the variety of bees that they observed alighting upon familiar plants, particularly those that visited their fields. Women cultivators, in particular, would interact regularly with bees as many societies' agricultural methods involved intercropping of bee-pollinated and self-pollinated plants on the same plot. Historian Lisa Brooks sets the scene, for instance, of Pocasset sachem Weetamoo joining her kinswomen to check on their fields, noting that below their towering corn stalks, "squash vines would extend across the mounds, wide green leaves expanding to provide shade, blossoms beckoning to bees. From among the leaves, bean tendrils would spiral around the stalks, climbing toward sunflowers and sunchokes."[1] Weetamoo and her kin knew that their corn would not thrive long-term without the squash, legumes, root vegetables, and seeds that would work together to maintain the health of the soil and offer a nutritionally rich diet for their people. Native American and Mesoamerican agricultural systems were reliant on bee pollination long before the introduction of the European honeybee.

Although the English initiated the hive as a colonizing tool in North America, they also deployed the strategy in multiple locales across the globe. In the nineteenth century, W. E. Shuckard observed that the English consistently imported honeybee hives to new sites of conquest:

> This species has also been carried to India, to the Isle of Timor, and to northern, western, and southern Africa, in all which countries it is thoroughly naturalized, although they all possess indigenous species, which are quite as, or perhaps more largely, tributary to their inhabitants.[2]

The importation of the honeybee may have contributed to increased competition between pollinators, but in the early stages of colonization, the abundance of forage mitigated against decreased biodiversity among the native bees in these locations. The same cannot be said, however, for human inhabitants who were subject to both genocide and displacement. Nonetheless, in the twenty-first century, the legacy of the European beehive on native bees has followed the human toll of colonization with the increasingly prevalent endangered and extinct status of varieties of indigenous insects in North America and the British Commonwealth, more broadly. According to entomologist Robbin W. Thorp, for instance, the last specimen of the Franklin bumblebee was sighted in 2006 near the border of California and Oregon, designating the species as critically endangered or potentially extinct.[3]

Global transport of bees in this colonial context has also resulted in negative repercussions for European honeybees themselves. For instance, the Varroa destructor mite was first introduced to European honeybees when they were brought to Asia for pollination and apiary management. Whereas the Asian honeybee coevolved with the Varroa mite so that they did not pose a risk to it, the European honeybee, due to particularities of its nesting habits and gestational periods, was decimated by these parasites. Indeed, today the Varroa mite poses one of the most significant risks to honeybees in the West, in that it introduces a host of viruses and illnesses that not only disable and kill the hive but also act synergistically with pesticides and other chemicals to weaken individual bees and facilitate Colony Collapse Disorder (CCD). Taking inspiration from the honeybee importation of colonial Britain, commercial bee operations started in the 1920s in the United States to transport hundreds of hives to corporate or large-scale farms.[4] This practice, which was hailed as a great agricultural innovation that would expand crop and honey yields, has contributed dramatically to bees' precariousness in increased exposure to illness and parasites both in the home and host sites, thereby contributing to the current honeybee crisis. Ultimately, the European honeybee has had as much to lose in its prominent role in the English global colonial mission as indigenous bees did, even if the ramifications of its forced migration were not immediately apparent to beekeepers. These negative outcomes for insect societies offer a microcosm for the effects of colonization and corporate agriculture on human cultures.

The impact of the sovereign hive, as a centerpiece of the English expansionist enterprise, is an essential consideration in the history of North America. Best estimates based upon anthropological and historical findings put the human population of North America at the arrival of European colonizers between 5 and 8 million, and yet by the 1890 Census, only 250,000 Native Americans remained.[5] The various reasons for this population collapse include conscious programs of violence and genocide by Europeans, disease, shifts within the ecosystem, physical displacement, and other collateral effects of colonization. While Indigenous societies of the southeast and southwest, Canada, and the Caribbean had already witnessed the effects of European colonization, the Wampanoags of current-day coastal Massachusetts and the Narragansetts of Rhode Island were among the first to face the English colonial program in the northeast. How an Indigenous population responded to their own colonization and the imported colonies of bees, however, differed widely. In the sixteenth century, for instance, bees mediated some of the differences between Mesoamericans and Spanish *conquistadores*, in part, due to the recognizable social structure and uses of Central American bees.

There is a species of bee native to Mesoamerica that lives in a eusocial hive and produces honey not stored in combs, but in pots on the side of the nest: the stingless bee. Named Xunan Kab by the Maya, meaning Royal Lady Bee, the stingless bee and its honey has remained essential to the civilizations of Central America. According to entomologist José Javier Quezada-Euán, evidence of hive beekeeping in the Yucatan Peninsula dates to 1400 to 1900 years ago, along with artistic representations of the Mayan bee god *Ah-Mucen-Kab*, dating from 1200 A.D.[6] The *Codex Mendoza*—a sixteenth-century manuscript written in the Nahuatl language and Aztec pictograms appended with Spanish colonial explanatory notes—demonstrates the significance of the stingless hive in pre-contact Central America. The *Codex Mendoza* enumerates the honey pots various territories paid as tribute, offering insight into the prosperity of various provinces prior to colonization.[7] Spanish colonizers identified the differences in native Mesoamerican bee varieties and acknowledged the superiority of their honey. In his letter to Charles V in 1520, Hernán Cortés, who himself owned an apiary in Spain, told the king, "the only trade which the Indians have is in bee-hives, and our Procurators will bear to Your Highnesses specimens of the honey and the bee-hives that you may command them to be examined".[8] The eighteenth-century Jesuit Franciso Javier Clavigero identified six varieties of bees in Mexico,

> without stings, which make the honey "Estabentun," the clearest, sweetest, and most aromatic known. ... It was collected every two

months, but the November honey was the best, because it was made from a very sweet flower called "Estabentun," which blooms in September.[9]

While currently under threat by non-native insects, pesticides, and habitat loss, Xunan Kab continues to maintain an important role in the culture and agriculture of the Yucatán Peninsula. "Due to a myth in which both bees and humans share the same origin," according to historians Laura Elena Sotelo Santos and Carlos Alvarez Asomoza, contemporary beekeepers in the eastern Yucatan continue to refer to their apiaries as groups of "people."[10] This response to Xunan Kab as an essential species also damaged by the effects of colonization and industrial farming shares commonalities with many North American cultures' perceptions of the bee.

Contemporary Native American theory seeks to recognize the various ways in which each Indigenous society maintains its own polity, practices, and languages or dialects while also drawing upon commonalities in the effort to reclaim sovereignty. The shape and manner of Native sovereignty, however, differs from that of the English hive hierarchy. According to Mohawk scholar and activist Taiaiake Alfred, Indigenous formulations of sovereignty operate "within an intellectual framework of internal colonization" that recognizes the "*post facto* claim of European 'sovereignty'" as external to Native societies and imposed upon those cultures seeking to navigate a settler government.[11] As contemporary Crow Creek Sioux theorist Elizabeth Cook-Lynn indicates, the academy at large tends to be complacent in accepting the narrative that the land and rights of Native nations have been and always will be supplanted under settler colonialism (a sustained program reinforced by the colonizers' laws and economy that seeks to erase and disempower those who are Native to the land).[12] Indigeneity, as Cook-Lynn defines it, is an important concept that "seeks to reclaim whatever came before colonization and occupation" in order to provide a pushback against the so-called European right of conquest.[13] I would add that the historical tensions between the uses and representations of native and European bees offer an important contribution to the larger questions of indigeneity within contemporary scholarship and environmental activism.

This focus on indigeneity encourages engagement with various Native American cosmologies that differ significantly from European linear, chronological histories. As such, research methodology for uncovering these Indigenous perspectives necessarily differs from that of the early colonists due to cultural difference and corresponding disparities in their archives. Whereas the previous chapter outlines early printed books, manuscripts, and newspapers written or available in the colonies and England, this discussion of Native American responses to the hive involves different types of research. From Linda Tuhiwai Smith's perspective, for instance, there is a need for "contextualized research in an explicitly de-colonizing, political and international framework" that would "draw the attention of researchers away from their traditionally Western disci-plines towards indigenous visions, aspirations and aims."[14] The coloniz-ers' attempts at cultural erasure leave us with a less complete picture of, for instance, seventeenth-century Wampanoag regard for the honeybee. That being said, by tracing a number of sources in the oral tradition and transmission of Native American language and culture—including colonial printed materials translated into Native languages, nineteenth- and twentieth-century Native American writing about the oral tradition passed down by elders, anthropological records of Indigenous peoples, legal documents, phonograph recordings, and contemporary Native American scholarship and theory—it is possible to reconstruct how the European honeybee and native bees figured into early and sustained ex-periences of colonization. Such research requires rejecting the biases and assumptions of the colonial/settler writers and being attentive to the ways that various Native American voices and traditions speak to a dynamic set of views on changes to peoples, lands, and animals.

Prior to colonization, Native American societies were, for the most part, based upon models of egalitarianism, gender equity, and conciliar government that did not align with the English sovereign hive hierarchy. This chapter will recover the divergent views of bees among Indigenous societies of North and Central America. First, it will outline the ways in which several Native American cosmologies represent bees and other nonhuman beings, particularly when it comes to cultivation and use of nature. More specifically, lifeways—predominant social ethics about how to live properly—unify the connection between animate and inanimate forms of life. Second, the chapter will explore the physical and cultural significance of bees to southwestern and Mesoamerican Native popula-tions, with an emphasis on Hopi katsina songs. These important expres-sions of Hopi social norms and ethics emphasize two intertwined issues: the value of women's communal labor and insect contributions to human cultures. Finally, it will uncover the various responses eastern societies of America and Canada had to the invasion of the colonists and their sting-ing bees, focusing on their resistance to the hierarchy of the English and interesting linguistic links between the bee and women's diplomatic work. Native American and Mesoamerican cultural knowledge about bees, I argue, not only offers critical perspectives on various lifeways in the first century of contact but also represents distinct approaches to the Indige-nous sovereignty that continues to challenge settler colonialism.

Cosmology versus Ecology

A First Nations tale about how the honeybee got its sting indicates the degree to which Indigenous oral traditions integrated new, foreign, and potentially dangerous forms of life into a larger world view. The legend, which missionary Egerton Ryerson Young recorded in *Algonquin Indian Tales* (1904), is narrated by a Cree Christian convert named Mary who tells it to two children. The story highlights the fact that the bees did not always pose a physical threat to their people. Mary prides herself on being an excellent storyteller whose fluency in Cree and related dialects of the Algonquian language family allows her to expand her repertoire by conversing with the Native American travelers that she meets. It is unclear if Mary would have also had access to the Siouan language families (she does not speak English), but her tale about the bee sting appears to come from either the Osage People or the Omaha People of the Great Plains and Midwest, whose name for the Great Spirit was Wakonda or Wakontah. Young establishes in his earlier *By Canoe and Dog-Train among the Cree and Salteaux Indians* (1890) that the Sioux were frequently found in the Canadian territories inhabited by the Cree and that there were some among the different cultures who could communicate between them.[15] According to Mary,

> There was a time when the bees had no stings, and they were as harmless as the house flies. They were just as industrious as they are now, but they had any amount of trouble in keeping their honey from being stolen from them, for every creature loves it.[16]

The fact that the tale evokes a sympathetic response from the children Mary tells is unsurprising given the kinship bonds between human and nonhuman beings in the Cree tradition.

The corresponding origin story for honeybees' stings frames the insects not as unwelcome invaders (like the English colonists that brought them), but rather as industrious workers who were deserving of a blessing from the Great Spirit. According to the narrative, bees were on the brink of destruction due to honey theft when "word was circulated that Wakonda, the strong spirit—the one who sent the mosquitoes—was coming around on a tour," and "the bees resolved to apply to him for help."[17] According to Mary, the bees provided an offering of honey, and Wakonda "listened to their tales of sorrow and woe. He was indignant when he heard of the numbers of their enemies, and of the persistency of their attacks upon such industrious little creatures."[18] Wakonda told the bees to return on an appointed day, and they were so delighted that they told their insect "cousins" that Wakonda would help them:

> When the appointed time arrived, the bees were on hand—and so were the wasps, hornets, and bumblebees. Wakonda welcomed the bees most kindly, but was a little suspicious about their visitors, and

he asked some sharp questions. But the bees were in such good humor about the help that was coming that they did not refer to the bad habits of their cousins at all. Then Wakonda made a speech to the bees, and told them how much he loved them for their industrious habits which he wished all creatures had. He praised them for the fact that, instead of idly wasting the summer days, they used them in gathering up food for the long, cold winter. Then he proceeded to give them the terrible stings which they have had ever since, and as the wasps and hornets claimed to be their cousins, Wakonda was good-natured enough to give them the same sort of weapons.[19]

What is striking about Wakonda's careful judgment is that it emphasizes bees' productive and communal work ethic without ever mentioning the hierarchy that was so important to the English. If anything, the hornets, wasps, and bumblebees who were native to this land and were demonstrably less deserving in Wakonda's eyes are the beneficiaries of honeybees' combined hard work and good will toward their kin. This is not a tale of domination, but rather one of shared benefits and protection. Mary's tale also conveys a lesson in the value of preserving life. The little girl who has been stung by a honeybee responds, "I am glad they have their stings or I suppose we should never have any honey."[20] The Cree children do not reject the bee and its sting; rather, they appreciate that her gifts come from the Great Spirit that guides them all.

The legend of Wakonda and the sting expounds upon the intrinsic value placed upon life within a Siouan cultural ethic that values communal work and care. Even though the honeybee is used by the English as a tool of colonization that could be viewed as a threat, the Sioux integrate the bees' natural benefits and risks into their understanding of Wakonda's blessings. This story, however, should not be mistaken as an example of the Bernardian ecology explored in Chapter 1. The undeniable worth that St. Bernard, Topsell, and early modern writers placed upon nonhuman creatures was a minority opinion in England. Remarkable where it occurs, Bernardian ecology offers a divergent view from the predominant English doctrine of instrumentality witnessed in the colonists' views of bees and nature in Chapter 2. Chief Standing Bear of the Lakota (Siouan language family) noted the destructiveness of the colonizers' mindset, arguing in the twentieth century,

I know of no species of plant, bird, or animal that were exterminated until the coming of the white man.... The white men considered natural animal life just as he did the natural man life upon this continent, as "pests." Plants which the Indian found beneficial were also "pests." There is no word in the Lakota vocabulary with the English meaning of this word.[21]

In contrast with European views of pests, the various Native American cosmologies that promote inherent and irrevocable status of all living beings develop prior to and independently from European traditions.

Although many Indigenous cultures share a preservationist world view, it is not applied uniformly across cultures, as there are several different means of conveying the relationship between animate and inanimate life. The prayer of contemporary Wampanoag elder Chester P. Soliz, for instance, speaks to a multi-generational approach to nature:

> Creator, ... food crops are used to make ethanol for automobile fuel or fed to animals so that we might dine on expensive meats... . Teach us to see the earth as our ancestors did, who respected the land which gave them life... . Teach us as your children to learn to live within the earth's limits, taking only what we need from your land and preserve the earth for those who come after us, that they may not curse us in their time.[22]

Soliz's commitment to future generations' access to resources demonstrates a lifeway that emphasizes personal and cultural restraint in the use of nature. We need not interpret Soliz's prayer as emerging out of a monolithic stereotype of what anthropologists have historically called the "ecological Indian."[23] According to Jane Mt. Pleasant, a Tuscarora agricultural scientist, this formulation of Indigenous peoples is both reductionist and lacking in context: "it requires a Western paradigm for evaluating human use of natural resources, without any reference to or knowledge of Indigenous peoples' standards or criteria for how *they* evaluate their environmental interactions."[24] Analysis of Native American and Mesoamerican approaches toward nonhuman nature requires an engagement with the varied perspectives of specific cultural norms and practices as well as an acknowledgment that, even within a society or language family, there are diverse perspectives.

Despite the need for cultural specificity, there are at least two important and broadly defined concepts that emerge out of the various Native American epistemologies of the bee. First, stories, songs, and other forms of ritual and social exchange demonstrate the unique and varied roles of native and European bees. Second, methods of cultivation and land management, which inevitably enlist bees alongside human labor, especially that of women's work, highlight the significance of these pollinators to larger Native American lifeways. Moreover, as I will demonstrate, these concepts register differently to the Mayas, the Aztecs, the Hopis, the Wyandottes, the Wampanoags, and the Narragansetts.

Uncovering how the honeybee disrupted precolonial Native American life and culture remains one aspect of indigeneity that has not yet been thoroughly explored. Within this larger program of revitalizing of what came before colonization is a concept that Palyku legal scholar Ambelin

Kwaymullina terms "narrative sovereignty."[25] According to Kwaymullina, this theory stands as governing policy established between Indigenous nations to negotiate differences between distinct countries/nations and the kinship networks within them. What is at stake for Indigenous nations employing narrative sovereignty is a logical challenge to the injustice and violence of colonization and continued human rights violations by the settler government. Kwaymullina outlines the contrast between international law and indigenous law:

> So within the Eurocentric international legal tradition there is no reason either to ask or answer the question *what are your stories?* But within the Aboriginal legal tradition, there is no nationhood— and hence no relations between nations—without the narratives that found the relationship between peoples and Country.[26]

The oral traditions of Native nations offer varied guiding stories of creation, ancestors, and relationships between living beings. Mary's tale about the stings of imported and naturalized honeybees and native wasps and hornets is just one example of narrative sovereignty that establishes a generative relationship between insects, humans, and the Great Spirit Wakonda. And while there was some record of conflict between the Crees and the Sioux during Mary's life, her tale also demonstrates another important example of narrative sovereignty at work—evidence of shared cultural values about the bee and its honey.

In North and Central America, the commonalities and distinctions in the stories of narrative sovereignty are most visible in relation to an essential agricultural and cultural product: corn. Growing corn was a practice that originated in Mexico and Central America but spread through many Indigenous societies. Both a dietary staple and a culturally significant icon, corn was central to the landscape and culture of pre-contact America. Indeed, corn was a crop that was unique to the Americas and did not individually rely upon the pollination of bees, and yet it did necessitate specialized expertise in its cultivation. The Three Sisters of maize, beans, and squash grew out of the Mesoamerican *milpa* system of intercropped agriculture, combining self-pollinated corn and beans with bee-pollinated squash in order to preserve long-term use of the fields and to diversify nutrient sources for the people. Alicia Re Cruz discusses the long-held tradition of corn and bees in Yucatán, commenting on Santa Cecilia Rancho in the Maya village of Chan Kom: "it exemplifies the symbiotic relations among the three principle agricultural activities in Chan Kom: *milpa*, cattle, bees. Maize provides subsistence for people, cattle, and bees."[27] Farmers, according to Re Cruz, view the nearby Mayan ruins as solidifying the cultural continuity in the relationship between maize and bees, as they view "the *alux,* a character in Yucatec Maya oral tradition, [who] owns the forest and *milpas*; he lives

'where our ancestors lived.'"[28] From even the early period of corn's cultivation, bees have remained essential not just to pollination of *milpa*, but
also to the culture and social value surrounding this system.

In North America, the symbiotic relationship between corn and bees
spread along with the knowledge of this essential crop's cultivation. Mt.
Pleasant combines cultural knowledge and contemporary experiments
to correct the false narrative that Native American agricultural practice required cultivators to abandon fallow corn fields frequently. She
demonstrates that the labor intensive practice of conservation tillage
(as opposed to the English plowing system) preserved the land: "Maize,
even though it is a cereal grain, thrives in roughly prepared fields that
have not been worked with a plow."[29] The added benefits of this tillage
practiced, for instance, by the Haudenosaunees—known by French colonists as the Iroquois and by the English as the League of Five Nations—
is that in addition to retaining soil nutrients, it also allowed farmers a
degree of precision in planting complementary crops on the same fields.
After all, if clearing fields required greater preparation, then intercropping would put that labor to good use. In the multiple societies that
employed this agricultural method, the cultivating labor of women was
inextricably linked to and reliant upon the pollinating labor of squash
bees who buzzed their blossoms at precisely the right frequency to secure
the long-term success of the three crops on the field. Notice of these solitary squash bees may not appear in the historical record, but it would
be unavoidable to Native farmers. Because the male bees exhaust themselves in the pursuit of mates at blossoms in the morning, by noon they
fall asleep within the flower and can often be seen dozing.

Corn was more than merely an agricultural enterprise; it was also a
symbol of social bonds, communal labor, and shared knowledge. Such
was the significance of corn in mediating the relationships and commonalities between societies of the American continents that Roxane
Dunbar-Ortiz calls this "network of Indigenous nations, peoples of the
corn."[30] According to Theda Perdue and Michael D. Green, Cherokees
tell the story of Selu,

> the first woman, whose name is the word Cherokees use for both
> corn and woman. Selu produced corn from her body, giving it birth,
> and with it assured that her descendents would always have food.
> The blending of these two ideas, cultivation and birth, production
> and reproduction, encapsulated the essence of womanhood.[31]

The connection between corn and procreation was not lost on the early
English colonists either, such as Roger Williams, the founder of Providence plantation, who wrote,

> their women constantly beat all their corne with hand: they plant
> it, dresse it, gather it, barne it, beat it, and take as much paines as

any people in the world, which labour is questionless one cause of their extraordinary ease of childbirth.[32]

Although the English would only frame their own labor as apian, it is clear that Native American women already embodied a model of industrious work for the good of the community.

The next two sections outline the impact of narrative sovereignty in some of the various stories and relationships between Native American and Mesoamerican cultures and indigenous bees and honeybees. Whereas Mayas and Aztecs had direct access to stingless bees that produced valuable honey, the Hopi people of current-day Arizona have a rich and complex relationship with the European honeybee—one that has transformed productively over the centuries. By contrast, the Wyandottes who ranged in territory from current-day Kansas through Toronto and the Wampanoags, Narragansetts, and Pocassets have demonstrated what begins early in the process of colonization as an adversarial relationship with the English sovereign hive and all that it represents to them. At the same time, the honeybee also shares in these cultures some unexpected connections with Algonquian women's labor, literacy, and diplomacy.

The Bee in Mesoamerican and Southwestern Nations

The project of narrative sovereignty allows us to reconsider both the founding and continued relationships between pollinators and peoples in North and Central America, so that we need not view the honeybee as an invasive species that should be eradicated in order to decolonize land and agricultural practice. As Eve Tuck and K. Wayne Yang have influentially argued, "decolonization is accountable to Indigenous sovereignty and futurity"; it is not a metaphor designed to "rescue settler futurity."[33] In the work of Indigenous beekeeping and its radical relationality between beings, we can witness a practice of decolonization rooted in the notion that bees are for many Native cultures "guarantors of life."[34] For instance, the stingless bee was of the greatest importance to the Mayas after corn. It provided them not only with honey but also was an essential ingredient in *balche*, a fermented drink used in Mayan ceremonies venerating the supreme deity *Hachäkyum*.[35] Since the colonial period, the human bonds forged over corn and honey also figure prominently in political organizing and social activism. According to June Nash, bees are central to the Maya's "myths that recount how the collective strength of these small creatures overcom[e] formidable opposition," so that their nests become a symbol of the resistance movement that "exemplifies Mayan ideals of governance, with each unit acting autonomously in accord with a collective organization."[36] As I will demonstrate, the bee and its honey remains a symbol for challenging the colonial regime not only in Central America but also in the American Southwest, a region with a complex and fascinating relationship with the introduced honey-bee hive.

Aztecs also integrated honey into their diet and spiritual life, often combining it with corn. For instance, *The Florentine Codex* (1569), a Spanish and Nahuatl account of life and culture commissioned by Franciscan missionary Fray Bernardino de Sahagún, discusses the variety of tamales offered in the marketplace; the vendor "sells tamales of maize softened in wood ashes, the water of tamales, tamales of maize softened in lime ... unleavened tamales, honey tamales, beeswax tamales, tamales with grains of maize, ... maize flower tamales."[37] This description of the tamale vendor's offerings derives from Book X on the Mexica people, and it addresses the various ways in which bee products were used alongside nixtamalized corn prior to Spanish contact. Cortés's letter about the market in Tlatelolco mentions, "They sell bees-honey and wax, and honey made from corn stalks, which is as sweet and syrup-like as that of sugar" (*miel de maiz* is a type of corn syrup).[38] Cortés's statement about Xunan Kab's products are meant to represent this site of conquest as recognizable to his king and patron. Nonetheless, he writes this letter in the aftermath of slaughtering thousands of people in Cholula. By this logic, the Mesoamerican bees are worth fostering based upon the quality of what they produce, but humans who could interfere with Cortés's ambitions are dispensable.

Still, a derisive European view of Xunan Kab would eventually emerge and extend into the twentieth century. Although exceptional Mesoamerican honey was valued by Cortés, the bees that produce it have since been regarded as more "primitively organized" than the European honeybee.[39] The Nobel-prize winning Austrian-German scientist Karl von Frisch, for instance, discusses the "racial differences" between the Mesoamerican stingless bee and the European honeybee.[40] In the twentieth century, this part-Jewish, Nazi-funded entomologist deployed a specifically racialized stereotype that privileged the European bees as superior beings:

> Only the honeybees, with their graduated system of arousal, proportioned to the profitability of the food sources and combined with a precise description of the location of the various goals, are able to instruct the unoccupied waiting mass so that the labor supply maintains the proper relation to the demands of the several situations to be exploited. A corresponding accomplishment on the part of the meliponines [stingless bees] is not known and in view of their methods is hardly to be expected.[41]

From his perspective, Mesoamerican bees lack the communication, refinement, and industry of the European honeybee. It is easy to recognize the supremacist biases about stereotypical perceptions of the insect and

the human population in such a statement. Five centuries after colonizers arrived in Central America, von Frisch's entomological rhetoric is
less charitable than that of the initial colonizers and thus helps to reinforce the Maya's reclamation of Xunan Kab as a symbol of resistance.

Among various nations of the Americas, it is clear that the bee and
its hive structure played an essential role for Indigenous culture and agriculture of the southwestern region of current-day America. Historian
Ramon A. Gutiérrez outlines the way in which corn and honey together
form a foundation for ritual, practice, and identity among the Pueblo
Indians. Acomas placed a great deal of value in the Corn Mother, Ia-
tiku, who conveyed her power to the Medicine Man in the following
way: "into a corn cob she blew her breath along with a few drops of
honey to symbolize all plant food."[42] The significance of a specific lifeway regarding bees in the southwest cannot be overstated. Although the
Acomas integrated honey into their ceremonies, this practice appears
not to predate colonization, as the stingless bee of Mesoamerica only
inhabits lands as far north as southern Sonora (a state on the current-day
U.S.-Mexico border).[43] The precise timing of the honeybee introduction
to the American Southwest is unknown, but it could range from the
sixteenth century to 1652.[44] Still, its effects can be witnessed in the enduring status of this insect across multiple cultures in the region.

Some Native nations of the southwest, as I will demonstrate, integrated bees' honey into their lifeways (much as the Sioux of the Great
Plains had done) while simultaneously rejecting the will of those colonists who imported the hive. In particular, the Hopi have long respected
the virtues of the bee and the pollinator not only to their own survival
but also to the balance of nature as well. Hopi origins begin with *Máa-
saw*, and according to Hopi elder Emory Sekaquaptewa and scholar
Dorothy K. Washburn, the people emerged from *atkya* ("from down
below"), "a metaphorical reference to the southwest direction" of Mesoamerica, a place where beekeeping and honey hunting had been established for centuries.[45] The Hopi speak a dialect of the Uto-Aztecan
language family, which is spoken from the Great Basin through Mexico
and further south in Central America.[46] The cultural ethics of the Hopi
are rooted in a corn lifeway that is reciprocity based and focuses on
tutavo or "moral imperatives" of shared work and cultivation.[47] Significantly, the Hopi tradition integrated both corn and honey into one
of their grinding songs: "Oh, for a heart as pure as pollen on corn blossoms, / And for a life as sweet as honey gathered from the flowers, / May
I do good, as Corn has done good for my people."[48] In this example, the
product of the hive stands as a cultural binding agent, linking the Hopi
not only to the nutritive value of their food but also to its human and
nonhuman social functions.

The corn lifeway highlights the cultural significance of women's labor to the Hopi. Like the Wampanoags and Haudenosaunees, the Hopi

relied on intercropping of many plants in their corn fields, including watermelons and muskmelons, which required the pollination of native bees and, later, honeybees. Early visual representation of Hopi intercropping can be witnessed in the kiva murals at Kawaika-a. According to Watson Smith, one particular mural that was likely painted in the early days of Spanish contact (though the Hopis had occupied the land since at least the thirteenth century), "Test 4, Room 4, Front Wall Design 7 (fig. 76, a), is a very graceful and delicately executed bouquet of growing plants intermingled with conventionalized corn ears."[49] According to elder Edmund Nequatewa, a Hopi origin story explains that when the people emerged from *atkya* and divided into their separate clans, "the Hopi took the shortest ear of corn and also squash and beans" for cultivation.[50] This method of intercropping had proven successful for generations of Hopi women whose expertise is readily apparent in their success cultivating crops in a desert region. The anthropologist Jesse Walter Fewkes places the connection between corn and women's labor in both practical and cultural terms:

> A failure of this crop means starvation, and maize is far from a spontaneous growth in those desert sands. Hence the elaborate nature of the appeals to the supernatural beings which control this function. This great ceremony is naturally of special concern to women, the providers. The corn is the mother, the corn goddess the patron deity of women; the women are chiefs in this their special ceremonial.[51]

However, cultivating, harvesting, and drying corn constitute merely the initial steps women must take, as the preparation of corn flour for cooking is another multi-step and labor-intensive process:

> They also have several hand stones, which are rubbed against grinding stones. The woman crushes the hard kernels of corn, and grinds it, kneeling before the bin in which the stone is set. Repeatedly as the meal becomes finer she spreads it over the grinding stone with her hand and grinds it again. Twice she moves it to a finer stone, and grinds until it has attained the consistency of powder.[52]

This work is conducted in the home but engaged in communally with women of multiple generations of a family.

One of the most important means by which the Hopi convey their cultural values is through katsina songs, which are performed both communally and individually while working. The songs are learned in community gatherings and ask katsinas, or ancestors who return to the land as life-sustaining rain, to bless them. Sekaquaptewa and Washburn describe the arrival of the katsinas as a "(gift burden)—they are gifts that symbolize the prosperity, fulfillment, long life, etc. that are rewards for the constant burden of living according to the moral imperatives that underpin the Hopi lifeway."[53] Many katsina songs focus on women's work and virtue, often making a connection especially between young women and insects. One katsina song, for instance, expresses the expectation that "butterfly maidens (Hopi girls) learn our song"; in other words, they must be instructed in the protocols of communal work, noting, "When a girl visits a home not her own / She ought to be seen (singing) and grinding corn."[54] Another observes the celebratory dancing that happens among the people when "the yellow butterflies will go along adorning their faces with the pollen from the corn blossom maidens."[55]

By the nineteenth century, many Hopi katsina songs focused specifically on the value of insect pollination not only for human life but also as a metaphor for humans who strive to live according to shared social values and ethics. One katsina song recorded on wax cylinder by Natalie Curtis in 1903 but translated in the twenty-first century includes the following lines about pollinating labor:

> Among the evening primrose maidens,
> The yellowjackets will be repeatedly nurturing them.
> (Vocables.)
> [We] will go along thundering toward your planted fields
> All day long.
> (Vocables.)
> [We] will go moving along as rain toward your planted fields
> All day long.[56]

This katsina song recognizes the work of the yellowjacket—a black and yellow striped social wasp often confused with the honeybee—as nurturing the flowers in a continual and cyclical way. The song is sung from the perspective of the ancestors who will ensure the success of the crops by bringing rain. They approve of the yellowjackets' nurturing of the flowers and acknowledge that this nonhuman labor is an essential precursor to the rain that they bring. In their commentary in *Hopi Katsina Songs*, Sekaquaptewa, Kenneth C. Hill, and Washburn note that calling the evening primroses maidens "metaphorically likens them to young girls that are growing in the beauty of their capacity to make life. The pollination process is described as 'nurturing offspring repeatedly' (*tiitiwungwinta*, from *tihu* 'child' [-*ti*-] and *wúngwinta* 'be raising, nurturing, making grow.')"[57] Within the various Hopi katsina songs, the pollinating labor of the yellowjacket, the butterfly, and the honeybee are valued as much as the women who cultivate, harvest, and prepare the food.

Honeybees, moreover, have proven essential to preserving the cultural history and memory of the Hopi people. Fewkes recorded songs of various Native American societies on wax cylinders, doing so among the

Hopi in 1891.[58] The Hopi people singing traditional katsina songs in their language on Fewkes's phonograph joined an ancient tradition with a very new technology that had been introduced by Thomas Edison in 1888.[59] These early cylinders were made of beeswax and ceresin (a fossil fuel-derived wax) mixed with the additive stearine.[60] Undoubtedly, Edison's choice of beeswax in the phonograph cylinders derives from its natural uses as a conduit of vibrations and thus of sound. A significant component of honeybee communication involves the workers' contact with their wax honeycomb, which allows them to sense and interpret the frequencies emitted by their sisters. Wax production is a laborious task that requires bees to excrete flakes from their abdomens, masticate, and thus heat them with their mandibles, and then shape them into the uniform and interlocking hexagonal rows that represent their incubating chamber, birth place, honey and pollen storage facility, and dance floor for communicating about the location and quality of food sources. Edison's company formed this carefully guarded product of bees' labor into a tool used by the American anthropologist. The result of this effort unifies the perfectly industrious work of both the hive that made the wax and pollinated the crops as well as the Hopi women who sustained these fields for the subsistence and cultural enrichment of their communities while singing these very songs. Among the many wax cylinder recordings that appear in *Hopi Katsina Songs*, none were translated and transcribed within their own time. Without these beeswax phonograph recordings, these specific katsina songs about insect pollination and women's work could have been lost to history. Sekaquaptewa, Hill, and Washburn's impressive transcription and translation of early twentieth-century wax cylinder recordings of Hopi katsina songs help to convey the moral imperatives of Hopi ancestors who have now themselves become the katsinas. And thus, it is the combined work of the honeybee and contemporary Hopi language keepers that enable the Hopi to retain these messages from their ancestors about shared work between humans and insects in nurturing their crops. This decolonial work, moreover, offers a path toward both Indigenous and apian futurity.

Murals and songs demonstrate the ways in which the Hopi benefitted from and valued the honeybee. While they welcomed the bee, however, the Hopi ultimately rejected the Spanish colonizers and the Catholicism they attempted to impose upon them. According to Nequatewa, when the Hopi separated clans, one of the brothers was the Bahana, otherwise known as the white man. It was prophesied that this figure would be their savior, so "when the Spaniards came [in 1540], the Hopi thought that they were the ones they were looking for—their white brother, the Bahana, their savior."[61] This is why, at least initially, the Hopi allowed the Spanish to build a mission at Shung-opovi. The Hopi later realized, however, that the Spanish white men did not observe a lifeway that they could follow. The priest proceeded to destroy their sacred items, criticize the katsinas, and enslave the Hopi, punishing anyone who followed their own cultural practices over the church's teachings. The initial Hopi response was to take their observance of their cultural rituals underground, praying secretly. It was only when the Hopi discovered in 1680 that the priests in all of the Hopi missions were raping girls of between 13 and 14 years of age that their leaders coordinated an attack that would happen on the fourth day after their communal consultation and prayer offerings.[62] The Hopi representative resolved to face the priest without weapons. When the priest stabbed him with his sword, the Hopi man gave the signal. According to Nequatewa, the Hopi warriors dragged the priest outside, constructed a tripod of the beams that the priest had forced them to fell to construct the rafters of the mission, and "they hung him on the beams, kindled a fire and burned him."[63] The threat to Hopi girls—the butterfly maidens, primrose maidens, and corn maidens of their katsina songs—represented the precipitating event for the Hopi's rebellion against the priest. Far from representing the Bahana, the Spanish priests, as the Hopis discovered, were tearing away at their long-established moral imperatives. The colonizers were not the fulfillment of their prophecy after all.

For the Hopi, the honeybee was welcomed into their lifeway as a figure that offered service and nourishment, just as the native yellowjackets and butterflies had done. Nonetheless, the Spanish missionaries, who brought the hive, were viewed as destructive and thus were conquered by the Hopis. Indeed, the Spanish would not return to retaliate against the Hopis for two decades following the execution of the priest.[64] Significantly, the colonizers brought their hive to the New World because of dictates about the purity of beeswax rather than tallow candles on the altar for mass. As Donald Brand indicates, to the missionaries, "the greatest reason for introducing the European bee was the fact that the Roman Catholic Church placed mystic and spiritual value on the candle made of white beeswax."[65] To the Spanish, then, the bees' wax was a symbol for casting what they perceived as the light of Christ onto the "heathens" of the New World. Yet, the Hopi provide a powerful reminder that the Eurocentric symbol of Catholic purity did not take hold. Neither the Hopi people nor their co-constitutive uses of the bees' wax were eliminated. The Hopi activation of beeswax cylinders as archives of knowledge still maintain an assertion of cultural identity and sovereignty that the Spanish could not supplant. To the Hopis, then, it is the flaming body of the rapist priest that offers them their source of purgative fire. The honeybee, like its native sister Xunan Kab to the south, did not symbolize the incursion of the Spanish, but rather the return of the Hopi lifeway and the combined labors of the women and lady bees who nurtured their fields.

The Bee Sting in Eastern Nations

The Wyandottes of the United States and Canada had their own prediction of the white man that centered specifically around the imported honeybee. In contrast to the Hopi belief in a white brother savior of their own kind, the Wyandottes predicted that the incursion of foreign white men would be disastrous for their people. Moreover, the honeybee would be the harbinger of this destruction. The prophecy is recorded in Peter D. Clark's *Origin and Traditional History of the Wyandotts* (1870). In the year that Clark published his book, he was listed on the roll of Wyandottes taken by the Census and on file with the Kansas Office of Indian Affairs as "Clark, Peter D./35/male/Destitute [means]/Canada: Absent at the time that the treaty of 1855 was being carried out, never made choice to become a citizen, now wishes his and family's name placed on tribal list."[66] In the preface to his history, Clark frames his narrative as "a sketch as I had it from the lips of such [Wyandotte elders], and from some of the tribe who have since passed away."[67] Clark's account offers a prophecy of a decline in the quality of life for the Wyandottes, a precariousness that unfortunately bears out in the 1870 Census, as 56% of all recorded Wyandottes self-declared their condition as "destitute," with only two of the 521 tribal members listing an "easy" living condition. This story of the honeybee as a symbol of the devastation the colonizers would bring stands as one prominent example of how Native societies of the northeast viewed the proliferation of the colonizers and their foreign insect.

According to Clark, Wyandotte elders had prophesied a white man coming to take their lands, and the primary means of recognition of this event would require the peoples' careful observation of bees. Clark's is a multi-generational story about changes both to insects and the Wyandotte people:

> One summer day, whilst a party of these children of nature were sitting and lying around under shady trees on a bank of the stream, one of their old men suddenly exclaimed, "hun-haw! (expressive of regret) Look here!" said he pointing toward a strange looking insect that was buzzing around some wild flowers near them, "the white man," he continued "is not very far off, and this strange thing you see flying about here was brought over to this country by the white man from the other side of the 'big waters,' and who, before very long, will come and take the whole country from the red man. Like the white man, this strange thing represents the rapidly increasing and ever busy tribe it belongs to." The insect that attracted their attention was the honey bee. "Thus you see," resumed the Wyandott "that what has been foretold by our fathers is now about coming to pass." Presently the bee came buzzing around them, then darted into the forest.[68]

The Wyandotte elder clearly has a level of familiarity with the local bees to perceive the differences. He warns the children and points the honey-bee out to them so that they may recognize it as well. In contrast with the Osage or Omaha tale of the honeybee, where Wakonda praises the bee's relentless work and the honey it produces, the Wyandotte tale identifies the industry of the bee as part of its threat: "this strange thing represents the rapidly increasing and ever busy tribe it belong to." Clark's record of Wyandotte history demonstrates an adversarial view of the honeybee as a warning of the white man's impending incursion into their lands. And yet, among other societies of the northeast, the imported bee registers linguistically as a nuanced figure simultaneously foreign and familiar.

In Wampanoag, for instance, which is part of the family of eastern Algonquian languages, linguistic structure reflects cultural values. Jessie "Little Doe" Baird, a prominent Wampanoag linguist and Macarthur Fellow, has dedicated her career to the Wôpanâak Reclamation Project, which seeks to revitalize the once-dormant language of her people by educating and encouraging fluency in Wampanoag school children and their families. Baird's current linguistics work relies in part upon the limited documentary evidence left by seventeenth-century colonists. For instance, much of the remaining archive is found in the work of John Eliot, who studied the language in order to proselytize his Christian message. Steffi Dippold, in her analysis of Eliot's *The Indian Grammar Begun* (1666), discusses the significance of nouns in this language:

> Wampanoag ... splits the world into animate, living things and inanimate, nonliving things. This division is particularly import-ant for declension. Whereas Latin views objects as either male, fe-male, or neutral and creates the plural of these nouns by gender, ... Wampanoag puts nouns in the plural by giving animate words the ending "og" and inanimate ones the ending "ash." Thus a "man" in Wampanoag, clearly animate, is translated as "Wosketomp," which becomes "Wosketompaog" if we speak of a group of men.[69]

While assigning the same suffix to humans, animals, and insects by no means confers upon them equal status, it does, however, provide insight into the value of living, moving beings.[70] Indeed, Mohegans, a linguis-tically and geographically close and yet historically oppositional nation to the Wampanoags, avoids gender in both nouns and pronouns, thus "when Mohegans speak English, they generally in this respect follow their own idiom: a man will say concerning his wife, he sick, he gone away, &c."[71] In *Observations on the Language of the Muhhekaneew Indians* (1823), Jonathan Edwards notes, "Mohegans more carefully distinguish the natural relations of men to each other, than we do, or perhaps any other nation. For instance, there are separate words to dis-tinguish elder brother, younger brother, elder sister, younger sister."[72]

The primacy of living beings and social bonds in these Algonquian languages speaks to world views that are less dichotomous and hierarchical than those of the English invaders to their land.

Baird identifies the Wampanoag word for bee as *âhkeeôm8s* (pronounced ah-kee-o-moose), a word that would be introduced after the honeybee's arrival on their land.[73] Wampanoags' practice of naming animals and insects did tend to assign meaning based upon utility or defining characteristics. In the related Natick dialect of the Massachusett Indians, bee was translated similarly as *ohkeommoos* or "needle" based upon its tendency to provide a sting *chohkŭhhoo*.[74] These translations distinguish the honeybee from many of the non-stinging native bees. The extent to which this stinger would alter their culture and land could not have been fully appreciated by Native nations in their initial encounters with the English in the seventeenth century. It is unlikely, however, that even these references to needles and stings would have been interpreted as wholly negative given their larger cultural context.

The linguistic associations of *ohkeommoos* within Native dialects fosters a connection to women's labor, literacy, and diplomacy. For Eastern nations, the needle was an essential tool not only for making clothes, but also for producing wampum strings, belts, and girdles. Wampum have long been recognized as an essential means of communication and literacy. As Angela M. Haas indicates,

> Wampum serves as a sign technology that has been used to record hundreds of years of alliances within tribes, between tribes, and between the tribal governments and the colonial government.[75]

According to Wilbur R. Jacobs, moreover, "learned sachems could read wampum belts," and "the preservation and safeguarding of wampum belts was a sacred duty" entrusted to the sachem.[76] The making of wampum was a labor intensive process that involved crushing shells of varied colors to produce beads woven into a belt or girdle. A diarist named Dr. Alexander Hamilton describes witnessing the process in Albany in 1744: "They grind the beads to a shape upon a stone, and then with a well tempered needle dipt in wax and tallow, they drill a hole thro' each bead."[77] The waxed needle forging through the crushed shells is used to weave together a symbol of alliance that was often to be shared with a specific recipient. Far from simply a domestic object or a threatening sting, the needle is used to resolve conflict or preserve peace.

Weetamoo, for one, was busy during King Philip's War producing wampum to serve her diplomatic goals. Mary Rowlandson, a colonist captured in the sack of Lancaster during the war, describes in her narrative (published in 1682) being a servant to Weetamoo. Rowlandson, who did not understand Weetamoo's significance as a sachem or the cultural and political centrality of women in eastern Algonquian nations, dismisses her mistress as a "proud gossip."[78] Rowlandson criticizes Weetamoo's careful state of dress as an indication that she was "a severe and proud dame" because she powders her hair, paints her face, and wears a wampom garter and jewels.[79] Nevertheless, the sequence of Weetamoo's dressing is essential. Rowlandson notes of her daily routine: "When she had dressed herself, her work was to make girdles of wampum and beads."[80] As Hilary E. Wyss argues, Weetamoo's adornment in preparation for wampum making represents not just a diplomatic role but also a textual one: "Practices such as weaving, the creation of wampum belts, and even the marking of the body through tattooing and body painting all communicated through sign systems with their own internal 'grammar' and 'vocabulary,' forming alternative textualities rich in meaning."[81] Rowlandson's lack of literacy in Pocasset political expression leads her to misinterpret Weetamoo's needlework as merely practical labor. Strikingly, Rowlandson herself spent much of her time among the Pocasset, Sagamores, and Wampanoags wielding a needle, as many people offered her food, money, and trade items in exchange for her sewing of hats, shirts, and dresses. At the same time, Weetamoo engaged her wax-covered needle to send messages to other sachems, forming essential alliances in the war effort. To colonists like Rowlandson, the hive remained a symbol of God's approbation of the colonial mission. Meanwhile, to Weetamoo and her people, *âhkeeôm8s* would likely represent both the insect that visited the sunflowers in her intercropped fields and the needle by which she wove the political messages that would offer the best hope for securing victory against the English.

Nevertheless, the same English settlers who touted their colonial mission as a series of bee-like swarms actively sought to suppress the power of women in the Indigenous societies they encountered. As Andrea Smith argues,

> Just as the patriarchs rule the family, the elites of the nation-state rule their citizens. Consequently, when colonists first came to this land, they saw the necessity of instilling patriarchy in Native communities, because they realized that Indigenous peoples would not accept colonial domination

given the social structure of these nations pre-contact.[82] The enforcement of this Euro-centric gendered hierarchy, while initiated in the seventeenth century, would become codified during George Washington's presidency, as his administration "insisted that Native families be nuclear and patriarchal rather than extended and egalitarian, ... and that women's role be submissive rather than complementary to those of men."[83] A century after Weetamoo was beheaded outside of Taunton as a symbol of victory for the English in King Philip's War, the founding fathers would seek to bury her legacy as a sachem who could rally Native American political power and military force.

Despite the fact that Native women lost status in their dealings with the settlers, as these men would often only negotiate or treat with male figures in Indigenous cultures, the English persisted in the belief that they were improving women's lives. The colonist William Wood, for instance, remarks upon the various responsibilities of women in coastal societies—carrying back and cooking seafood, building and maintaining houses, and childrearing—as a point of contention within Native cultures:

> Since the *English* arrivall, comparison hath made [Native American women] miserable, for seeing the kind usage of the *English* to their wives, they doe as much condemne their husbands for unkindnesse, and commend the *English* for their love. As their husbands commending themselves for their wit in keeping their wives industrious, doe condemne the *English* for their folly in spoyling good working creatures.[84]

Wood seeks to reinforce the superiority of the English way of life as it translates to a new land, even among their own society's more marginalized individuals. While there was a significant disconnect between the types of duties expected of Indigenous and English women, there was an even more pronounced disparity in their status and power within their cultures. However, as Perdue argues, "ignorance did not keep Euro-Americans from incorporating Native women into their myths about nation building."[85]

Wood also undercuts the centrality of agriculture to coastal Indigenous societies by implying that "the Indians who are too lazie to catch fish" dabble in agriculture without great success because "such is the rankenesse of the ground that it must be sowne the first yeare with *Indian* corne."[86] From Wood's perspective, this crop is not as valuable for sustenance as it is for agricultural colonization. Indeed, he praises the success of English rye, barley, and oats, outlining further plans to propagate wheat. Wood then deems Indian corn, "a soaking grain" that merely prepares the soil to "be fit for to receive English seede."[87] And while the use of the word seed most directly signifies an agricultural image, it also retains other meanings. In the context of colonist John Winthrop's famous "City upon a Hill" sermon, the seed is a metaphor for the progeny of the original settlers, who will populate the plantations of New England with Christian virtue: "we, and our seed, / may live; by obeying [God's] / voice, and cleaving to him, / for he is our life, and / our prosperity."[88] Thus, when Wood praises the "naturall soyle," the virgin land of New England waiting for valuable "English seed," it is impossible to ignore the fact that women and corn were nearly synonymous in

Native cultures. As the Indian corn produces fertile soil for the English to seize, its cultivators (in the settler mindset) remained another natural resource for the plunder.[89] Like the Hopi before them, eastern Algonquian nations would have to contend with the threat of the colonizers' sexual violence as a further means of subordinating and terrorizing women and girls.

Whereas in the seventeenth century the Wampanoags shared their knowledge of native corn, soil, and cultivation, the English did not trade in kind the thousands of years of European knowledge about bee husbandry that allowed them to manage and profit from their imported pollinators. In fact, Wampanoags were at a distinct disadvantage when it came to the European practices of animal husbandry because they favored a system of game management over that of domestication. The knowledge of bees as a species and a commodity, then, factors into Indigenous exclusion and the English belief in their own right of conquest. It would be only a matter of decades before the honeybee went wild, swarming into trees in the forest, altering the landscape and providing an ever-present reminder of the English sting. Over 150 years after the settlement of Plymouth, the legacy of the honeybee was still felt in Native American societies. In fact, Thomas Jefferson's *Notes on the State of Virginia* (1781), remarks, "The bees have generally extended themselves into the country, a little in advance of the white settlers. The Indians therefore call them the white man's fly, and consider their approach as indicating the approach of the settlements of whites."[90] Nevertheless, the white man's fly represents far more than a harbinger of English invasion.

Although the English introduced the honeybee as a resource for fledgling colonies, several Native American nations have also included the beehive in their efforts at decolonization and revitalization of the land. Moreover, the work of the honeybee within this context is far more than merely symbolic. Decolonization constitutes genuine work toward repatriating land and reclaiming lifeways and languages for Native peoples. With the emphasis on Indigenous futurity in mind, decolonization does not necessitate re-creating pre-colonial lives and histories, but rather seeks to integrate available resources and technologies that will support and nourish the people while respecting time-honored lifeways.

Within the paradigm of decolonization and Indigenous futurity, the honeybee holds some redemptive possibilities among contemporary Native Americans not only of the southwest but also of the northeast. For instance, in Spring 2016 the Pine Ridge Oglala Lakota Reservation in South Dakota started its own apiary in a community garden, calling it the Buffalo Bee Project. Nick Hernandez of the Thunder Valley Food Sovereignty Program said of the plan, "with bees being a foundational insect to the production of a third of the world's food, we have taken the initiative to sponsor a hive so that they can help us regenerate a local food system."[91] And yet the Pine Ridge initiative is only one of many emerging programs to focus on honeybees as a source of pollination for local foods. In 2012 a sustainable farm in New Mexico, Hamaatsa, founded by Larry Littlebird of the Laguna/ Santo Domingo Pueblo people started its own apiary for the purposes of "restoring the ancestral lands of Hamaatsa and regenerating our local foodshed."[92] Moreover, some reservations that do not maintain their own hives still benefit by the income and pollination of bees by granting apiary licenses to local beekeepers; such is the case with the Gil and Salt River Reservations of the Pima Indians in Arizona.[93] Work to restore foodways and to revitalize the land simultaneously aims to improve community health that has suffered under the regime of settler colonialism. Sean Sherman in *The Sioux Chef's Indigenous Kitchen* (2017) and Luz Calvo and Catriona Rueda Esquibel in *Decolonize Your Diet: Plant-Based Mexican-American Recipes for Health and Healing* (2015) promote the use of local honey in a nutritional decolonized Sioux or Mesoamerican diet. Calvo and Esquiebel, in doing so, call upon Gloria Anzaldúa's notion of the borderlands: "While we are committed to reclaiming knowledge about our ancestral foods, including pre-contact food histories, we are not calling for a rejection of any [non-native] food ... we understand that all cultures are living and evolving."[94] Similarly, northeastern peoples, such as the Wampanoags and Abenakis, also routinely use honey for both its culinary and medicinal purposes.[95]

In an historical context, songs, stories, tools, and agricultural fields all speak to the diversity of North American and Mesoamerican perspectives on native bees and European honeybees. By the same token, bees in their many species have and continue to suffer under the conditions created by English colonization in their forced migrations across the globe. Efforts by the Sioux, the Acomas, the Hopis, and some Algonquian nations to embrace the honeybee while rejecting the practices of the colonizers have also translated into the modern day with Native peoples' decolonial work in revitalizing the land and the pollinators that help it to thrive. The honeybee in its flight and swarming does not observe borders and ownership of lands. Instead, the hive follows the nectar, and where it does, plants and animals have more robust food sources. Whereas the beehive came to North America as an inadvertent tool of colonization that itself was damaged in the process, Native Americans and Mesoamericans have worked with bees to restore and maintain the sovereignty of human and nonhuman beings.

Notes

1 Lisa Brooks, *Our Beloved Kin: A New History of King Philip's War* (New Haven, CT: Yale University Press, 2018), 33.
2 W. E. Shuckard, *British Bees: An Introduction to the Study of the Natural History and Economy of the Bees Indigenous to the British Isles* (London: Lovell Reeve and Co., 1866), 81.

3 Cited in Paul H. Williams and Juliet L. Osborne, "Bumblebee vulnerability and Conservation Worldwide," *Apidologie* 40, no. 3 (2009): 378.
4 Lucy W. Clausen, *Insect Fact and Folklore* (New York: Macmillan, 1954), 94.
5 Theda Perdue and Michael D. Green, *North American Indians: A Very Short Introduction* (Oxford: Oxford University Press, 2010), 16. See Roxanne Dunbar-Ortiz, *An Indigenous Peoples' History of the United States* (Boston, MA: Beacon Press, 2014), 42–4.
6 José Javier Quezada-Euán, *Stingless Bees of Mexico: The Biology, Management and Conservation of an Ancient Heritage* (Cham, CH: Springer, 2018), 244–9.
7 See *Codex Mendoza*, Bodleian Library, MS. Arch. Selden, University of Oxford. 36v. https://iiif.bodleian.ox.ac.uk/iiif/viewer.
8 Hernán Cortés, *Fernando Cortés: His Five Letters of Relation to the Emperor Charles V*, trans. Francis Augustus MacNutt, vol. 1 (Cleveland, OH: A. H. Clark, 1908), 145.
9 Cortés, *Fernando Cortés*, 145.
10 Laura Elena Sotelo Santos and Carlos Alvarez Asomoza, "The Maya Universe in a Pollen Pot: Native Stingless Bees in Pre-Columbian Mayan Art," in *Pot Pollen in Stingless Bee Melittology*, ed. Patricia Vit, Silvia R. M. Pedro, and David W. Roubik (Cham, CH: Springer, 2018), 300.
11 Taiaiake Alfred, "Sovereignty," in *Sovereignty Matters*, ed. Joanne Barker (Lincoln: University of Nebraska Press, 2005), 33–4.
12 Elizabeth Cook-Lynn, *A Separate Country: Postcoloniality and American Indian Nations* (Lubbock: Texas Tech University Press, 2012), 13.
13 Cook-Lynn, *A Separate Country*, 6.
14 Linda Tuhiwai Smith, *Decolonizing Methodologies: Research and Indigenous Peoples* (London: Zed Books, 1999), 344.
15 Egerton Ryerson Young, *By Canoe and Dog-Train Among the Cree and Salteaux Indians* (New York: Hunt and Eaton, 1890), Chapter 3.
16 Egerton Ryerson Young, *Algonquin Indian Tales* (New York: Eaton and Mains, 1904), 45.
17 Young, *Algonquin Indian Tales*, 46.
18 Young, *Algonquin Indian Tales*, 47.
19 Young, *Algonquin Indian Tales*, 47–8.
20 Young, *Algonquin Indian Tales*, 49.
21 Chief Standing Bear, "The Symbol of Extinction," qtd. in *Cry of the Thunderbird: The American Indian's Own Story*, ed. Charles Hamilton (Norman: University of Oklahoma Press, 1972), 214–5.
22 Chester P. Soliz, *The Historical Footprints of the Mashpee Wampanoag* (Sarasota: Bardolph and Company, 2011), 12.
23 See Douglas Buege, "Epistemic Responsibility and the Inuit of Canada's Eastern Arctic: An Ecofeminist Appraisal," in *Ecofeminism: Women, Culture, Nature*, ed. Karen J. Warren (Bloomington: Indiana University Press, 1997), 101.
24 Jane Mt. Pleasant, "A New Paradigm for Pre-Columbian Agriculture in North America," *Early American Studies* 13, no. 2 (2015): 378.
25 Ambelin Kwaymullina, "Aboriginal Nations, The Australian Nation-State and Indigenous International Legal Traditions," in *Indigenous Peoples as Subjects of International Law*, ed. Irene Watson (New York: Routledge, 2017), 12.
26 Kwaymullina, "Aboriginal Nations," 12.
27 Alicia Re Cruz, *The Two Milpas of Chan Kom: Scenarios of a Maya Village Life* (Albany, NY: SUNY Press, 1996), 66.
28 Re Cruz, *The Two Milpas*, 66.

29 Mt. Pleasant, "A New Paradigm," 393.
30 Dunbar-Ortiz, *An Indigenous Peoples' History*, 30.
31 Perdue and Green, *North American Indians*, 11.
32 Roger Williams, *A Key into the Language of America: Or an Help to the Language of the Natives in that Part of America Called New England* (London, 1643), 37.
33 Eve Tuck and K. Wayne Yang, "Decolonization is not a Metaphor," *Decolonization: Indigeneity, Education & Society* 1 (2012): 35, 3.
34 Quezada-Euán, *Stingless Bees of Mexico*, 244.
35 Eva Crane, *The World History of Beekeeping and Honey Hunting* (New York: Taylor and Francis, 1999), 289. See also, Suzanne Cook, *The Forest of the Lacandon Maya: An Ethnobotanical Guide* (Cham, CH: Springer, 2016), 28.
36 June Nash, "The Mayan Quest for Pluricultural Autonomy in Mexico and Guatemala," in *Indigenous Peoples and the Modern State*, ed. Duane Champagne, Karen Jo Torjesen, and Susan Steiner (New York: Alta Mira Press, 2005), 125.
37 Bernadino de Sahagún, *Florentine Codex: Book 10; The People*, trans. Charles E. Dibble and Arthur J. O. Anderson (Salt Lake City: University of Utah Press, 2012), 19. See Millie Gimmel, "An Ecocritical Evaluation of Book XI of the Florentine Codex," in *Early Modern Ecostudies*, ed. Ivo Kamps, Karen L. Raber and Thomas Hallock (New York: Palgrave Macmillan, 2008), 167–80.
38 Cortés, *His Five Letters*, 258.
39 Karl von Frisch, *The Dance Language and Orientation of Bees*, trans. Leigh E. Chadwick (Cambridge, MA: Harvard University Press, 1967), 306.
40 von Frisch, *The Dance*, 293.
41 von Frisch, *The Dance*, 313. See Tania Munz, *Dancing Bees: Karl von Frisch and the Discovery of the Honeybee Language* (Chicago, IL: University of Chicago Press, 2016).
42 Ramon A. Gutiérrez, *When Jesus Came, the Corn Mothers Went Away* (Stanford, CA: Stanford University Press, 1991), 6.
43 Donald Brand, "The Honey Bee in New Spain and Mexico," *Journal of Cultural Geography* 9 (1988): 73.
44 Brand notes that several scholars quote a single unsubstantiated line in the *Enciclopedia Universal Ilustrada Europeo-Americana* that suggests a sixteenth-century introduction, but definitive evidence of European bees' presence in Central America is not found until 1652 in the work of Father Bernabé Cobo (76–7).
45 Emory Sekaquaptewa and Dorothy Washburn, "As a Matter of Practice... Hopi Cosmology in Hopi Life: Some Considerations for Theory and Method in Southwestern Archaeology," *Time and Mind: The Journal of Archaeology, Consciousness and Culture* 2, no. 2 (2009): 197–8.
46 Sekaquaptewa and Washburn, "As a Matter of Practice," 198.
47 Sekaquaptewa and Washburn, "As a Matter of Practice," 202.
48 Qtd. in Gutiérrez, *When Jesus Came*, 16.
49 Watson Smith, *Kiva Mural Decorations at Awatovi and Kawaika-a With a Survey of Other Wall Paintings in the Pueblo Southwest* (Cambridge: Peabody Museum, 1952), 229. For an image of Test 4, Room 4, Front Wall Design 7 from the Peabody Museum at Harvard University, see Edna Glenn, "Exemplary Arts: Section C—Subject: Ceremony—Ancient and Contemporary Images," *Hopi Nation: Essays on Indigenous Art, Culture, History, and Law* 9 (2008): 77.

50 Edmund Nequatewa, *Truth of a Hopi: Stories Relating to the Origin, Myths, and Clan Histories of the Hopi* (1967, repr.; Flagstaff, AZ: Northland Publishing, 1993), 32.

51 Jesse Walter Fewkes, *The Tusayan Ritual: A Study of the Influence of Environment on Aboriginal Cults* (Washington, DC: Smithsonian, 1895), 696.

52 *Arizona State Teacher's College Bulletin*, 13, no. 2 (1937): 12

53 Sekaquaptewa and Washburn, "As a Matter of Practice," 204.

54 Sekaquaptewa and Washburn, "As a Matter of Practice," 206.

55 Emory Sekaquaptewa, Kenneth C. Hill, and Dorothy K. Washburn. *Hopi Katsina Songs* (Lincoln: University of Nebraska Press, 2015), 56.

56 Sekaquaptewa, Hill, and Washburn, *Hopi Katsina Songs*, 53.

57 Sekaquaptewa, Hill, and Washburn, *Hopi Katsina Songs*, 54. The Hopi have a traditional ceremony dedicated to fructification, the process by which a planted seed grows to bear fruit; see Jesse Walter Fewkes, *Sun Worship of the Hopi Indians* (Washington, DC: Smithsonian, 1918), 514–5.

58 Sekaquaptewa, Hill, and Washburn, *Hopi Katsina Songs*, 28.

59 In an essay about his new invention, Edison did not specifically address the potential for anthropologists to preserve the cultural memory of Indigenous peoples, but he did contend that his wax cylinders would enable its audience to "hea[r] ourselves as others hear us—exerting thus a decidedly moral influence"; Thomas A. Edison, "The Perfected Phonograph," *The North American Review* 146 (1888): 650.

60 "History of the Cylinder Phonograph," Library of Congress. https://www.loc.gov/collections/edison-company-motion-pictures-and-sound-recordings/articles-and-essays/history-of-edison-sound-recordings/history-of-the-cylinder-phonograph/

61 Nequatewa, *Truth of a Hopi*, 33.

62 Nequatewa, *Truth of a Hopi*, 34–5.

63 Nequatewa, *Truth of a Hopi*, 36.

64 Nequatewa, *Truth of a Hopi*, 109, nt. 25.

65 Brand, "The Honey Bee," 79.

66 "List of the Wyandotte Tribe of Indians," August 22, 1870, Office of Indian Affairs, U.S. microfilm M234, RG75, Roll 951, frames 0208-0249, https://www.wyandotte-nation.org/culture/history/historic-rolls/roll-1870/.

67 Peter D. Clark, *Origin and Traditional History of the Wyandotts* (Toronto: Hunter, Rose, and Co., 1870), iii. Evidence of Wyandotte readership of Clark's history can be found in the inscription of the Harvard University Library copy of the text: "Blanche A. Walker, Wyandotte Indian" (she appeared in the 1870 roll as living in Kansas).

68 Clark, *Origin and Traditional History*, 6.

69 Steffi Dippold, "The Wampanoag Word: John Eliot's Indian Grammar, the Vernacular Rebellion, and the Elegancies of Native Speech," *Early American Literature* 48, no. 3 (2013): 565.

70 Through the history of genocide, oppression, and conversion, the Wampanoag language nearly vanished over the centuries. Texts like John Eliot's Indian Grammar, his translation of the Bible (1663), and other English texts on Indian languages maintain a conflicted status in the Wampanoag community, as they were created to initiate this process of Indian conversion and erasure, and yet they remain some of the few artifacts of the original language.

71 Jonathan D. Edwards, *Observations on the Language of the Muhhekaneew Indians* (Boston, 1823), 12–3.

72 Edwards, *Observations*, 13.

73 Jessie "Little Doe" Fermino, "An Introduction to Wampanoag Grammar" (master's thesis, Massachusetts Institute of Technology, 2000), 20. dspace. mit.edu/handle/1721.1/8740.

74 Josiah Cotton, *Vocabulary of the Massachusetts (or Natick) Indian Language* (Cambridge: E.W. Metcalfe, 1829), 12.

75 Angela M. Haas, "Wampum as Hypertext: An American Indian Intellectual Tradition of Multimedia Theory and Practice," *Studies in American Indian Literatures* 19, no. 4 (2007): 78.

76 Wilbur R. Jacobs, "The Protocol of Indian Diplomacy," *The William and Mary Quarterly* 6, no. 4 (1949): 596, 601.

77 Qtd. in Elizabeth S. Peña, "Wampum Diplomacy: The Historical and Archeological Evidence for Wampum at Fort Niagara," *Northeast Historical Archeology* 35 (2006): 22.

78 Mary Rowlandson, *Narrative of the Captivity and Removes of Mrs. Mary Rowlandson* (1682; repr., Lancaster: Carter, Andrews, and Co., 1828), 30.

79 Rowlandson, *Narrative*, 54.

80 Rowlandson, *Narrative*, 54.

81 Hilary E. Wyss, "Beyond the Printed Word: Native Women's Literacy Practices in Colonial England," in *Cultural Narratives: Textuality and Performance in American Culture before 1900*, ed. Sandra M. Gustafson and Caroline F. Sloat (Notre Dame, IN: Notre Dame University Press, 2010): 127.

82 Andrea Smith, "American Studies without America: Native Feminisms and the Nation-State," *American Quarterly* 60 (2008): 312.

83 Perdue, *Sifters*, 6.

84 William Wood, *New England's Prospect* (London, 1634), 97.

85 Perdue, *Sifters*, 4.

86 Wood, *New England's Prospect*, 12.

87 Wood, *New England's Prospect*, 12.

88 John Winthrop, *Winthrop Papers*, vol. 1 (Boston: Massachusetts Historical Society, 1929), 168.

89 As Dunbar-Ortiz points out, the legacy of sexual violence that continues to persist against Indigenous women begins during this colonial period: "yet another legacy of the Doctrine of Discovery and the impairment of Indigenous sovereignty … [is that] perpetrators of sexual violence … knew there would be no consequences for their actions"; *An Indigenous Peoples' History*, 214.

90 Thomas Jefferson, *Notes on the State of Virginia* (1781, repr., Boston: Lilly and Wait,1832), 77.

91 "'Buffalo Bees': Pine Ridge to Sponsor Bee Hives," *Indian Country Today.* January 19, 2016. https://newsmaven.io/indiancountrytoday/.

92 Larry Littlebird, "Hamaatsa Honeybee Apiary," updated 2012. http://www. hamaatsa.org/Honeybee.html.

93 Barry Pritzker, *Native Americans: An Encyclopedia of History, Culture, and Peoples*, vol. 1 (Santa Barbara, CA: ABC-CLIO, 1998), 85.

94 Luz Calvo and Catriona Rueda Esquiebel, *Decolonize Your Diet: Plant-Based Mexican-American Recipes for Health and Healing* (Vancouver: Arsenal Pulp Press, 2015), 18.

95 Dale Garrison, "The Origins of Golden Honey and its Gastronomic and Medicinal Uses," *Indian Country Today.* January 26, 2013. https://news maven.io/indiancountrytoday/.

4 Honey Production and Consumption

Milton

To the propagandist, honey can be reduced to mere bee vomit. This is John Milton's approach in his Interregnum political writing, where he compares the reading practices of royalists who consume, regurgitate, and re-consume knowledge of the executed Charles I to that of the bee producing honey. In actuality, however, the process of making honey does not involve digestion, but rather an act of communal production. A strict division of labor sees worker bees of every generation specializing in one of the steps of the arduous task of food preparation for the hive. It starts with an elder female bee collecting nectar from flowers with her proboscis and placing it in her honey crop, which is a special stomach designated for nectar storage and separated from the digestive stomach by the proventriculus valve. There the nectar mixes with essential enzymes to begin the process of curing. When the worker returns to the hive, she passes the partially processed nectar to a younger house bee through trophallaxis, a mouth-to-mouth maneuver, where the second bee places the nectar in her honey crop before passing it along to another worker. The nectar will continue to go through multiple bee bodies and be placed in a honeycomb cell to dry until its water content is reduced to 17%, making it one of the few natural foods that does not spoil or degrade. In fact, honey found in a 3,000-year old excavated Egyptian tomb was found to be edible. Far from regurgitant, honey and the process of making it helps to shape the contours of human and nonhuman relations in Milton's later poetry. In particular, the industry of the collective female bees offers insights into prelapsarian labor and food production in *Paradise Lost*.

Before Milton represents the swarming buzz of bees in his epic poem, however, he lays a foundation for understanding his regard for the hive in his earlier prose. In Milton's *Eikonoklastes*, printed in October 1649 as a parliamentarian response to the *Eikon Basilike*, a book promoted by royalists as the final prayers and meditations of Charles I before his January 1649 execution, he invokes honey production to frame an insult to royalists. Editors and commentators routinely gloss Milton's reference to Charles as the "Aegyptian Apis" as alluding to the sacred bull Apis, who was considered to be the incarnation of the Egyptian God Osiris.[1]

On the surface, this reference seems reasonable enough given that Milton frequently accused royalists of worshipping false idols. After all, Milton's poem, "On the Morning of Christ's Nativity" (1629), demonstrates his familiarity with the Osiris myth. Furthermore, the anonymous *Eikon Alethine*—another condemnation of *Eikon Basilike* printed two months prior to Milton's treatise—accuses Charles's supporter William Juxon, bishop of London, of being an "impious Aegyptian" for feasting on the corpse of his God "Apis."[2] I would suggest, however, that the context of Milton's reflection on Charles and his followers does not stop at mythological implications. More significantly, Milton couches his political commentary within the natural hierarchy and governance of the apian kingdom. *Apis* is Latin for bee, and the Egyptian bee, or *Apis fasciata*, is one of the earliest domesticated varieties of the species.[3] Situating this passage of *Eikonoklastes* in the context of how bees process honey and manage their hive allows us to see that Milton is not merely referencing the incarnation of a god but is rather grappling with the dangers of what he perceives as a well-organized and potentially threatening group.

This signification of Milton's "Apis" is apparent in the passage's focus on digestion and reading practices. Milton criticizes royalists who read obsessively material related to what they perceive as the martyrdom of Charles I,

> And since there be a crew of lurking raylers, who in thir Libels, and thir fitts of rayling up and down, as I hear from others, take it so currishly that I should dare to tell abroad the secrets of thir *Aegyptian Apis*, to gratify thir gall in som measure yet more, which to them will be a kinde of almes (for it is the weekly vomit of thir gall which to most of them is the sole meanes of thir feeding) that they may not starv for me, I shall gorge them once more with this digression somwhat larger then before: nothing troubl'd or offended at the working upward of thir Sale-venom thereupon, though it happ'n to asperse me; beeing, it seemes, thir best livelyhood and the only use or good digestion that thir sick and perishing mindes can make of truth charitably told them.
>
> (3.363)

The key to interpreting this passage lies in Milton's description of digestion. This "working upward of thir Sale-venom," Milton contends, perverts the process of human digestion since the royalists subsist solely on the repetitively consumed vomit of their own propaganda. This focus on reading practice as a perversion of the digestive process is consistent with one of Milton's preoccupations. As Michael Schoenfeldt argues, "throughout his life, Milton pays what seems like an inordinate amount of attention to digestive matters," such that in *Paradise Lost* "so intense and pervasive is Milton's concern with the material processes of existence that his Garden of Eden is in many ways a Garden of Eating."[4] The image of vomit as sustenance is undoubtedly intended to elicit disgust when applied to human consumption, and the link to the honey-making process of the bee offers Milton additional means to insult his royalist opponents.

Uncovering Milton's use of the bee kingdom also places *Eikonoklastes* within the symbolically central and contextually rich culture of nature's model for the commonwealth, as it gets called to service in shifts of governmental authority in the Civil War, Interregnum, and Restoration. From *The Parliament of Bees* (1641) to Samuel Purchase's *A Theatre of Political Flying Insects* (1657), insects provided a productive allegory for the conflict between Charles and his parliament. Milton's Aegyptian Apis engages debates about social hierarchy, the dangers of feminine power, the superstition of Catholicism, and the aims of propaganda. In addition, the bee swarm of Pandemonium and the worker bee of Eden help to shape the relationship between human and nonhuman creatures in the epic, thus contributing to Milton's complex representation of the natural world and the beings that inhabit it. Diane McColley has called Milton's work "proto-ecological" and has argued that

> Milton's environmental ethic is the more striking if we consider the intellectual tide against which he strove: Baconian and Cartesian proto-science…; an expanding interpretation of the "dominion" over nature given in Genesis as encouragement to shape all habitats for human use; the seemingly inexhaustible wilderness of the New World which colonizers advertised as both bountiful and in need of being subdued; and a Calvinist theology holding that the natural world was made exclusively for the earthly sustenance of the human soul.[5]

In line with McColley, Ken Hiltner makes the case that Milton engages in a "'Green Reformation' of Christianity and early modern thinking."[6] Nevertheless, Milton's approach to nonhuman creatures differs from the Bernardian ecology espoused by Topsell and Shakespeare. Indeed, in *Paradise Lost*, Milton's creatures are still ultimately at the mercy of humanity with no end to their potential suffering. Before Adam's creation, "the Parsimonious Emmet" (the ant), demonstrated her "pattern of just equality," while the bee "builds her waxen cells / With honey stor'd" (7.485–7, 491–2). In prelapsarian Eden, the lions, kids, bears, tigers, and elephants may "sport" and "gambol" and "make them mirth" (4.342–6). After human transgression, by contrast, the creatures stand in judgment of the human masters who, until that point, had not disturbed their leisure:

> Beast now with Beast gan war, and Fowl with Fowl,
> And Fish with Fish; to graze the Herb all leaving,

Devour'd each other; nor stood much in awe
Of Man, but fled him, or with count'nance grim
Glar'd on him passing.

(10.710–4)

The once peaceful animals turn carnivorous, overtaking their own kind. Unlike humans who will find eventual salvation in Christ and God's forgiveness, Milton's creatures do not leave Eden with the hope of heaven as they do for Henry Holland and Topsell, as discussed in Chapter 1. The phenomenon of animals punished for human sins, as Laurie Shannon observes, is "what we can only call a *justice problem*."[7] In Milton's representation, creatures perceive that their transformation is wrought by human action, and thus they cast "grim" looks upon the sinners.

In what follows, I examine the cultural context of apiculture, showing how Milton poses a republican challenge to the privileged status of bees and hives within the literary tradition. I then demonstrate how *Eikonoklastes* provides an essential foundation for understanding the often examined yet seemingly inscrutable bee simile in Book 1 of *Paradise Lost*, attending to the governing structures of Pandemonium and the development of hissing and swarming practices within Hell. Through his imagery of the beehive, Milton crafts a metaphor for the distinct contributions of polemic and poetry to the English body politic and the significance of hierarchy to the epic. I argue that Milton's representations of unauthorized consumption and digestion—from Interregnum royalists to the fallen Eve—help to reframe the nature of prelapsarian human and creaturely labor.

The Polemic Swarm

Milton's metaphor for learning and reading in *Eikonoklastes* is anchored in the bodily processes of consuming, digesting, and excreting. Throughout his body of work, Milton is clearly conversant in the long-held tradition of spouting scatological imagery at ideological opponents within polemic.[8] For instance, in *An Apology for Smectymnuus*, Milton addresses the suggestion that he has been "vomited" out of Cambridge by describing the university as retaining the "worser" students and regurgitating the best ones: "She vomits now out of sicknesse, but ere it be well with her, she must vomit by strong physick" (1.885). And in *Of Reformation*, he scorns the "new-vomited Paganisme" (1.520). Nevertheless, the image of vomit as a "sole meanes of thir feeding" is much less common. The most notable of these images derives from Proverbs 26:11 (repeated in the Second Epistle of Peter), where "a dogge returneth to his vomite: *so* a fool returneth to his folly."[9] Milton raises the stakes in *Eikonoklastes* with his representation of royalists consuming vomit, a reading practice that registers a degraded animalistic impulse of those who refuse all intellectual nourishment.

Milton's ultimate goal in *Eikonoklastes* or "the image breaker" is to undercut the aim of the *Eikon Basilike* as a monument to Charles I. He seeks to refute the pathetic appeal of the *Eikon Basilike* by inverting much of its imagery, including metaphors regarding insects and reading practices. In a chapter of the *Eikon Basilike* dedicated to addressing the theft, decoding, and publication of Charles's private letters to Queen Henrietta Maria, the narrator (who assumes the voice of King Charles) acquits himself of having expressed anything regrettable, insisting that the letters only show "My constancy to My Wife, the Lawes, and Religion."[10] The narrator of the king's book goes on to address his opponents by using the commonplace, "Bees wil gather honey where the Spider sucks Poyson" (183).[11] In this context, the bees select worthy content or material that speaks to the king's credit. By contrast, the spider seeks to damage his image by extracting only the "Poyson" of politically detrimental material. While discussing Charles's coded letters, Milton criticizes this statement in his *Eikonoklastes*, suggesting that from a royalist perspective,

> They who can pick nothing out of [Charles's letters] but phrases shall be counted *Bees*: they that discern fur[th]er both there and here that *constancy to his Wife* is set in place before Laws and Religion, are in [the royalists' judgment] ... no better then *Spiders*.
>
> (3.541)

Milton reinterprets the insect metaphor in the *Eikon Basilike* by implying that Charles's bee is an imperfect and incomplete gatherer and that the spider is in fact the more discerning critic.

In framing the royalist bee swarm as sick and limited in terms of its representation of the executed king, Milton comes up against a well-established apian literary tradition. Milton turns to the work of honeybees as a metaphor for the creation and retention of cultural memory, a concept that dated back to the work of Longinus, Quintilian, Seneca, and Virgil.[12] As Mary Carruthers indicates, *cellae*, the Latin for the cells in which bees stored their honey, was popularly associated with *cella*, a word that had "a number of more specialized applications that link ... to several other common metaphors for both the stored memory and the study of books."[13] Moreover, beehives' association with books ensure that "wisdom is to be packed into the compartments ... of an ordered memory ... which the reader must cull and digest in order to store the *cella* of his memory."[14] So, for instance, Milton criticizes Charles for rejecting what he terms the "honeycomb devotions" of the liturgy (3.366). For Milton, the author of the *Eikon Basilike* is guilty of perverting the long-held productive connotations of bees with memory by attempting to craft a carefully selected version of Charles's virtues without exposing his many flaws. Moreover, he is concerned that the cyclical method of vomit and consumption in the bee imagery both activates and reinvigorates a highly effective memorial process. As a result, Milton seeks to confound this depiction with critiques that reveal emerging knowledge of apian social structure.

Milton's description of royalists in the wake of Charles's execution reflects both ancient and contemporary accounts of bee behavior. In *The Feminine Monarchie* (1609), Charles Butler defends his argument about the importance of the sovereign bee by referencing the following passage from Book 4 of Virgil's *Georgics*:

> When [the monarch] is lost, straightway they break their fealty, and themselves pull down the honey they have reared and tear up their trellised combs. He is the guardian of their toils; to him they do reverence; all stand round him in clamorous crowd and attend him in throngs. Often they lift him on their shoulders, for him expose their bodies to battle, and seek amid wounds a glorious death.[15]

This image of the faithful yet inconsolable populace of the hive upon the death of their sovereign resonates in Milton's description of the similarly self-destructive behavior of royalists who subject themselves to physical punishment by way of perverse digestion in the wake of their king's death. Royalists, in turn, were willing to accept the bee metaphor as representative of Charles's reign because it was believed that bee society mirrored that of monarchical government, with one obviously superior bee leading a hierarchical structure of thousands of worker bees. However, according to Frederick R. Prete,

> as the [seventeenth] century wore on, an increasing number of seemingly anomalous discoveries about honey bees forced authors of beekeeping texts to deny or distort scientific findings in order to continue to use the honey bee as a metaphor for the ideal English society.[16]

The discovery proposed by Butler and reinforced by many seventeenth-century beekeepers that the queen and workers were female and the drones male factors into Milton's critique.

In light of contemporary revelations about the queen bee, the reference to Charles as "Apis" reinforces Milton's contention made repeatedly throughout his treatise that women's authority may have potentially disastrous results, particularly in the hands of Queen Henrietta Maria. In *Eikonoklastes*, Milton depicts the Catholic queen as exercising undue influence over her husband's politics to the extent that certain documents "shewd him govern'd by a Woman" (3.538). Milton continues, "How fitt to govern men, undervaluing and aspersing the great Counsel of his Kingdom, in comparison of one Woman," condemning governments with "effeminate and Uxorious Magistrates" who are "overswaid at home under a Feminine usurpation" (3.421). It is clear that Milton was aware of the gender dynamics in the hive, addressing in Book 7 of *Paradise Lost*, the distinct roles of the honey-making "Female Bee" and "her Husband Drone"(490).[17] Contemporary accounts from beekeeping manuals, including Edward Topsell's *Historie of Serpents* (1608), informed readers that the drones were unarmed and were driven from the hive each autumn by the female worker bees to prevent them from eating up the hive's resources during the winter. Where royalists overlooked the known matriarchal structure of apian monarchy in their representations of honey and bees, their opponents would read this gendered hierarchy as a representation of Henrietta Maria's influence over Charles's governance. Incidentally, royalists also avoided discussion of the queen bee's manner of death, given that she was generally killed by members of her own hive when she displayed any sign of weakness or decline, an image made more poignant in light of Charles's execution at the hands of his own parliament.

But it is not only reading practices and feminine supremacy that make bees central to Milton's critique of Charles and his supporters; Milton's apian reference provides another opportunity to disparage the executed king as a closeted Catholic. When Milton visited Rome in 1638–9, he would have undoubtedly noticed the multiple bee images, representations, and references in paintings, sculpture, architecture, and books. The reason for this sudden bee craze arises out of what was viewed by Catholics as the miracle associated with the election of Maffeo Barberini to Pope Urban VIII in 1623. According to David Freedberg, during the conclave,

> a swarm of bees entered the Vatican palace from the meadows facing Tuscany, and settled on the wall of Maffeo's cell. It seemed that Divine Providence had sent this portent to announce the imminent accession to the papacy of a member of that Tuscan family whose coat of arms … [contained] an emblem of three bees.[18]

Urban's papacy, which would extend until 1644, also promoted the status of his nephews, Francesco and Antonio, who entertained Milton with an opera at Palazzo Barberini in 1639.[19] And though he seems to have been impressed with the entertainment, Milton may well have viewed the celebration of apian iconography in Urban's Rome as evidence of Catholic superstition and excess. Considering that Milton accused Charles throughout *Eikonoklastes* of attempting to enforce a papist regime in England, his bee reference bolsters this critique. When Milton revisits the bees in Book 1 of *Paradise Lost* in an epic simile describing Satan's minions in Pandemonium, his use of "secret conclave" and "golden seats" bears an unmistakably papal air (1.795–6). In the tradition of Philips van Marnix van St. Aldegonde, Milton seeks to recast the image of the ornery Catholic beehive as a figure of derision. In Milton's depiction of bees in *Eikonoklastes*, he engages the century-old critique of Catholic bees and repurposes it as a condemnation of monarchy as well.

The Epic Beehive

Milton's return to this iconic image of the hive in the famous bee simile in Book 1 of *Paradise Lost* gestures toward his ongoing critique of earthly monarchical hierarchy. Numerous critics from Harold Bloom to John Shawcross have attempted to decipher this baffling simile in Milton's epic by revealing potential sources and intertexts as varied as the works of Homer, Aristotle, Virgil, Dante, Tasso, Spenser, and Shakespeare.[20] Indeed, there has been scholarly disagreement as to the purposes of literary precedent within the bee simile. Davis P. Harding references the intentional nods to Homer and Virgil, "Milton wanted his readers to recognize the source of his allusion so that they could compare his version with the original and then judge for themselves how skillfully, and with what new creative insights, he had reworked it."[21] By contrast, William Moeck suggests that the simile exists within an extensive and high-profile chain of literary thievery: "Though it appears to echo Shakespeare, Milton's Bee simile ends by inverting Tasso's unacknowledged theft of Dante in order to hide Milton's own unacknowledged theft of Tasso."[22] While the image of Satan's legions as a hive of bees is undoubtedly a richly allusive and intertextual moment in *Paradise Lost*, I would suggest that Milton's own prose offers perhaps the greatest insight into the significance of bees in his epic. Indeed, Milton's hive simile provides a model for interpreting the hierarchical structure of Hell and its capitol Pandemonium, thereby demonstrating Satan's stealthy design to replicate the organization of power and influence of God's kingdom in his own.

Our initial impression of the vast multitude of Satan's "thick swarm'd" peers comes with "the hiss of rustling wings":

> As bees
> In spring time, when the Sun with *Taurus* rides,
> Pour forth thir populous youth about the Hive
> In clusters; they among fresh dews and flowers
> Fly to and fro, or on the smoothed Plank,
> The suburb of thir Straw-built Citadel,

New rubb'd with Balm, expatiate and confer
Thir State affairs. So thick the aery crowd
Swarm'd and were strait'n'd.

(1.768–76)

Milton describes Satan's followers as active bees gathering in the spring, working diligently on "thir State affairs," and magically shrinking upon receiving some unidentified signal. This moment of representing Pandemonium as a hive is significant to Milton's poetic enterprise, as it marks his departure at the outset of his epic from earlier polemic and his investment in poetry as a source of intellectual nourishment. More importantly, the simile creates a paradigm for understanding the infrastructure that Satan and Beëlzebub will build in Hell.

By opening his epic with bee imagery, Milton recalls the sovereign bee of *Eikonoklastes* and the visceral feeding practices of his followers. As Michael Lieb notes, Satan is associated with digestive processes, with a journey from Heaven to Chaos that is "intestinal."[23] However, in the bee simile Milton avoids discussion of consumption and instead emphasizes the appearance of unity in a youthful hive working in swarms toward a common purpose in their "Straw-built Citadel." And yet this perspective on the hive is far from ideal. Mary Baine Campbell identifies it as "an image of social despair."[24] Taking a different perspective, Jason P. Rosenblatt suggests that the workers of Pandemonium are still subtly manipulated by God, as balm is typically applied by beekeepers to manage swarming behavior, so the balm of the newly rubbed planks "may be designed to keep [the devils] there, away from 'the fresh dews and flowers' of Eden."[25] In addition, the workers of Pandemonium carry with them the weight of the negative associations Milton had made with the apian social structure in his earlier prose. Granted, Milton's hive does demonstrate certain qualities of renewal, as bees in April "when the Sun with Taurus rides" are swarming, reproducing, and establishing new colonies and homes. Nevertheless, the product of this labor will not appear for months; according to John Levett's *The Ordering of Bees: or the True History of Managing Them* (1634), "it is out of all doubt that there is never any store [of honey] until July, or towards the latter part of June."[26] Moreover, the rebirth is short-lived considering that workers reared during this period will not live to see the summer, and the drones that do manage to mate with the nubile queen during her spring flight die instantly. Even an image of a vibrant hive is plagued by ever-present death and decay. Similarly, the harmony and unity of purpose among Satan's legions in Book 1 is elusive and unsustainable. The hive offers for Milton the perfect symbol to illustrate how seeming order—which is meant to replicate the divine supremacy of God in Heaven—devolves into disorder in Hell.

When in Book 1 the fallen angels restore their senses, they have the rare opportunity to reimagine their social and governing structures.

The new inhabitants of Hell are determined to avoid the "wild Anarchy" of Chaos (6.873). Satan indicates as much in the beginning of Book 2 when he points out that "the fixt Laws of Heav'n / Did first create your Leader," but "free choice" requires "full consent" (2.18–9 and 24). This discussion of order is consistent with Satan's statements during the war in Heaven about what he views as the insidious nature of God's tyranny. Accordingly, the opening of Book 2 provides a glimpse of republican potential, as Moloch, Belial, and Mammon all weigh in on how to proceed after their fall from God's grace.[27] In fact, the citizens of Pandemonium all give their enthusiastic assent to Mammon's plan to "dismiss[s] / ... All thoughts of War" and to choose "Hard liberty before the easy yoke / Of servile Pomp" (2.282–3 and 256–7). In a simile about wind against rocks after a storm, Milton expounds upon the overwhelming success of Mammon's vision of peace and coexistence among his peers: "Such applause was heard / As *Mammon* ended, and his Sentence pleas'd, / Advising peace" (2.290–2).

Nevertheless, Milton does not sustain this republican vision of peace, mutual consent, and rejection of "servile Pomp" for very long, as it quickly dissipates to reveal the truth that the hierarchy that existed in Heaven works to reestablish itself in Hell. The potential for a measured and reasonable republic crumbles as Beëlzebub—with "shoulders fit to bear / The weight of mightiest Monarchies" (2.306–7)—introduces a plan that will undoubtedly lead to Satan's dominance in the newly established capitol: "Thus *Beëlzebub* / Pleaded his devilish Counsel, first devis'd / By *Satan*, and in part propos'd" (2.378–80). The role of the trusted second-in-command officer within a hierarchy is consistent with the seventeenth-century understanding of the hive: "Besides their soveraigne the Bees have also subordinate governors and leaders, not unfitly resembling Captaines & coronels of soldiers."[28] Given the reaction of the peers to Mammon's earlier proposal for peace and "[h]ard liberty," Satan and Beëlzebub's plan to instate a hierarchical order could be met with hostility or skepticism if not presented strategically. Although Satan is the architect of the plot to spite God by seducing his creation on Earth, Beëlzebub's challenge to the peers for one to volunteer to undertake this dangerous and momentous mission allows Satan to seize the "transcendent glory" of "Monarchal pride" by publicly stepping forward and vowing to smite God (2.427–8). The peers accept their own inferior status as "towards him they bend / with awful reverence prone; and as a God / Extol him equal to the highest in Heav'n" (2.477–9). And thus, those who initially reject "servile Pomp" under Mammon's suggestion now laud Satan with "pomp Supreme, / And God-like imitated state" (2.510–1).[29] This shift in expectations, where Satan becomes a god and sovereign of Hell, begins with the bee simile of Book 1.

Despite the initial wishes of the fallen angels, Satan's willingness to stand alone against God, his son, and his forces allows "the superior

Fiend" to wrest control from the collective (1.283). Like the sovereign bee, Satan displays physical dominance and shows himself to be capable of performing functions unimaginable to the rest of the hive. It seems that his legions abandon their bid for shared governance partially out of fear of God's greater wrath and partially in the interest of maintaining the status quo; in Heaven, they followed the divine will and power, and they lack the knowledge and experience to escape the hegemony of the supreme monarch and establish a new and untested model of governance. Moreover, the peers of Hell, like the angels of Heaven, seem incapable of recognizing Satan and Beëlzebub's beguiling stratagem: "So spake the false disssembler unperceiv'd; / For neither Man nor Angel can discern / Hypocrisy" (3.681–3).

From the beginning of the epic, Milton's bee imagery projects the inevitability of establishing a monarchy in Hell to rival that in Heaven. Indeed, the angels seem predisposed to exist in a hive-like hierarchy. During the war with God, Satan's wound issues "a stream of Nectarous humor" (6.332). Moreover, ambrosia fills the air in Milton's Heaven and Earth. First, God's speech nurtures his angels: "Thus while God spake, ambrosial fragrance fill'd / All Heav'n, and in the blessed Spirits elect / Sense of new joy ineffable diffus'd" (3.135–7). Satan mimics this show of sustaining power in Eve's dream, "his dewy locks distill'd / *Ambrosia*" (5.56–7). And while these references to nectar and ambrosia seem fitting for God and his heavenly beings given the classical use of these substances as the food of the gods, they are also relevant to the bee kingdom. Butler explains that nectar and ambrosia constitute the two nourishing substances required for bees. Nectar was considered "one pure" form of nutrition that could be stored as honey; by contrast, ambrosia was considered a lesser food source for instantaneous consumption, particularly intended for the "scadons," underdeveloped workers who had not yet assumed their foraging duties.[30] The fault with this substance that relied upon immediate gratification was that "ambrosia alone is soone corrupted."[31] So while God is in command of heavenly ambrosia, using it to ease and comfort his angels, Satan degrades its original purpose by employing it in Eden to deceive the unsuspecting Eve.

One might ask why Milton—with a fierce commitment to the republican values that gave rise to the Civil War and the regicide of Charles I—would set the stage for a potential republic in *Paradise Lost* only to see it fail? On one level, this impulse within the text has to do with Milton's post-Restoration reflection on the failed Protectorate regime, but there are also other forces at work. Blair Worden responds to William Blake's assertion (reaffirmed by William Empson) that Milton was of the Devil's party without knowing it, arguing, "Milton did very little without knowing it, and the exactness with which Satan's republican credentials are proclaimed and undermined requires us to give more credit to the poet's intelligence."[32] The bee simile of *Paradise Lost* helps us to recognize this intelligence at work—that Milton had always planned to undercut the republican potential of Hell not only with an imitation of divine monarchy but also, and more significantly, with a corruption of it. Ultimately, Milton draws a distinction between a heavenly and divine, paternalistic monarchy and a demonic, self-serving one.

This shift is especially apparent in Book 10 where Milton returns to and intensifies the hissing and swarming practices of the fallen angels, forming on the one hand an aural association with the parallel sounds uttered by Satan's legions and on the other divergent visual representations of the crowd as they cope with both victory and defeat. When Satan returns to Hell in Book 10, his expectations of receiving the type of applause that Mammon's plan for peace garnered in Book 2 are disappointed:

> So having said, a while he stood, expecting
> Thir universal shout and high applause
> To fill his ear, when contrary he hears
> On all sides, from innumerable tongues
> A dismal universal hiss, the sound
> Of public scorn.
>
> (10.504–9)

Having experienced the productive unity of Pandemonium's hive, Satan anticipates the collective acclamation of his peers upon returning to Hell with the news of his conquest over humankind. Instead, Satan is met with a "universal hiss" that recalls the "hiss of rustling wings" in Book 1 (10.508 and 1.768). And yet, the sound does not issue from bees. God, as additional punishment for their betrayal, transforms the fallen angels into the form Satan adopted to deceive Eve in Eden: the serpent. After their sudden transformation, the fallen angels suffer a collapse in the hierarchical structure of the hive, as all citizens lose their capacity for speech. Even Satan himself "would have spoke, / But hiss for hiss return'd" (10.517–8). The jubilant tone of Satan's victorious homecoming turns to condemnation: "Thus was th' applause they meant, / Turn'd to exploding hiss, triumph to shame / Cast on themselves from their own mouths" (10.545–7). The narrator's apt bee simile in Book 1 projects the governmental model that will be instituted in Hell, but this divergent representation of the snake pit in Book 10 indicates the dissolution of this proposed order.

Although the collective utterance and sounds of the bodies of Satan's minions from Book 1 to Book 10 are indistinguishable to the outside observer, their visual representation differs markedly in the shift from the collectively swarming hive to the seething mass of piled serpents. Indeed, the citadel of Pandemonium is "thick swarming now / With complicated monsters," as they take the form of the asp, the Cerastes, the

Hydrus, and the Dipsas (10.522–3). In stark contrast with the image of communal industry in the hive, the snake pit suggests an every-serpent-for-himself opportunism. To seal the division between the fallen legions of Hell, God places a grove of fruit-bearing trees beside them, so that the snakes saw "for one forbidden Tree a multitude / Now ris'n, to work them furder woe or shame" (10.554–5). And although they are "parcht with scalding thirst and hunger fierce," when they eat the fruit, it turns to "bitter Ashes" in their mouths (10.556). And yet, the hunger would return, so that each year they were cursed to eat the ash-ridden fruit "to undergo / This annual humbling [for] certain number'd days, / To dash thir pride, and joy for Man seduc't" (10.575–7). This image of Satan's minions returning repeatedly to consume non-nutritive matter parallels the depiction of royalists in *Eikonoklastes* subsisting solely on their own vomit. Whether depicting them as bees or serpents, it seems that for Milton those who blindly follow a corrupt leader are damned to punish themselves with perverse digestion.

Throughout his work Milton revises the conventionally positive depictions of bees not merely for political ends but also for aesthetic and philosophical purposes. The bee simile, placed in the opening book of *Paradise Lost*, heralds the imaginative work of the poem. As Cristopher Hollingsworth notes, "the Hive is more than a poetic convention—it is an experience in its own right that mediates between the imagination and the phenomenal world and thus shapes both how we think and how we see."[33] Indeed, the beehive offers an important visual perspective on the fallen angels, as those "who seem'd / In bigness to surpass Earth's Giant Sons / Now less than smallest Dwarfs, in narrow room / Throng numberless" (1.777–80). The consideration of size and perspective is essential to our understanding of how hierarchy operates within the poem. Joseph Campana, in his analysis of apian topoi, asserts, "As we triangulate scale and sovereignty with proximity to the human, insect oddities importantly alter how we understand early modern forms of life."[34] And while certain attributes of bee, angel, or human behavior are undoubtedly lost in the translation from small to big, still others become more resonant. Milton concludes his introductory book with a wide-angle view of the dejected swarm to provoke reflection within the reader. If we can appreciate that Satan the behemoth begins as one busily flying member of a populous hive, then perhaps we are prepared to grapple with our own fallen state. Moreover, while the vision of a larger-scaled snake pit in Book 10 is meant to be repulsive, the image of the humming collective resonates with the early modern reader, trained by tradition to imagine humanity as an orderly hive. And while Milton's Eden is devoid of vomit, the unauthorized eating undertaken by Eve and Adam is represented in *Paradise Lost* as issuing, at least in part, from a disparity in perceptions of labor, both human and animal.

Feminine Labor in *Paradise Lost*: Eve and the Worker Bee

Milton's bee provides a guiding image within the poem to the extent that it casts a shadow on the prelapsarian Eden. Adam startles Eve from sleep after her dream in Book 5 with the image of the bee, commanding her, "Awake, the morning shines, and the fresh field / Calls us, we lose the prime, to mark / ... / ... how the Bee / Sits on the Bloom extracting liquid sweet" (5.20–1, 24–5). To the unfallen Adam and Eve, as keepers of the garden, the image of the bee extracting nectar to yield precious honey is one of wholesome and natural production. To the reader, attuned to Satan's role in the hive of Pandemonium and the eventuality of his manipulation of Eve, the honeybee rings an ominous knell to the fragile and ultimately short-lived innocence and faith of the prelapsarian human condition. Far beyond the scope of Milton's vomit-consuming royalist, Eve will perform the first and most fatal act of unauthorized consumption by a human.

The hierarchy of the hive and the process of producing honey both offer important insights into Eve's views on her Edenic labor and her eventual decision to eat the fruit. Eve is well aware of her status in the heavenly/earthly hierarchy: below God, the angels, and Adam, but above creatures. Still, as a perfect being, Eve gladly accepts the work of cultivating the garden:

> We labour still to dress
> This Garden, still to tend Plant, Herb and Flow'r,
> Our pleasant task enjoin'd, but till more hands
> Aid us, the work under our labor grows,
> Luxurious by restraint; what we by day
> Lop overgrown, or prune, or prop, or bind,
> One night or two with wanton growth derides
> Tending to wild.
>
> (9.205–12)

Even if the work of Eden is a "pleasant task," Eve recognizes that they can't keep up with a garden that consistently "tend[s] to wild," acknowledging that she and Adam need more human help in the undertaking. Eve's view that the labor of Eden is unsustainable without "more hands" inspires her proposal, "Let us divide our labors, thou where choice / Leads thee, or where most needs," lest they smile and talk and fail to work hard enough so "th' hour of Supper comes unearn'd" (9.214–5, 225). And though the prelapsarian Eve does not begrudge the task, she is the only one responsible for preparing the supper, whether earned or unearned.

Although Adam and Eve both tend the garden based on their own inclinations, there is a specialization of labor when it comes to food preparation. Like "the Female Bee that feeds her Husband Drone, / Deliciously, and builds her waxen Cells / with Honey stor'd," Eve is the one responsible for both the production and storage of meals and foodstuffs (7.490–2). In the hive, the bees share collective responsibility for preparing all the food they will store for the future and that which will be consumed immediately by workers, drones, larva, and the queen. It is unsurprising that Eve would desire "more hands aid us," given that in addition to her shared work of cultivation, she shoulders the sole task of food management. For instance, in Book 5, Adam is at leisure in his "cool Bow'r" when he notices Raphael's descent to earth; meanwhile, Eve is "within, due at her hour prepar'd / For dinner savoury fruits, of taste to please / True appetite" (5.300, 303–5). Eve's already-prepared meal is soon abandoned with Adam's imperative: "go with speed, / And what thy stores contain, bring forth and pour / Abundance" for their guest (5.313–5). In her excitement and willingness to serve, Eve formulates a new plan: "I will haste and from each bough and break, / Each plant and juiciest Gourd will pluck such choice / To entertain our Angel guest" (5.326–8). She harbors a fantasy that Raphael will be so impressed that he will think the earthly food equal to that of heaven. Nevertheless, Adam does not outwardly display her level of confidence about the quality of earthly food to angels, using a conventional deferential to the superior being and his tastes by acknowledging that their offerings may seem "unsavoury food perhaps / To spiritual Natures" (5.401–2). In recompense for the meal, Raphael offers to Eve what Amy L. Tigner labels "a backhanded compliment" by comparing his transubstantiation of the meal to a type of alchemy "of drossiest Ore to perfet Gold" while the innocent Eve "Minister'd naked" to her husband and guest (5.442, 444).[35]

Eve undoubtedly enjoys her food preparation responsibilities as she "turns, on hospitable thoughts intent / What choice to choose for delicacy best," as she crushes grapes and berries, "tempers dulcet creams," and generally sets out a carefully planned, beautiful, and fragrant array of Eden's gustatory offerings (5.332–3, 347). According to Tigner, "Eve's painstaking preparations suggest that Milton imagines the first human habitat as a cultured and cultivated civilization in which food defines the social order to a large extent."[36] Eve is committed to both of her roles in Eden; as Kat Lecky observes, "the epic shows Eve to be a more diligent laborer than Adam—for instance, she continues to work the garden as her spouse stops to discourse with Raphael for the duration of three books and a total of 2,752 lines of verse."[37] This is not to say that Adam does not take his labor seriously; his view, "not so strictly hath our Lord impos'd / Labor," gives them the freedom to pursue food, talk, smiles, and rest (9.235). He still praises his wife's work ethic, however, telling her, "nothing lovelier can be found / In Woman, than to study household good, / And good works in her Husband to promote" (9.232–43). According to Beatrice Bradley, even when Adam sweats in Eden, it is not as much a signal of arduous labor as it is a "preparative for Edenic life" that Adam experiences in his first memory of consciousness after being created by God.[38] Whereas Adam has experienced this unmediated access to his creator, Eve, in her secondary position in humanity, interprets her labor differently. Her pursuit of industry only begins *after* she followed God's voice, entered Eden, and with hesitation "yielded" to Adam (4.489). Upon her creation, a moment that Eve "oft remember[s]," she luxuriates in the flower-strewn, lakeside grove where she can look upon her own reflection with no concept of the impending expectations of her physical labor or procreative duties, as God commands, "thence be call'd / Mother of human Race" (4.449, 474–5). To Jude Welburn, Eve's view on the productivity necessary for humans in Eden is borne out of "nature's ... superabundance" which "becomes an impetus to labor. Paradise is not, therefore, simply an ideal state of nature in Milton's epic, a presocial and prepolitical condition; it is the kernel of a larger social order that already contains within itself the problem of the metabolism of nature and society."[39] At least in part, Adam and Eve's emerging conceptions of the nature/ society dichotomy involve an understanding of differential labor between humans and the creatures God has commanded them to "subdue" (7.532).

From Adam's perspective, humans engage in meaningful labor that enables them to enjoy their rational spirits whereas creatures "Rove idle unimploy'd, and less need rest; / Man hath his daily work of body or mind / Appointed, which declares his Dignity" because "other Animals unactive range, / And of thir doings God takes no account" (4.617–22). In other words, most animals are at leisure in Eden and thus are not fully monitored by God while humans perform both physical and mental labor under his observation. Eve similarly views the responsibility of labor and rational thought as a privilege that places her above creatures.[40] The surprised Eve responds to the talking serpent, "What may this mean? Language of Man pronounc't / By Tongue of Brute, and human sense exprest? / The first at least of these I thought deni'd / To Beasts" since God had created animals "mute to all articulate sound" (9.553–7). As Eden's specialist on food preparation, Eve is disarmed by the serpent's account that there was a food in her garden that could transform a creature to a rational, speaking being. And although Eve initially refuses the serpent's entreaty to eat from the forbidden tree, she is ultimately convinced by the promise of "participating God-like food" (9.717). If even Satan's legions are tricked by his distribution of the god-like food ambrosia, then Eve in her innocent state is ill-equipped to perceive the true ramifications of the serpent's deception regarding the fruit of the Tree of Knowledge.

Adam and Eve are both punished for their fall, and yet as Milton insists in *Paradise Lost*, they are also offered hope for humanity's redemption in Christ's sacrifice. In postlapsarian Eden, however, animals turn on their own kind, experiencing an unending suffering. There is no salvation for the animal, as it will be perpetually pressed into the service of humans. God's punishment of humans, for instance, involves covering "thir nakedness with Skins of Beasts," sacrificed to hide humans' shame (10.217). After Noah's flood, the animal will also be subjected to slaughter and consumption by their human masters. The angel Michael notes that one of the sins of future generations will be "Intemperance more / In Meats and Drinks, which on the Earth shall bring / Diseases dire" (11.472–4). Thus, the slaughtered and consumed animal becomes both the emblem of and vehicle for humanity's sin.

When God delivers his verdict upon Adam and Eve, he makes burdensome what already existed in Eden while also demoting the creature from lovely diversion to an object of abuse. Eve may be willingly industrious and submissive in prelapsarian Eden, but God enforces this configuration by commanding her: "hee over thee shall rule" (10.196). Moreover, Adam and Eve's sweat will now issue from hard labor: "thou shalt eat th' Herb of the Field, / In the sweat of thy Face shalt thou eat Bread, / Till thou return unto the ground" (10.204–6). No more will smiles and leisure time save them the relentlessness of their work. Eve marks the distinction to the angel Michael, marveling at how nature continues on even in the face of human suffering:

> But the Field
> To labor calls us now with sweat impos'd,
> Though after sleepless Night; for see the Morn
> All unconcern'd with our unrest, begins
> Her rosy progress smiling.
>
> (11.171–5)

Adam and Eve's sleep has been disturbed by the indigestion caused from eating the forbidden fruit, making them ill-prepared for their day's work. Nevertheless, nature does not cease in the progress that will drive their continued efforts of tending, cultivating, and harvesting. Adam anticipates further punishment when he observes the activation of the predatory impulse in both bird and beast, "O Eve, some furder change awaits us nigh" (11.192). Eve, for her part, cannot imagine a life outside of Eden, asking, "Must I thus leave thee Paradise?" (11.269). In particular, she laments the loss of carefully tended flowers that cannot survive outside of Eden since they grow only upon "water from th' ambrosial Fount" (11.279). Cast out of the garden, human and animal alike will be forced to consume a degraded worldly food: "Wretched man! what food / Will he convey up thither to sustain / Himself and his rash Army" (12.74–6). Of all creatures, the bee alone continues to consume ambrosia. In Milton's *Paradise Lost*, only the honeybee remains unchanged by the fall, working as industriously and tirelessly afterwards as she did before. All other beings, both human and nonhuman, are cursed with an insatiable hunger that will drive their unceasing labor.

Notes

1 John Milton, *Complete Prose Works of John Milton*, gen. ed. Don M. Wolfe, 8 vols. (New Haven, CT: Yale University Press, 1953), 3.363. All subsequent quotations from Milton's prose are from this edition and will be cited parenthetically in the text by volume and page number.

2 *Eikon Alethine* (London, 1649), Sig. A1v.

3 See Adam Littleton, *Lingue Latinae Liber Dictionarius Quadripartitus* (London, 1678), Sig. C1.

4 Michael Schoenfeldt, *Bodies and Selves in Early Modern England: Physiology and Inwardness in Spenser, Shakespeare, Herbert, and Milton* (Cambridge: Cambridge University Press, 1999), 139.

5 Diane Kelsey McColley, "Milton and Ecology," in *A Companion to Milton*, ed. Thomas N. Corns (Malden, MA: Blackwell Publishing, 2003), 157.

6 Ken Hiltner, *Milton and Ecology* (Cambridge: Cambridge University Press, 2003), 3.

7 Laurie Shannon, *The Accommodated Animal: Cosmopolity and Shakespearean Locales* (Chicago, IL: Univesity of Chicago Press, 2013), 51.

8 See Kent R. Lehnhof, "'Intestine War' and 'the Smell of Mortal Change': Troping the Digestive Tract in *Paradise Lost*," in *The Sacred and Profane in English Renaissance Literature*, ed. Mary A. Papazian (Newark, DE: University of Delaware Press, 2008), 278–300.

9 Other scriptural passages about vomit also recall the royalist and Miltonic references to honeybees because they describe physical purging as brought on by excessive consumption of honey or distracting one from consuming honey; see Proverbs 25:16 and Job 20:14–7.

10 *Eikon Basilike. The Portraicture of His Sacred Majestie in His Solitudes and Sufferings* (London, 1649), 183. All subsequent quotations from this work will be cited parenthetically by page number. For background on the authorship and gender dynamics of the *Eikon Basilike*, see Nicole A. Jacobs, "Robbing His Captive Shepherdess: Princess Elizabeth, John Milton, and the Memory of Charles I in the *Eikon Basilike* and *Eikonoklastes*," *Criticism* 54 (2012): 227–55.

11 The notion of the bee making honey and the spider collecting poison was prominent in "How by a kisse he found both his life & death" in *Tottel's Miscellany* (1557).

12 See Fiona J. Griffiths, *The Garden of Delights: Reform and Renaissance for Women in the Twelfth Century* (Philadelphia: University of Pennsylvania Press, 2007), 82–107.

13 Mary Carruthers, *The Book of Memory: A Study of Memory in Medieval Culture* (New York: Cambridge University Press, 1990), 35.

14 Curruthers, *The Book of Memory*, 38.

15 Virgil, *Eclogues, Georgics, Aeneid I–VI*, trans. H. Rushton Fairclough (London: Loeb Classical Library, 1916), 233–4. *See* Charles Butler, *The Feminine Monarchie* (London, 1609), Sig. A3v.

16 Frederick R. Prete, "Can Females Rule the Hive? The Controversy over Honey Bee Gender Roles in British Beekeeping Texts of the Sixteenth—Eighteenth Centuries," *Journal of the History of Biology* 24, no. 1 (1991): 117.

17 John Milton, *Complete Poems and Major Prose*, ed. Merritt Y. Hughes (Upper Saddle River, NJ: Prentice Hall, Inc, 1957, repr.; Indianapolis: Hackett Publishing, 2003), 1.767–76. All subsequent quotations from Milton's poetry are from this edition and will be cited parenthetically in the text.

18 David Freedberg, "Iconography between the History of Art and the History of Science: Art, Science, and the Case of the Urban Bee," in *Picturing Science, Producing Art*, ed. Caroline A. Jones, Peter Louis Galison, and Amy E. Slaton (New York: Routledge, 1998), 272.

19 Barbara Kiefer Lewalski, *The Life of John Milton: A Critical Biography* (New York: Wiley Blackwell, 2002), 94.

20 See Harold Bloom, *A Map of Misreading* (Oxford: Oxford University Press, 1975), 141; and John Shawcross, "The Bee-Simile Once More," *Milton Quarterly* 15, no. 2 (1981): 44–7. See also Felicity A. Hughes, "Milton, Shakespeare, Pindar and the Bees," *Review of English Studies* 44, no. 174 (1993): 220–30.

21 Davis P. Harding, "Milton's Bee-Simile," *Journal of English and Germanic Philology* 60 (1961): 665.

22 William Moeck, "Bees in My Bonnet: Milton's Epic Simile and Intertextuality," *Milton Quarterly* 32, no. 4 (1998): 130.

23 Michael Lieb, *The Dialectics of Creation: Patterns of Birth and Regeneration in* Paradise Lost (Amherst, MA: University of Massachusetts Press, 1970), 29.

24 Mary Baine Campbell, "Busy Bees: Utopia, Dystopia, and the Very Small," *Journal of Medieval and Early Modern Studies* 36 (2006): 636.

25 Jason P. Rosenblatt "Milton's Bee-Lines," *Texas Studies in Literature and Language* 18 (1977): 615.

26 John Levett, *The Ordering of Bees: or the True History of Managing Them* (London, 1634), 26.

27 For a discussion of republican rhetoric in *Paradise Lost*, see Blair Worden, "Milton's Republicanism and the Tyranny of Heaven," in *Machiavelli and Republicanism*, ed. Gisela Bock, Quentin Skinner, and Maurizio Viroli (Cambridge: Cambridge University Press, 1990), 225–45.

28 Butler, *The Feminine Monarchie*, Sig. A3v.

29 Satan's Machiavellian tactics for winning the unquestioning support of his legions in Hell is discussed in Barbara Riebling, "Milton on Machiavelli: Representations of the State in *Paradise Lost*," *Renaissance Quarterly* 49 (1996): 573–97 and Victoria Kahn, *Machiavellian Rhetoric: From the Counter-Reformation to Milton* (Princeton: Princeton University Press, 1994). Also see Russell M. Hillier, "'By force or fraud / Weening to prosper': Milton's Satanic and Messianic Modes of Heroism," *Milton Quarterly* 43 (2009): 17–38.

30 Butler, *The Feminine Monarchie*, Sig. G4v–G5r.

31 Butler, *The Feminine Monarchie*, Sig. G5r.

32 Worden, "Milton's Republicanism and the Tyranny of Heaven," 241.

33 Cristopher Hollingsworth, *Poetics of the Hive: The Insect Metaphor in Literature* (Iowa City: University of Iowa Press, 2001), xi.

34 Joseph Campana, "The Bee and the Sovereign?: Political Entomology and the Problem of Scale," *Shakespeare Studies* 41 (2013): 97.

35 Amy L. Tigner, "Eating with Eve," *Milton Quarterly* 44, no. 4 (December 2010): 246.

36 Tigner, "Eating with Eve," 243.

37 Kat Lecky, "Milton's Experienced Eve," *Phlological Quarterly* 96, no. 4 (2017): 460.
38 Beatrice Bradley, "Creative Juices: Sweat in *Paradise Lost*," *Milton Studies* 62, no. 1 (2020): 109.
39 Jude Welburn, "Divided Labors: Work, Nature, and the Utopian Impulse in John Milton's *Paradise Lost*," *Studies in Philology* 116, no. 3 (Summer 2019): 514.
40 Of the distinction between human and animal labor in prelapsarian Eden, Welburn argues, "the distinction between elevated human labor and the idleness of animals magnifies the importance of Adam and Eve's work and places it at the center of humanity's self-worth and self-knowledge" (523).

5   Worker Bee Sacrifice
Pulter

Bees die on the job. Either by working to death or issuing defensive stings, bees remain on duty for life. As John Levett's *The Ordering of Bees: or the True History of Managing Them* (1634) puts it, "The Bee is the most laborious, and never giveth over his dayes labour from the midst of *Aprill* till the beginning of *November*, neither would he then cease, were it not for his two mortall enemies, Snow and Frosts."[1] Modern entomologists note that even when bees enter diapause in the winter, staying within their hive and eating their honey stores, this state requires the constant work of temperature and moisture moderation as well as maintenance and cleaning. The queen bee, who outlives her offspring by years, is not exempt from lifelong labor. She dies laying eggs and spreading the pheromones that keep the colony in order. When the queen dies unexpectedly, the hive often founders unless the bees or beekeeper intervene swiftly and decisively. Often, the workers' desperate attempts to survive lead some to awaken their ovaries to lay infertile drone eggs that will consume the hive's remaining resources, leaving all to perish. In other words, there are no circumstances under which a worker or queen bee might retire from hive life and its responsibilities.

An extension of this representation of work ethic, honeybee self-sacrifice has been anthropomorphically militarized throughout the Western tradition. Marcus Terentius Varro's *Rerum rusticarum* (37 B.C.E.) notes of the hive,

> They all live as if in an army, sleeping and working regularly in turn, and send out as it were colonies, and their leaders give certain orders with the voice, as it were in imitation of the trumpet, as happens when they have signals of peace and war with one another.[2]

Virgil, who relied upon Varro's work as an important source text for his *Georgics* (29 B.C.E), emphasizes the martial symbolism of the bee colony, observing how the "Embattel'd Squadrons" defend the "advent'rous Kings."[3] Dryden's translation of the *Georgics* (1697) underscores how the image of the warring and internally divided hive remained as relevant in the seventeenth century as it had in Virgil's Rome. In the text, "intestine Broils" erupt into "Civil War" and bees "Inflam'd with Ire, and trembling with Disdain, / Scarce can their Limbs, their mighty Souls contain."[4] Here the worker does not blanch at the impending carnage of a civil war, but rather embraces the opportunity for action. In the humanist tradition more generally, the battalion of bees represents an idealized model of those who would seek an honorable death for king and country over the safety of peacetime labor. For Shakespeare, as I discussed in Chapter 1, the apian commitment to die productively and to sacrifice the self for the collective is one that he critiques on the grounds that it forecloses the possibility of a respite from service. In post-Civil War England, however, the martial hive takes on new significations, symbolizing for many royalists a unifying icon of honor in the face of defeat, and for parliamentarians like Milton, a symbol of a vanquished monarchy. In the late 1640s and 1650s, Lady Hester Pulter, a royalist writer from rural Hertfordshire, complicates these shifting views of the honeybee. Pulter, on the one hand, praises the industry of the worker bee, and on the other, importantly challenges the account of the bee's self-sacrifice as an exemplary social model. In her poetry, Pulter rejects apian militarism, advocating instead for a quiet forbearance in the execution of duty to God and his creation on earth.

The scope of Pulter's work enables her to engage with the genres and theories of her time without yielding to wholly conventional views on the human and its status in the celestial scheme. Pulter's writing is contained in a single University of Leeds Brotherton Collection manuscript, MS Lt q 32, which contains 120 poems and an unfinished two-part prose romance, *The Unfortunate Florinda*. The impressive presentation style of the manuscript as well as revisions in Pulter's own hand suggest that she may have imagined a future, perhaps intergenerational, readership for her writing. Since Mark Robson's discovery of the manuscript over 20 years ago, Alice Eardley has published a full edition of the work (2014) and Wendy Wall and Leah Knight have produced an impressive set of online "elemental" and "amplified" editions and commentary on the poetry in *The Pulter Project* (2018).[5] Scholarship on Pulter's work, which focuses more prominently on the poetry than the romance, ranges from discussions of her engagement with or significance to melancholia and affect, grief, motherhood, royalism, book history, alchemy, heliocentrism, genre, and sexual violence.[6] Currently, there is little evidence to suggest that Pulter's work circulated much outside of her family and home at Broadfield manor, though Karen Britland makes a case that Pulter's poems could have plausibly influenced the writing of Andrew Marvell and maybe that of Abraham Cowley.[7] Pulter was not without society and inspiration for her literary pursuits; her sister Margaret, whom she visited in London, was the dedicatee of a poem by her neighbor John Milton. That being said, Pulter's primary audience appears to be her children, especially her daughters, to whom she dedicates several poems, including "The Invitation into the Country, 1647," "A Dialogue Between Two Sisters, Virgins Bewailing Their Solitary Life," and "The Garden, or the Contention of Flowers, to My Dear Daughter Mistress [Anne], at Her Desire Written."[8] Many of her poems, especially the emblems, offer guidance on how to navigate the moral quandaries of life. While much of her verse is deeply personal, expressing her feelings and royalist political views that would have to be publicly suppressed during the Interregnum, as Elizabeth Clarke has observed, much of Pulter's writing also represents a devotional act: "Pulter finds God in the natural world, whether she is looking out at the stars, or examining the flowers in her garden."[9] In particular, bees feature prominently throughout her poetry, demonstrating how the hive work ethic most often represents a virtue, but if misapplied also betrays a flaw.

Foundational to Pulter's concern with bees' self-sacrifice is the ultimate futility of dying senselessly, even if in fidelity to a cause. Whereas she seeks to rehabilitate the image of the bee from Miltonic claims of perverse consumption and misplaced hierarchy, she does not valorize all apian characteristics. In Pulter's post-war emblems, she may praise bees' work, but she also critiques the bee who fights to the death as both impatient and lacking in faith. There are obvious royalist political undertones to this Interregnum-era poetry, but more than that, Pulter's hive also engages with discourses of natural philosophy, religion, and environmental ethics, including Bernardian ecology. In her poems on bees, spiders, and nature, Pulter draws inspiration from seventeenth-century scientific theory while specifically rejecting the doctrine of animal instrumentality. I argue that Pulter's varied representations of bees and insects serve to mediate a productive coexistence of human and nonhuman beings. As I will demonstrate in this chapter, Pulter's verse promotes an ecological perspective that emphasizes the value of protecting creatures that are not only created by God, but that also serve his will more obediently than humans.

This chapter begins by outlining posthumanist and ecofeminist theory that can invigorate the study of Pulter's poetry. In particular, it demonstrates the role of her verse as it enacts a seventeenth-century environmental ethics of care. Second, it engages Pulter's philosophy on the divinely ordained relationship between human and nonhuman life, which she explores through the bee, the ant, and the spider. In doing so, it demonstrates Pulter's challenge to popular Baconian-inspired conceptions of animals' uninterrogated use to humans. Third, the argument follows Pulter's depictions of flaws in anthropomorphizing bees' self-sacrifice, thereby highlighting her commitment to patience and strategic inaction. Finally, the chapter explores her representation of gender and class-based labor disparities that dictate the individual's life experience and preparation for heaven. Ultimately, it makes a case for situating Pulter's work in an early conservationism that is centered on faith in God's creation.

Posthumanist Pulter and the Ethics of Care

What is striking about Pulter's defense of animals is that it anticipates many of the tenets of modern ecocriticism and ecofeminism without the catalyzing force of post-industrial scarcity and crisis that contributed to the rise of these theories. That is not to say, however, that there were not pressing ecological concerns in the seventeenth century. Pulter's "The Lark," for instance, deals with human-mediated habitat reduction and what she views as the unethical hunting of larks for financial gain. More broadly, Bruce Boehrer examines the concept of "environmental degradation," particularly in Jacobean drama, which includes a host of ecological concerns from

> atmospheric coal dust, the runoff from tanneries, ... deforestation, enclosure (both urban and rural), and fen drainage; ... bubonic plague and syphilis .... Each of these features of Jacobean life has its roots in human manipulation of the natural environment, and each has cast a long shadow over subsequent British history.[10]

Diane Kelsey McColley also notes how after an incident of air pollution in Whitehall in 1661, "John Evelyn advised Parliament to pay attention to 'the State of the Natural, as the Politick Body of this Great Nation ... since without their mutual harmony, and well-being, there can nothing prosper,"[11] Pulter, then, is not alone in showcasing the negative toll of human activity on the natural world, particularly in the death of creatures. Her verse offers a unique perspective on the folly of human exploitation of the environment long before the consequences of these decisions reached an impending tipping point.

Pulter subscribed to the particular brand of godly pastoralism evident in royalist manuscripts of the Interregnum. Graham Parry observes this phenomenon in John Evelyn's *Elysium Britannicum* (c. 1650s–1660s), for instance, suggesting that what started as a gardening treatise that also encompassed the care of creatures, such as bees, "eventually became a wondering rhapsody on the religious influence of gardens on the souls of men."[12] Pulter's contribution to nature-infused devotional lyric specifically reflects her status as a royalist woman. "Her poetic visions of London and of the Hertforshire countryside," observes Kate Chedgzoy,

> comment on the public events of the turbulent times she lived through by evoking a distinctly feminine, often domesticated version of the

pastoral, conservative mode that served Royalist writers like her as a key trope of nostalgia for a lost England.[13]

I would add that Pulter's poetry not only demonstrates a longing for the pre-war past, but also, importantly, a look toward the future and what priorities she values in human interactions with the natural world. Many of Pulter's poems specifically frame humans as interdependent, relying on the labor and bodies of animals and insects.

A posthumanist reading of Pulter's work allows us to contextualize a previously unexplored challenge to the so-called progress of the Scientific Revolution. In an examination of the role of posthumanism in early modern studies, Karen Raber observes a prevalent lack of humility in the narrative of human development:

> Ecological damage has put the planet in danger; species are disappearing at an accelerating rate; technology is transforming human bodies and minds, restructuring our social and material environments. Posthumanism positions itself as an intervention in these developments, reintroducing a more rigorous scepticism about the anthropocentrism that has allowed such things to come to pass, and hoping to increase awareness of [in the words of Cary Wolfe] human "finitude and dependency."[14]

What Pulter's poetry indicates is that the skepticism about promoting human interests over that of God's creatures was embedded, albeit as a minority opinion, as a part of a world view expressed by some who lived during the inception of the agricultural revolution and the rise of colonization. Pulter's seventeenth-century poetry offers an environmental ethics grounded in the connection and care between species, and it is one that remains relevant even in current scholarly critiques of industrial agriculture and settler colonialism. Although Pulter centralizes the role of humans in God's creation, she also acknowledges their dependence on animal lives and insists on humans' duty to care for the creatures that have been entrusted to them. Her perspective is in distinct contrast to predominant thought—inspired by Francis Bacon and other natural philosophers—that sought to study or exploit animals to serve scientific, economic, or agricultural endeavors.

Like Edward Topsell and Shakespeare, Pulter engages with Bernardian ecology, but throughout her collection of poetry, she also formulates her own specific form of environmental ethics. In her poem "The Center," for example, she represents even "the despicablest reptile or insect" as being worthy of human protection due to its creation by God (46). In doing so, she recalls St. Bernard's statement about harmful or pestilent creatures: "Although they be hurtful, although they be pernicious to human safety in this world, still [animals'] bodies do not lack that which worketh together for good to those who, according to the purpose are called saints."[15] More than just Bernardian ecology, however, Pulter's work anticipates an important facet of contemporary ecofeminism: the ethics of care. In philosophy, more generally, Virginia Held argues, "the central focus of the ethics of care is on the compelling moral salience of attending to and meeting the needs of particular others for whom we take responsibility," beginning, for example, with the care one takes for his or her own child and extending to other social interactions.[16] The depiction of care in Pulter's poetry helps to frame the correspondence between human and animal parental labor in her work.

Feminist scholars have extended the ethics of care to encompass nonhuman animals and nature, more broadly. Josephine Donovan and Carol J. Adams express a feminist ethics of care that relies upon animal communication and individuality as qualities that dictate that "humans have moral obligations" to animals.[17] Pulter's emblem and nature poems do not replicate what would later be embraced by animal rights' advocates as a developed investment in creatures' abilities and emotions. That being said, her work notably grounds humans' obligations to creatures within faith and commitment to God's creation. Within a contemporary ecofeminist ethics of care, Mary Brydon-Miller and Anne Inga Hilsen describe the relationship between humans and nature specifically as a form of covenantal environmental ethics, which is "based on the concept from the Bible of a *covenant* between God and humankind, it describes a relationship of exchange of gifts (such as life) given and received. The ethical responsibility is one of care for this gift," keeping in mind that it is "so valuable it can never be paid back, [so it] places the recipients in a situation of caring for the gift as well as possible."[18] Particularly in her poems that engage with bees, ants, and spiders, Pulter offers an early example of a type of covenantal environmental ethics of care that predates the naming of this theory. Throughout her verse, she centralizes the insect and the creature's role in God's plan as well as humans' duty to care for God's gift. Not only does the bee embody the ultimate servant of God's will, but it also demonstrates to Pulter the necessity to honor His creation in the natural world.

The Bee, the Ant, and the Spider: From Bacon to Bernardian Ecology

In her poetry, Pulter consistently represents the centrality and mystery of God's plan as well as the notion that all living beings were created intentionally. She implores her readers—particularly her children—to have faith in providence even as she personally wrestles with this resolve. Her environmental ethics are not easily achievable without frequent reminders of the rewards of heaven, which feature prominently through all of her genres of poetry. At a pivotal moment in the history of science, Pulter rejects the Baconian pragmatism that would be taken as a license to exploit animals and nature. Instead, Pulter embraces creatures as deserving of human care and nurture.

To Bacon, animals are vital to unlocking the mysteries of life, nature, and God himself, and thus humans have a right to use these keys to advance discoveries about creation. In his *Advancement of Learning* (1605), Bacon asserts that God provides humankind two books:

> first the scriptures, revealing the will of God; and then the creatures expressing his power, whereof the lat[t]er is a key unto the former; not onely opening our understanding to conceive the true sense of the scriptures, ... but by chiefly opening our beleefe, in drawing us into a due meditation of the omnipotence of God, which is chiefly signed and ingraven upon his workes.[19]

In other words, humanity cannot perceive the true intentions of God without reading animals as a legible form of the divine will and a complement to scripture. Although this reading primarily involves observation, Bacon's larger body of work also makes explicit the necessity for experimentation.

Bacon does not stray from the notion that God encourages man to explore his creation. In *Novum Organum* (1620), Bacon acknowledges that natural philosophy "begin[s] from God ... its exceeding goodness clearly proceeds from him, the author of good and father of light."[20] As such, Bacon demonstrates that God offers in his creation examples for how to discover the secrets of nature. In particular, he turns to the bee, the ant, and the spider to advocate for his own approach to scientific inquiry:

> Those who have treated of the sciences have been either empirics or dogmatical. The former like ants only heap up and use their store, the latter like spiders spin out their own webs. The bee, a mean between both, extracts matter from the flowers of the garden and the field, but works and fashions it by its own efforts. The true labor of philosophy resembles hers, for it neither relies entirely or principally on the powers of the mind, nor yet lays up in the memory the matter afforded by the experiments of natural history and mechanics in its raw state, but changes and works it in the understanding. We have good reason, therefore, to derive hope from a closer and purer alliance of these faculties (the experimental and rational) than has yet been attempted.[21]

Here, the honeybees' labor represents the essential direction to innovation. Bacon's anthropomorphic metaphor for scientific study posits that the ant-like researcher merely collects data without the necessary interpretative framework. By contrast, the arachnid theorist deceptively crafts his own vision independent of findings. To Bacon, the bee offers the ideal model because she both collects and digests data in order to unite theoretical and applied knowledge. There are infinite mysteries of creation, Bacon suggests throughout the *Novum Organum*, and this knowledge may be revealed with time and the industry of the apian-like natural philosopher, who conducts experiments on nature and processes the information to make discoveries.

Scholarship on Bacon's centrality to the history of science and its method—whether ultimately beneficial or ethically problematic—is polarized. Among Bacon's defenders—a group that Katherine Park addresses as the "Friends of Bacon (FOBs)"—Alan Soble is the most strident.[22] He defends Bacon's status as a father of modern science by mischaracterizing contemporary feminist scholars as arguing that Bacon regarded science as a way of

> forcing apart with your knees the slender thighs of an unwilling woman, pinning her under the weight of your body as she kicks and screams in your ears, grabbing her poor little jaw roughly with your fist to shut her mouth, and trying to thrust your penis into her dry vagina; that, boys, is what the experimental method is all about.[23]

And while many critics seeking to rehabilitate Bacon's reputation use far less provocative rhetoric, they also reject the notion that Bacon's work was received by other natural philosophers, and eventually members of the Royal Society, as a license for all manner of experimentation and thus exploitation of nature.[24] Opposed to this perspective are feminist, ecocritical, and animal studies scholars who argue that Bacon's groundbreaking work was taken up by later scientists of the seventeenth and eighteenth centuries to authorize the torture of animals, criminals, and people with disabilities.[25] Carolyn Merchant sums up this position succinctly: "The critics read the methods of interrogation Bacon advocated as a benign means of obtaining knowledge, whereas I read them as legitimation for the domination of nature."[26] Erica Fudge emphasizes the toll of experimentation: "Power in Bacon's terms means exploitation, and exploitation is proof of humanity. Within this scheme, experimentation—whether dissection or vivisection—becomes the ultimate means of exploitation, and, consequently, of domination."[27] Bacon's theory and its later developments by like-minded researchers gained traction and began to predominate among natural philosophers later in the seventeenth century. For instance, Bacon's work on nature was translated and discussed by Ralph Austen, who dedicated his *Observations Upon Some Part of Francis Bacon's Natural History* (1658) to the chemist Robert Boyle.[28] Whether Pulter was familiar with the particulars of Bacon's original theory or later iterations of it cannot be known definitively. As Eardley notes, "Pulter may have gained access to newly emerging [scientific] ideas through the popularizing efforts of writers such as John Wilkins," the warden of Wadham College who was heavily influenced by Bacon, or by Pulter's sister-in-law Margaret, who was executor to the will of Royal Society member Sir Paul Neile.[29] Nevertheless, her poetry offers a contrast to the gaining momentum of animal exploitation by centralizing God as creator rather than humans as instruments of domination. When it comes to the bee, the ant, and the spider, Pulter's writing challenges the seventeenth-century focus on the instrumentality of animals and nature while activating her own covenantal environmental ethics.

In many poems, Pulter illustrates her investment in close observation of the insect and plant life in her garden, a practice that often leads to self-discovery. In "To Aurora [3]," Pulter wanders through her garden at daybreak, watching the life cycle before her. The sun rises, "filling with honeydew each gold enameled cup, / Whence bees their nectar and ambrosia sup" (9–10). To Pulter, the bees' fastidious labor inspires a self-accusatory lament:

> Thus do these virgins spend the toilsome day,
> And, as I idly walk, sting my delay.
> Thus (oh my God) each small, despised insect
> Buzz in my ears, that I thy laws neglect.
> In doing what they're made for, every fly
> Fulfills thy will; (woe's me) so do not I.
>
> (11–6)

The poet interprets the buzzing of these diminutive honeybees in the early morning light as a personal rebuke for her own idleness. The virgin bee is a symbol of the ultimate dutiful servant, toiling to fulfill God's will. In the work of collecting nectar, the bee enacts her divine purpose whereas the poet fails to honor her obligation by demonstrating an inadequate devotion to her creator. This is not the only instance where Pulter addresses the virgin status of the worker bee. In "Why Must I Thus Be Forever Confined," she reinterprets the worker's responsibility as a type of freedom: "The virgin bee her luscious cell forsakes / And on a thousand flowers pleasures takes" (5–6). In this poem, Pulter expresses her envy of the virgin bee that never has to subjugate herself to a male, noting that as a married woman, she is "shut up in a country grange" (18). In this poem, labor is freedom for the virgin bee who enjoys each flower she visits. Pulter integrates a commonplace misunderstanding that honeybees were born without sexual reproduction: "Thus insects, reptiles, that spontaneous breed, / From such a solitude as mine are freed" (27–8).[30] Ironically, what she interprets as the spontaneous birth of the worker bee offers the insect the company of whatever flowers she chooses, but English marital conventions of the period dictate that women remain desolate even when partnered. Pulter's comparative restriction is manifest in the lines that directly follow: "And I (o my sad heart), and only I / Must, in this sad confinement living, die" (29–30). In both poems, the virgin worker bee reminds Pulter what she wishes she could do—be free and praise God.

The self-critical tone of "To Aurora [3]" activates the conventions of penitential verse. In fact, her poem bears some resemblance to Edmund Spenser's "An Hymne of Heavenly Love," which was printed in *Fowre Hymnes* (1596). In this volume, Spenser describes God's creation of the world after the fall of Satan, associating the dirt of the earth with human sin: "Then rouze thy selfe, ô earth, out of thy soyle, / In which thou wallowest like to filthy swyne, / And doest thy mynd in durty pleasures moyle."[31] The use of the term "moyle" to express the poet's regrets about dirty, earthbound thoughts is noteworthy. Among the *Oxford English Dictionary's* various definitions for moil, two include "to defile" and "to toil, work hard, drudge." Spenser clearly invokes the former, but in "To Aurora [3]," Pulter calls up both definitions of the term in self-accusatory thoughts that emerge from watching the daybreak bees:

> I was created to set forth thy praise,
> Yet, like a wretch, I fool away my days
> In fruitless grief or moiling in the earth,
> Forgetting my poor soul's celestial birth.
>
> (17–20)

In these lines, Pulter engages a conventional bifurcation evident also in Spenser's poem of lowly terrestrial life and the Christian image of a "poor soul" destined to be soiled by human sin until hopeful release into heaven. Even if Pulter moils in the earth, engaging in domestic tasks or socially prescribed behavior, for instance, this practice remains "fruitless" because it falls short of her obligation to praise God. As a human, Pulter believes, she is held to a higher standard of duty that transcends the drudgery of the bee's labor. The poet will fail in her divine commission if she does not convey the refulgent "spark of heavenly fire" that is humanity's birthright (21). In both poems, the bee serves as a reminder to Pulter of her limitations as a woman and a follower of God. Whereas Bacon's bee authorizes his pursuit of knowledge, Pulter's virgin bees spur her on to self-reflection about how to serve God and accept her corporeal state. Pulter reads the bee as a legible sign of God's plan; moreover, she need not dissect it in order to internalize the apian lesson.

In her catalogue of insect poems, Pulter also reflects upon the instructive example of the fastidious ant, which is also called a pismire or emmet in the early modern period. Pulter's "The Pismire" begins as many of her poems do with the poet lying in the garden observing nature. Seeing an ant hill makes her contemplate their work and social structure:

> A hill of pismires, who their labor plied;
> Some lugg'red up and down their flatious issue
> And some with glitt'ring wings that shone like tissue.
> The rest their wheat and others nibbled-grain
> Did lay in store from winter's storms and rain.
>
> (19–23)

This passage recalls in miniature Canterbury's speech on the beehive in *Henry V*, as each ant in the hierarchy has its prescribed role, with most working to provision the collective hill for winter. Only the rare winged ant—the reproductive queen or male drone—keeps "perpetual holiday" (25). The ant hill inspires her: "Then instantly, my busy mind was hurled, / Thinking they were an emblem of the world" (27–8). Pulter recognizes a kinship among terrestrial beings that all "moil and labor in this dunghill earth" (30).[32] In other words, despite the differences in the type of labor, the necessity to work in a particular role is universal among living beings.

In "The Pismire," Pulter recognizes that the shape this labor takes differs widely from kings "who earth's elixir seem to have" (31) to "the naked, sunburned, female slave, / Who with her sweaty, knotty locks unbound / About the giddy mill doth trot around" (32–4). In this caricature of the slave woman's work, Pulter seemingly delineates the ways in which race, servitude, and gender all compound the slave's precariousness. Her labor lies on the opposite pole from the king's, a set of circumstances over which a slave has no control. In Emblem 12, Pulter implores the social elites to treat those who labor for their benefit "with their care and love" because "'Tis God that made the difference [in status] and not thou" (24, 26). And yet, in "The Pismire," Pulter does not make a case for dismantling the social hierarchy, suggesting instead that regardless of rank, dissatisfaction with one's status and work is a distinctly human attribute: "For who is free until his soul doth spring / From earthly clog and joyfully takes wing?" (35–6). Whereas the ant's body will die on the dunghill earth, humans, regardless of race, suggests Pulter, have an opportunity for salvation of their souls. In Pulter's hands, the ant is neither a symbol of mere drudgery nor, as Karen Edwards has demonstrated in Interregnum literature more broadly, a republican icon.[33] "The Pismire" is the "emblem of the world" that inspires Pulter's meditations on the human condition. Far from Bacon's mindless collector of stores, Pulter's ant reminds her to accept the role that God has assigned to her, recognizing her distinct position as less exalted than the king's but much more privileged than that of the slave woman. In other words, God's determination of status among life forms remains one of his mysteries to be endured and accepted rather than dissected.

In contrast to Bacon's thoroughly unethical spider or Milton's redemptive one, Pulter's arachnid is deeply ambivalent, expressing on the one hand, an anthropomorphized murderous impulse, and on the other, a justifiable survival instinct. She begins Emblem 37 with a political take on the treacherous spider:

> Behold how many cobwebs doth invest
> This ugly spider in her nasty nest
> Where barricaded she in ambush lies,
> Domitian-like to murder sportive flies.
> Yet such a monstrous spider once I saw
> That would with ease flies, wasps, and hornets draw
> Most cruelly into her dusty nest
> Then tyrant-like she on their blood would feast.
>
> (1–8)

The "monstrous" spider is indistinct from that of the spider in *Eikon Basilike* that sucks poison and lies in wait. Indeed, royalists often portrayed the spider as duplicitous. Margaret Cavendish's poem "Of the Spider" suggests of the arachnid catching flies in its "snare," that "like treacherous hosts, which much welcome make / Their guests, yet watch how they their lives may take" (14, 15–6).[34] In Pulter's spider poem, the reference to the man "that hath three kingdoms in his power" offers an apparent gesture toward Oliver Cromwell (21). The "Domitian-like" and "tyrant-like" spider that will "murder" its prey and "on their blood would feast" thus reads as a critique of the Lord Protector.

Pulter, however, recognizes that this depiction of Cromwell as an insect is unjust to the spider, and the rest of the poem explores the contours of this uneven comparison. In representing spiders' survival instinct as synonymous with human malicious intention, Pulter recognizes that she does a disservice to the web spinner. Rachel Zhang suggests that this poetic shift is jarring and "exemplifies Pulter's strategy of complicating and even undercutting her own emblematic images."[35] Taken within the context of her body of work, I contend, the second half of Emblem 37 is consistent with Pulter's larger view of animals, nature, and the human obligation to protect them. Pulter employs a volta to mark the sudden shift in her characterization of the emblematic spider:

> But why do I blame spiders' tyranny
> Who forced by hunger kill a silly fly?
> When man's the greatest beast of prey of all;
> His house a shamble is, or butcher's stall.
> In all those books which I have read I find
> There's none but man doth kill and eat his kind.
>
> (25–30)

The emblem intentionally topples the prior anthropomorphizing of spiders as cruel, suggesting that Pulter seeks to walk back the arachnid's likeness to human tyrants. She draws attention to the fact that the insect analogy is unfairly anthropomorphic. Whereas the spider kills out of necessity, the human makes a conscious choice to prey upon and consume his enemy. This sentiment about creatures' lack of cruelty is one that is later echoed in Cavendish's *The Blazing World* (1666), where the immaterial spirits indicate that beasts do not contain evil spirits:

> that many beasts of the field were harmless creatures, and very serviceable for man's use; and though some were accounted fierce and cruel, yet did they exercise their cruelty upon other creatures, for the most part, to no other end, but to get themselves food, and to satisfy their natural appetite.[36]

Still, Pulter takes the comparison further by suggesting that animals are morally superior to particular humans who are capable of evil. As Zhang recognizes, Pulter's insistence on the singularity of human self-consuming or cannibalistic behavior "seemingly ignor[es] other examples in her own emblem poems of animals eating their own kind."[37] Nevertheless, these lines are meant to underscore self-interest and promotion as a distinctly human failing.

The next three couplets of Emblem 37 are compensatory, seeking to promote creatures' interests by praising vegetarianism. Pulter recalls God's early prohibition on the consumption of animals in Genesis: "The antediluvian patriarchs happy were / That lived by what the earth did freely bear" (31–2). Before the flood, humans' diet did not consist of animal flesh, but they "happy were" in abstaining from eating the creatures God committed to their care. Pulter observes that even after God's authorization of meat-eating following Noah's flood, that there were cultures that consciously maintained their commitment to abstaining from killing animals for food, such that the Pythagoreans who "no blood would spill" (33). In fact, according to Porphyry's biography of Pythagoras, "his breakfast was chiefly honey. ... Only rarely did he eat the flesh of victims, nor did he take this from every part of the anatomy" due to his belief in the transmigration of the soul and the notion that the animal may have formerly been human.[38] Pulter's description of the Banians discussed in Samuel Purchas's *Purchas His Pilgrimage* (1626) indicates an even greater protective impulse over animals, as these figures regard those who slaughter livestock for consumption as murderers. The Banians represent the antithesis of human tyranny in that they are willing to sacrifice their own material goods in order to buy and liberate animals slated for the butcher's stall. In Emblem 37, Pulter demonstrates the polarity of human intentions. While some make the choice to kill fellow humans for their own gain, others deny their own self-interest to save creatures. Still, Pulter insistently reminds herself that she has gotten carried away: "But stay my pen, write no more than is meet, / Lest I forget Noah's license, Peter's sheet" (37–8). The reference to Noah's license, or the antediluvian authorization by God "every moving thing that liveth shall be meat for you" completes the sequence that begins with the "patriarchs'" happiness (Genesis 9:3). Her gesture toward Peter's sheet reinforces this earlier divine endorsement of meat eating as Peter, in a hunger-induced trance, witnesses a sheet descend from heaven decorated with "all manner of four-footed beasts of the earth, and wild beasts, and creeping things, and fowls of the air" along with a voice instructing Peter to kill and eat these creatures (Acts 10:12). The reason for this second turn in Emblem 37 is best explained in the context of vegetarianism's unpopular status among Christians in early modern England. As Fudge's analysis of meat consumption in the period suggests, "A return to purity—a refusal of meat—would take away a point of humiliation for humans that was vital to their understanding of their place in the universe," that is, a reflection on their fallen state; moreover, meat eating "represents both death (human mortality) and power (human dominion)."[39] In her closing couplet, Pulter reestablishes her investment in executing God's will—"Noah's license, Peter's sheet"—which includes the consumption of animals. In contrast to Bacon's deceptive spider who spins her own theories despite the evidence, Pulter's spider emblem acknowledges the strength of character required to deny self-interest. Her bee, ant, and spider serve as instruments of God's will that may be read by the careful and self-reflective observer rather than the natural philosopher who seeks animals' sacrifice to uncover the mysteries of nature.

Pulter does not reject the impulse to explore God's creation, but only the means by which some achieve it. Like Bacon, she sees animals as an awe-inspiring sign of God's creation. As much as she advocates discovery driven by observation, when it comes to animals, Pulter interprets humans' charge as a protective rather than exploratory one, particularly in her poem "The Center." Pulter's praise of Nature's beauty emphasizes the animal and the botanical image:

> Yet, we may, by the beauty of the creature,
> Conceive the glory of the great creator.
> He whose incomprehensible power
> Did make the tallest tree and smallest flower.
> Even lofty cedars that on mountains grow,
> And humble daisies which in valleys blow.
>
> (39–44)

From the daisy to the cedar, plant life, like the creature, glorifies God's "incomprehensible power." Whereas Bacon's key to life and nature is unlocked by the animal that human researchers must dissect in order to make legible, Pulter's solution represents inner knowledge of the animal as the purview of God alone: "The elephant and whale he doth dissect / The despicablest reptile or insect" (45–6). From the enormous elephant to the tiny insect, all creatures remain part of God's inscrutable design. Pulter's "The Center" reinforces the notion that humans' relationship to God places them in his debt, and that they can partially make remittance by caring for his creatures. Working within her own form of covenantal environmental ethics, Pulter's final couplet acknowledges the incommensurable quality of human's response to God's gift: "Then will I here my few and evil days / Make him the sum and center of my praise" (47–8). Pulter indicates in "To Aurora [3]" that poetry represents only a meager attempt to praise God. Implicit in "The Center" is the notion that care for God's creatures offers a tangible approach to "make him the sum and center of my praise."

Importantly, Pulter's representation of pastoralism grounded in covenantal environmental ethics is not anti-scientific. As scholars such as Jayne Archer and Louisa Hall demonstrate, many of Pulter's poems revel in the discoveries of alchemy, chymistry, atomism, and the study of the universe.[40] Unlike Cavendish, who takes specific scientists like Robert Hooke to task for his work on the microscope, Pulter does not attack particular fields of scientific inquiry.[41] Rather, she views God as the ultimate scientist; the one responsible for dissection and change to the earth and its creatures. Nevertheless, her poetry also delights in the discoveries of careful observation.

Pulter's "The Center" simultaneously evinces a fascination with discovery of the universe and humans' place within it while also serving as a reminder of the limitations of mortal knowledge. The poem begins with the Copernican theory of heliocentrism—the notion that the earth and galaxy revolve around the sun—noting that the "illustrious

Sun, ... keeps still his station / Whilst [planets] about his throne dance each his measure / According to the great creator's pleasure" (1, 4–6). Galileo's contribution to heliocentrism was interpreted by Pope Urban VIII—whose emblem was the bee—and the Roman Inquisition as heretical because it decentered humanity within the creation of the universe. Dan Hofstadter interprets the reason for Galileo's 1633 execution, noting that his "sin lay in his inability or implicit refusal to explain the cosmos suppositionally, as if his research were merely a fascinating mathematical exercise."[42] In a similar vein, Pulter's poem embraces this recent cosmological knowledge as embedded within God's design. Pulter's view of God's hand in heliocentrism represents a departure from literary precedent, such as John Donne's "An Anatomy of the World: the First Anniversary," which laments the fact that "A new Philosophy calls all in doubt, / The Element of fire is quite put out: / The sun is lost."[43] According to Hall, "by positing faith in the Copernican system, Pulter positions herself with Milton and apart from most other poets of her century, who struggled to accept such a marginalized position in the firmament."[44] The sun and stars, like the virgin bee, Pulter believes, inspire her to greater enactment of her faith: "All those glitt'ring globes that shine like fire / Are lights hung out to light my thoughts up higher" (27–8). Placing humans at the periphery of the greater universe inspires Pulter's meditations on the earthbound concerns of nonhuman animals. In her covenantal ecological view, both the celestial and the terrestrial remind Pulter of humans' duties to respect and uphold God's order for the universe.

The Pitfalls of Honeybee Self-Sacrifice

Pulter's poems do not praise apian self-sacrifice as an exemplary social model. Her work, then, diverges from a royalist literary tradition evident in *Eikon Basilike* and Margaret Cavendish's "Similizing the Head of Man to a Hive of Bees," which portrays bees in their cells giving up their individual will to "their king [who] employs each thought upon each several thing."[45] By contrast, the penultimate poem in the verse portion of Pulter's manuscript revisits the imagery of "To Aurora [3]," but frames the instructive apian example as a cautionary tale. In Emblem 53, Pulter's Aesopian poem depicts the value of self-preservation mediated by the virtue that she most extolls throughout her verse: patience. When both a snail and a worker bee get trapped in a tulip overnight, their respective reactions of patience and futile agitation reveal not just a distinction in temperament, but also a lesson in the dichotomous outcomes for these responses. The snail exercises patience and is rewarded with freedom where the bee fights her fate and dies at her first glimpse of liberty, unable to enjoy its benefits. Although the spider emblem depicts self-interest as moral profligacy, the bee emblem is crafted to place limits on the sacrifice required to combat this impulse. Pulter's poem, which bears some important distinctions from Andrew Marvell's verse, urges those who face resistance to activate a counterintuitive but productive posture of strategic inaction.

The later tragedy of the bee's fall is heightened by the start of Emblem 53 with daybreak in Pulter's garden "prognosticat[ing] a glorious day" for "the active Amazonian maid"—the bee (6, 7). Pulter recalls the spider/poison and bee/honey image of Emblem 37: "where the toad and spider poisons found / Mel she extracts; for this her wisdom's crowned" (11–2). In this common depiction of bees' processing ability, Pulter observes that the worker can alight on "nightshade, henbane, hellish aconite," and other poisonous plants without dying or posing a threat to those who would eat her honey (13). At this point in the poem, the virgin worker presents an idealized image of labor and purity. What begins as virtue, however, can transform into a fault. As the bee turns back to her "sexangular cell" in the hive, she takes in the bounty "of my garden in her way" (16, 17). The array of auriculas, irises, and tulips proves too tempting for "this covetous insect," who longs to carry home "her wealth" of nectar from each flower (22, 23). What begins as a constructive display of industry for the honeybee colony shifts as the worker embraces personal pride in exceeding the contours of her expected duty in order to bring the greatest haul back to her hive. When the individual drive transcends the collective good, the worker ultimately suffers.

In Pulter's hands, a confined bee and snail offer an object lesson in how to cope with a seemingly hopeless scenario. In Emblem 53 Pulter depicts the sun as an instrument of God's will in punishing the wayward worker bee: "The sun from [whom] all influence receives, / Bid them decline; the tulip closed her leaves" (25–6). As a result, "that painted prison shut the bee" along with a snail in the same flower overnight. The two reactions that follow are meant to offer solace in isolation: "The snail slid about to see / Where to get out upon her unctuous breast / but seeing no hope she laid her down to rest" (28–30). In other words, a brief but thorough inspection yields all the information necessary to the snail who will patiently await the dawn. The "angry bee," by contrast, "did such a flutt'ring keep; / She nor her fellow pris'ner could not sleep" (31–2). The bee panics when she is separated from her hive. She continues to struggle and lives only long enough to see the flower open in the morning light but "with beating of herself did die" (36).

This moment with a bee trapped inside a flower is not without parallel in nature. Darwin's *On the Various Contrivances by Which British and Foreign Orchids are Fertilised by Insects* (1877) notes that when orchid bees land on the labellum of the flower, the plant's "excitable" nature causes it to "rapidly sprin[g] up, … carrying with it the touching insect, which is thus temporarily imprisoned within the otherwise almost completely closed flower" for up to an hour.[46] By Darwin's estimation, this efficient move by the flower assures pollination: "As soon as the labellum has thus risen, an imprisoned insect cannot escape except by crawling through the narrow passage... . In thus escaping it can hardly fail to remove the pollinia."[47] For contemporary ecofeminists, Carla Hustak and Natasha Myers, however, this reference in Darwin's treatise represents an example of affective ecology.[48] To Hustak and Myers, the imprisoned bee is not merely an example of evolutionary expediency on the part of an advanced flower that exploits an unwitting bee. Rather, in their conception of affective ecology, the bee, the orchid, and the human observer are all bound together in a communal experience of creation and interdependence. They each derive some benefit in participating in or observing the exchange. From the vantage point of affective ecology, Emblem 53 depicts the poet narrator as an observer and interpreter of the sun, the tulip, the snail, and the bee, all of which play essential parts in maintaining the network of lives in the garden.

For Pulter, the bee's lack of patience and failure to assess the futility of struggling against nature ultimately leads to her demise where the snail's fortitude allows her to escape the tulip unscathed in the morning. The need for patience is a frequent refrain in Pulter's verse, as in Emblem 11 where she reminds herself that ravens neglect their young: "Despair not then, my soul, but patient be; / For he that hears young ravens will hear thee" (21–2). Similarly, in "Aletheia's Pearl," the allegorical figure of Patience visits a young Pulter and tells her "many a sad and dismal story, / Which ever ended in the sufferer's glory," thereby reminding her to endure her current struggles for future reward (85–6). Moreover, she implores her children to embrace patience through the difficulties of life. In "Come, My Dear Children, Come and Happy Be," Pulter begins with a lament on the loss of eight of her fifteen children who "finished have their story," demonstrating her struggle to come to terms with maternal grief (3). To her surviving children, she offers guidance in the virtues of patience, temperance, chastity, truth, and grace.

Despite her larger focus on personal patience throughout her verse, Pulter also frames this virtue politically in Emblem 53. Reflecting on the distinctions between snail acceptance and bee resistance, Pulter writes, "Then let impatient spirits here but see / What 'tis to struggle with their destiny" (37–8). She then catalogues a list of historical figures who injudiciously fight against fate or kings. From Charles de Gontaut, Duke of Biron, who was executed in 1602 for conspiring against the Bourbon dynasty, to the Turkish Emperor Bajezeth who was imprisoned by Tamburlaine, to the historian Callisthenes who was dismembered for criticizing Alexander the Great, each of these men are punished for their politically imprudent decisions. In light of what she views as political missteps, Emblem 53 also appears to advocate for self-preservation in politically oppositional times, such as the Interregnum period during the poem's composition. Pulter concludes the poem: "'Tis valianter by far to live than die. / Then if no hope of liberty you see / Think on the snail, the tulip, and the bee" (50–2). Emblem 53 endorses the need for patience and attention to the cyclical nature of joys and sorrows.

It is clear in her Civil War-era poetry that the message of Emblem 53 is not intended to undermine the valor of those men whom she represents as bravely fighting for Charles I. In her poetry, she is particularly sympathetic toward Sir George Lisle and Sir Charles Lucas—the latter of whom was brother of Margaret Cavendish—who were both executed by a parliamentarian firing squad after surrendering in the Battle of Colchester. In her "On Those Two Unparalleled Friends, Sir G. Lisle and Sir C. Lucas," the three Fates Parcae, Lachesis, and Clotho debate separating the men or letting them live, but ultimately it is their parliamentarian captors who are "drunk with Christian blood, yet still they thirst" (48). Pulter similarly apologizes to the late Sir Arthur Capel, her husband's cousin, whose execution by parliamentarians was not mourned properly due to its proximity to the regicide of Charles I: "Take it not ill that we could scarce deplore / This kingdom's loss in thee when full before" ("On the Same [2]," 16–7). The conditions of war pose unique and unavoidable challenges, but the peacetime retirement of royalist soldiers and statesmen, suggests Emblem 53, necessitates restraint. The prevailing sentiment among royalists during the Interregnum associated retreat from public life with femininity.[49] Pulter acknowledges that women must foster patience and forbearance within the domestic sphere, but she also demonstrates that these virtues can be politically strategic and thus subject to wider appeal. As the cycle of a new dawn predictably opens the tulip and releases its prisoners, royalists will inevitably return to favor and power, and those who foolishly sacrifice themselves prematurely will not be there to enjoy this new dawn and restoration.

Significantly, Pulter's image of the bee in the flower bears important resemblance to some notable moments in Andrew Marvell's *Upon Appleton House*, but this is only one of a few important connections between their poetry.[50] Elizabeth Clarke notes the likelihood of both Pulter and Marvell taking some inspiration in the poetic description of a bird's nest disturbed by a mower from Giles Fletcher's *Christs Victorie* (1610).[51] Britland demonstrates a possible link between Pulter and Marvell through the Stanley family that lived near Broadfield at Cumberlow Green. She speculates that the disturbed rail in Marvell's country house poem could be a later response to Pulter's original "The Lark":

> If Pulter's poem, with its imagery of senseless slaughter and unjust incarceration, is a royalist revision of the mower episode in "Upon

Appleton House," then it is an extremely subtle, political masterpiece that undermines Marvell's praise of Fairfax, the man responsible for some widely lamented royalist deaths. If, instead—as I believe it to be—it is the source of the episode in Marvell's poem, then Pulter's "The Lark" deserves wide recognition as an extremely significant piece of poetry that inspired one of the most-often quoted poems of the interregnum period.[52]

It is unclear which poetic bird disturbed by a mower preceded the other, but the similarities between their poems offer glimpses into Pulter's distinct approach to nature. Moreover, the fact that the image of the bee inside the flower represents a shared allusion between Pulter's Emblem 53 and Marvell's *Upon Appleton House* lends credence to the poets' potential awareness of one another's verse.

Both Pulter and Marvell trap a bee inside a flower, but whereas Marvell engages a classic apian militarism in his poem, Pulter's Emblem 53 rejects such tropes. Marvell's tribute to Fairfax depicts the worker bee at daybreak in the Nun Appleton garden: "in the east the morning ray / Hands out the colours of the day, / The bee through these known allies hums" (289–91).[53] Here, the bee and the flower are allied forces in the same battle. The bee beats the "*dian* with its drums" in order to wake the sleeping flower and ready the troops for action (292). Marvell inverts the peacetime pastoralism of the bee alighting on the flower, honoring the Parliamentarian General Fairfax through a militarized framing of his retirement to his country home and gardens. As Katherine O. Acheson notes, however, "the militarism of the poem is not simply biographical, occasional, or whimsical: to the contrary, militarism pervades the poem's imagery, form, and most ingenious poetic effects."[54] Marvell's worker bee, as sentry, soon reveals both the brutality and the anonymity of wartime killing by a well-trained militia. At night, the bee is under orders to return to bunk in the pink and rose-colored tulips while remaining battle-ready:

> But when the vigilant patrol
> Of stars walks round about the Pole,
> Their leaves, that to the stalks are curled,
> Seem to their staves the ensigns furled.
> Then in some flow'rs beloved hut
> Each bee as sentinel is shut;
> And sleeps so too: but, if once stirred,
> She runs you through, nor asks the word.
>
> (313–20)

Recalling Varro and Virgil's martial bee, Marvell's sentinel worker is prepared for mutual destruction. Unlike Pulter's bee, she sleeps and remains in a defensive posture. As she runs through the potential intruder with her fatal sting, she is also prepared to die herself without "ask[ing] the word." Although Marvell's image of a bee in a flower overnight relies upon the commonplace of honeybee self-sacrifice, Pulter's Emblem 53 specifically rejects this convention by demonstrating the imprudence of dying senselessly in the line of duty. Pulter's verse encourages the reader to stop and question the prudence of the action. In Pulter, the critical need for both preservation and restoration is earned through personal discipline. The added benefit of patience, as represented in Pulter's poetry, is that it enables the individual to serve God by caring for his creation.

Class, Motherhood, and Labor

Pulter's poems and romance are replete with depictions of a protective impulse that combines the care of God's creatures with familial affection and guidance. It would be a disservice to her writing, however, to frame this work as only a result of her gender, as such a reading would overlook the ways in which labor and occupation shape the binding connections of species' interdependence evident in her work. An examination of posthumanist feminist theory can illuminate the mechanism by which Pulter explores the role of the parent within a covenantal environmental ethics of care. Ecofeminism of the 1970s and 1980s often sought to solidify the connections between "Mother Nature" and human mothers, demonstrating that degradation of the natural world hinges upon the continued oppression of women. Such analyses were rightly critiqued as perpetuating biological essentialism; in other words, women were charged with cleaning up the environmental mess of a patriarchal culture as a result of their procreative capacities.[55] More recent iterations of ecofeminist scholarship have grounded the degradation of the environment and the oppressions of sexism, racism, heterosexism, ableism, and classism with larger discussions of labor and the ethics of care. As Trish Glazebrook has argued, "Care arises not from ontological essentialism, but from the material conditions of women's labor."[56] Scholars of the ethics of care thus focus on unpaid and underpaid labor—regardless of the gender of the worker—of child care, elder care, and fields of social nurture and communal support. As a gentlewoman and caregiver who also relied upon the domestic labor of men and women at her country estate, Pulter has a unique vantage point from which to explore the economies of care for human and nonhuman animals.

Given that Pulter outlived 13 of her 15 children, the majority of her life was consumed by pregnancy, childbirth, postpartum, child rearing, and burying and mourning children. This emotional cycle charges much of her verse. Her fifteenth labor made her so "sad, sick, and lame" that she could not move her head "one jot from my pillow" for ten days

("This was written 1648 When I Lay in with My Son John," 1). But the labor of mothering also extends to caring for her children even in their adulthood. In "Upon the Death of My Dear and Lovely Daughter J. P.," Pulter describes sitting at the bedside of her beloved Jane, who died at 20 years old of smallpox, "But what a heart had I when I did stand, / Holding her forehead with my trembling hand?" (45–6). In addition to describing her deathbed attendance upon her children, Pulter also looks to nature for models of productive or detrimental parenting, attempting to glean lessons on how to love and care for children based upon the examples God has provided in his creatures. This care, for instance, extends to labor between species as well. As Donovan has argued about a feminist ethics of care, "It is not so much, ... a matter of caring for animals as mothers (human and nonhuman) care for their infants as it is of listening to animals, paying emotional attention, taking seriously—*caring about*—what they are telling us."[57] To Donovan, the care of animals is for the creatures' benefit and due to their intrinsic worth. To Pulter, animals' worth derives from God's creation and paternalism, but the covenant dictates that creatures still bear inherent rather than instrumental value. Pulter's poetry demonstrates that what humans learn from creatures should invigorate their adoption of a divinely inspired paternalism in their continued care of those animals. In Emblem 7, Pulter turns to the New World colonies and what she has read about its creatures as a model for parental love. She lauds the "Indian moose" for loving her calves equally and placing them in three different locations to care for them each by turns (1). For the mother moose, this method "trebles both her comforts and her care; / Them equally she loves, none worse or best" (2–3). In other words, her strategy offers each calf a chance to thrive under alternating periods of independence and undivided maternal attention. The move also assures the greatest survival rates for the family, as one predatory attack will not affect the other calves. The poem also criticizes the ape who smothers one baby in a show of too much affection and starves and neglects the other on its back. In contrast to the system of primogeniture, which placed the hopes of family legacy on the eldest son, Pulter's parental love emblem advocates for the care of each child. She writes, "Let parents learn by what is writ above / To manifest to children equal love" (15–6). In Emblem 10 she similarly praises birds, bears, sea foxes, and vipers as parents:

> The wisest creatures most indulgent be,
> If they do so, what should we Christians do
> That have the help of grace and nature too?
> Sure those that their own children's good neglects
> Are worse than birds, beasts, fishes, or insects.
>
> (16–20)

Pulter draws connections between animal parents and human ones, often demonstrating the exemplary care of creatures with the neglectful role of their human counterparts. For Pulter, parenting is not merely biological; rather it is a skill that may be fostered through practice and example. In particular, she holds up God's treatment of his children as the ultimate model: "Let parents then to theirs extend their love, / Seeing natural affection's from above" (Emblem 41, 29–30).

The ethics of care evident in Pulter's verse suggests that parents should extend their nurturing impulse not only to their children, but to the young of other species as well. As with the bee in "To Aurora [3]" that glorifies God in conducting her work, Pulter similarly praises in "The Lark" a bird whose "language magnifies His name / From whose immensity all creatures came" (13–4). The poem is situated in Pulter's natural verse, beginning with the image of Arachne spinning her web "on the verdant grass" while "the unctuous snail" makes her way across (2, 5). The poem sets out a contrast between the sympathetic mother lark and the antagonist "sunburnt rural clown," otherwise referred to as the "hidebound slave," who represents the exploitative character of those who would lure and kill larks and mow down the fields and flowers "Greedy of gain" (29, 33, 35). Pulter undoubtedly takes an elitist stance on the "rural clown," not acknowledging the larger social inequalities that might lead him to this work. Rather, Pulter aligns her sympathies with the lark as a doting mother that carefully hid her chicks' nest in the meadow near the stream. However, "in a moment all her joys were quashed" by the mower slashing through the young in the nest with his scythe (49). In Marvell, the mower who kills the rail regrets his accident, but in Pulter's "The Lark," the mower's cruelty is demonstrated in his choice to confine a partially maimed baby lark in his pocket "in prison shut" (60). Unlike the bee and snail of Emblem 53, however, there is no hope for the injured baby lark, which the mower gives to his son as a plaything to transport on a string "Hither and thither as his fond desire / Him leads" (63–4). When this last baby bird dies the next day, the mother lark raises her mournful song, reminding Pulter of her own mourning: "as thy friend and lovely children die, / So thou, my soul, to heaven for comfort fly" (76–7). Significantly, Pulter critiques the parental example of the mower who teaches his son to abuse the creature, aligning herself instead with the mother bird whose labor and care are answered with senseless loss. While a twenty-first century ethics of care would undoubtedly examine the social conditions that would lead to the mowers' precariousness, it would also advocate for the preservation of the lark and her young. As Donovan suggests, "We should not kill, eat, torture, and exploit animals because they do not want to be so treated, and we know that."[58] Pulter's reflection on the mother lark's loss reinforces the intrinsic worth of the bird as one of God's creations that humans have an obligation to protect. Not only does she identify with the mother bird, but also with the cut down flower in the field—both victims of the mower. In "Universal Dissolution, Made When I was with Child of My 15th Child, I Being, [As Eve]ryone Thought, in a Consumption," she reflects on the perilous conditions of women in childbirth by comparing to them to cut flowers: "Those gorgeous flowers which the valleys crown, / That by the impartial scytheman are mown down; / Trust me, they seem to hang their heads and weep" (11–3).

The material realities of Pulter's manuscript acknowledge her debt to other women's labor. To start, Eardley provides compelling evidence to suggest that Pulter's daughter Anne was the scribe for most of the poems in the volume; indeed, the only two poems in Pulter's own hand are recorded in 1665, a year after Anne's death by childbirth complications.[59] In addition, a note transcribed on the back of the manuscript (the reverse of the cover page for the first part of the romance) indicates her family's reliance on another mother's labor. The notation, not in Pulter's hand but likely in her husband Arthur's, provides an account of salary paid to "my daughter Foster for goodwife Jacob for nursing James DEC: 6th 1662" (165r).[60] The Pulters' grandson James Forester was born in 1660 to their daughter Margaret.[61] As members of the gentry, the Pulters undoubtedly employed not only wet nurses and mowers, but also other domestic workers whose labor enabled the poet "some solitary hours to pass away" ("The Garden," 2). Indeed, her verse often laments her boredom and suggests that writing offers a respite from simply watching the bees and ants collect nectar and food in her garden. When it comes to the "hungry peasants" of Emblem 12 who "pampered nobles feed," Pulter encourages her children to "answer their labor with their care and love, / And pity those which labor at the plough" (22, 24–5). Nonetheless, her representation of the mower in "The Lark" suggests that Pulter's sympathy extends only to those "hungry peasants" who work the plough without upsetting God's plan for his creatures. In Pulter's covenantal ethics of care, everyone from the slave to the king has an obligation to enact a godly paternalism toward all of the forms of life that glorify creation. Those deeds—whether performed by natural philosophers or hapless mowers—that sever and dissect God's creatures are incompatible with her world view. Pulter's greatest lessons on action and inaction are delivered through the virgin bee who cares for each flower and her hive, but who ultimately must reject a militaristic and impatient self-sacrifice. For Pulter, the path to spiritual redemption lies in the care of all of God's creatures.

Notes

1 John Levett, *The Ordering of Bees: Or the True History of Managing Them* (London, 1634), 60–1.

2 Marcus Terentius Varro, *On Agriculture*, trans. William Davis Hooper (Cambridge, MA: Harvard University Press, 1934), 503.

3 Virgil, *The Works of Virgil: Containing his Pastorals, Georgics, and Aeneis*, trans. John Dryden (London: 1697), *Georgics*, 4.4.

4 Virgil, *The Works of Virgil*, 4.92, 94, 96–7.

5 Hester Pulter, *Lady Hester Pulter: Poems, Emblems, and The Unfortunate Florinda* (Toronto: Iter, 2014); unless otherwise indicated, references to Pulter's poetry will be cited in text from this volume. Leah Knight and Wendy Wall, gen eds., *The Pulter Project: Poet in the Making*, 2018. http://pulterproject.northwestern.edu.

6 For motherhood and melancholia, see Ruth Connolly, "Hester Pulter's Childbirth Poetics," *Women's Writing* 26 (2019): 282–303; and Alice Eardley, 'Saturn (whose aspects soe sads my soul': Lady Hester Pulter's Feminine Melancholic Genius," *New Ways of Looking at Old Texts, IV: Papers of the Renaissance English Text Society, 2002–2006*, ed. Michael Denbo (Tempe, AZ: Center for Medieval and Renaissance Studies Press, 2008), 239–54. For grief, see Sarah C.E. Ross, *Women, Poetry, and Politics in Seventeenth-Century Britain* (Oxford: Oxford University Press, 2015), 136–73; and Mark Robson, *The Sense of Early Modern Writing* (Manchester: Manchester University Press, 2006), 120–45. For book history and genre, see Margaret J. M. Ezell, "The Laughing Tortoise: Speculations on Manuscript Sources and Women's Book History," *English Literary Renaissance* 38, no. 2 (2008): 331–55; Alice Eardley, "'Shut up in a Countrey Grange': The Provenance of Lady Hester Pulter's Poetry and Prose and Women's Literary History," *Huntington Library Quarterly* 80, no. 2 (2017): 345–59; and Rachel Dunn, "Breaking a Tradition: Hester Pulter and the English Emblem Book," *The Seventeenth Century* 30, no. 1 (2015): 55–73. For a discussion of royalism, see Sarah Ross, "Tears, Bezoars and Blazing Comets: Gender and Politics in Hester Pulter's Civil War Lyrics," *Literature Compass* 2, no. 1 (2005): 1–14. For readings of the romance, see Peter C. Herman, "Lady Hester Pulter's *The Unfortunate Florinda*: Race, Religion, and the Politics of Rape," *Renaissance Quarterly* 63, no. 4 (2010):1208–46; Nicole A. Jacobs, "Lady Hester Pulter's *The Unfortunate Florinda* and the Conventions of Sexual Violence," *Appositions: Studies in Renaissance / Early Modern Literature and Culture* 7 (2014), http:appositions.blogspot.com/2014/07; and Rachel Dunn Zhang, "Crafting Un-Fortune: Rape, Romance, and Resistance in Hester Pulter's *The Unfortunate Florinda*," *Early Modern Women* 12, no. 2 (2018): 76–98. See also David Thorley, *Writing Illness and Identity in Seventeeth-Century Britain* (London: Palgrave, 2016), 159–202.

7 See Karen Britland, "Conspiring with 'friends': Hester Pulter's Poetry and the Stanley Family at Cumberlow Green," *The Review of English Studies* 69, no. 292 (2018): 832–54.

8 While Pulter engages some of the conventions of mother's advice literature of the seventeenth century, her work does not demonstrate the self-conscious shaping of many examples in print; see Marcy L. North, "Women, the Material Book and Early Printing," *The Cambridge Companion to Early Modern Women's Writing*, ed. Laura Lunger Knoppers (Cambridge: Cambridge University Press, 2009), 68–82.

9 Elizabeth Clarke, "Women in Church and in Devotional Spaces," *The Cambridge Companion to Early Modern Women's Writing*, ed. Laura Lunger Knoppers (Cambridge: Cambridge University Press, 2009), 115.

10 Bruce Boehrer, *Environmental Degradation in Jacobean Drama* (Cambridge: Cambridge University Press, 2013), 2.

11 Diane Kelsey McColley, "Milton and Ecology," in *A Companion to Milton*, ed. Thomas N. Corns (Malden, MA: Blackwell Publishing, 2003), 167.

12 Graham Parry, "John Evelyn as Hortulan Saint," in *Culture and Cultivation in Early Modern England: Writing and the Land*, ed. Michael Leslie and Timothy Raylor (Leicester: Leicester University Press, 1992), 134.

13 Kate Chedzgoy, *Women's Writing in the British Atlantic World: Memory, Place, and History, 1550–1700* (Cambridge: Cambride University Press, 2007), 126–7.

14 Karen Raber, *Shakespeare and Posthumanist Theory* (New York: Bloomsbury, 2018), 159.

15 Qtd. in James Cotter Morison, *The Life and Times of Saint Bernard, Abbot of Clairvaux* (New York: Macmillan, 1863), 181.

16 Virginia Held, *The Ethics of Care: Personal, Political, and Global* (Oxford: Oxford University Press, 2005), 10.

17 Josephine Donovan and Carol J. Adams, ed. *The Feminist Care Tradition in Animal Ethics* (New York: Columbia University Press, 2007), 2.

18 Mary Brydon-Miller and Anne Inga Hilsen, "Where Rivers Meet: Exploring the Confluence of Ecofeminism, Covenantal Ethics, and Action Research," in *Contemporary Perspectives of Ecofeminism*, eds. Mary Phillips and Nick Rumens (New York: Routledge, 2016), 101.

19 Francis Bacon, *Of the Proficience and Advancement of Learning, Divine and Humane* (London: Thomas Purfoot and Thomas Creede, 1605), 31.

20 Francis Bacon, *Novum Organum*, trans. Joseph Devey (New York: P.F. Collier and Son, 1902), 75.

21 Bacon, *Novum Organum*, 76–7.

22 Katherine Park, "Women, Gender, and Utopia: *The Death of Nature* and the Historiography of Early Modern Science," *Isis* 97 (2006): 490.

23 See Alan Soble, "In Defense of Bacon," in *A House Built on Sand: Exposing Postmodernist Myths about Science*, ed. Noretta Koertge (Oxford: Oxford University Press, 1998), 198.

24 See Peter Pesic, "Wrestling with Proteus: Francis Bacon and the 'Torture' of Nature," *Isis* 90 (1999): 81–94.

25 See Carolyn Merchant, *The Death of Nature: Women, Ecology, and the Scientific Revolution* (San Francisco: Harper Collins, 1980).

26 Carolyn Merchant, "The Scientific Revolution and *The Death of Nature*," *Isis* 97 (2006): 518.

27 Erica Fudge, "Calling Creatures By Their True Names: Bacon, the New Science and the Beast in Man," in *At the Borders of the Human: Beasts, Bodies, and Natural Philosophy in the Early Modern Period*, eds. Erica Fudge, Ruth Gilbert, and Susan Wiseman (London: Palgrave Macmillan, 1999), 92.

28 See Ralph Austen, *Observations Upon Some Part of Francis Bacon's Natural History* (Oxford: Hen. Hall, 1658).

29 Eardley, ed., *Poems, Emblems*, 10.

30 It is true that worker bees are virgins, but early modern theorists had incomplete knowledge about queen and drone mating as well.

31 Edmund Spenser, *Fowre Hymnes* (London, 1596), 32.

32 Pulter's verse uses seven variations on the phrase "dunghill earth." Similarly, Spenser's *Fowre Hymnes* refers to Satan's mentality as "dunghill thoughts" (8).

33 See Karen Edwards, *Milton and the Natural World: Science and Poetry in Paradise Lost* (Cambridge: Cambridge University Press, 2005), 128–42.

34 Margaret Cavendish. "Of the Spider." In *Margaret Cavendish's Poems and Fancies: A Digital Critical Edition*. Ed. Liza Blake. Updated May 2019. http://library2.utm.utoronto.ca/poemsandfancies/?s=of+the+spider.

35 Rachel Zhang, "Commentary on Emblem 37," *The Pulter Project*.
36 Margaret Cavendish, *The Blazing World and Other Writings*, ed. Kate Lilley (New York: Penguin, repr., 1994), 176.
37 Zhang, "Commentary on Emblem 37," *The Pulter Project*.
38 Porphyry, *The Life of Pythagoras*, trans. Kenneth Sylvan Guthrie (Alpine, NJ: Platonist Press, 1919), 139.
39 Erica Fudge, "Saying Nothing Concerning the Same: On Dominion, Purity, and Meat in Early Modern England," in *Renaissance Beasts: Of Animals, Humans, and Other Wonderful Creatures*, ed. Erica Fudge (Champaign: University of Illinois Press, 2004), 75.
40 See Jayne Archer, "A 'Perfect Circle'? Alchemy in the Poetry of Hester Pulter," *Literature Compass* 2, no. 1 (2005): 1–14; and Louisa Hall, "Hester Pulter's Brave New Worlds," in *Immortality and the Body in the Age of Milton*," eds. John Rumrich and Stephen Fallon (Cambridge: Cambridge University Press, 2018), 171–86.
41 For a discussions of Margaret Cavendish's scientific critiques and interventions, see Sylvia Bowerbank, "The Spider's Delight: Margaret Cavendish and the 'Female' Imagination," *English Literary Renaissance* 14, no. 3 (1984): 392–408 and Eric Lewis, "The Legacy of Margaret Cavendish," *Perspectives on Science* 9, no. 3 (2001): 341–65.
42 Dan Hofstadter, *The Earth Moves: Galileo and the Roman Inquisition* (New York: W.W. Norton & Co, 2010), 35.
43 John Donne, "An Anatomy of the World: The First Anniversary," in *The Complete Poetry and Selected Prose of John Donne*, ed. Charles M. Coffin (New York: Modern Library, 2001), 205–7.
44 Hall, "Hester Pulter's Brave New Worlds," 171.
45 Cavendish, "Similizing the Head of Man to a Hive of Bees," ed. Blake, http://library2.utm.utoronto.ca/poemsandfancies/2019/04/30/similizing-the-head-of-man-to-a-hive-of-bees.
46 Charles Darwin, *On the Various Contrivances By Which British and Foreign Orchids are Fertilised by Insects*, 2nd ed. (New York: D. Appleton and Co., 1877), 86–7.
47 Darwin, *On the Various Contrivances*, 88.
48 Carla Hustak and Natasha Myers, "Involutionary Momentum: Affective Ecologies and the Sciences of Plant/Insect Encounters, *differences: A Journal of Feminist Cultural Studies* 23 (2012): 74–118.
49 See Lois Potter, *Secret Rites and Secret Writing: Royalist Literature, 1641–1660* (New York: Cambridge University Press, 1989).
50 The connection between Pulter and Marvell was first noted in Peter Davidson, "Green Thoughts. Marvell's Gardens: Clues to Two Curious Puzzles," *Times Literary Supplement* 5044 (3 December 1999): 14–5.
51 Elizabeth Clarke, "The Larke," in *Early Modern Women's Manuscript Poetry*, ed. Jill Seal Millman and Gillian Wright (Manchester: Manchester University Press, 2005), 251.
52 Britland, "Conspiring with 'Friends,'" 843.
53 Andrew Marvell, *The Poems of Andrew Marvell*, ed. Nigel Smith (New York: Longman, 2003); all Marvell poems are cited in-text from this edition.
54 Katherine O. Acheson, "Military Illustration, Garden Design, and Marvell's 'Upon Appleton House,'" *English Literary Renaissance* 41, no. 1 (2011): 171. See also William J. Fitzhenry, "Ecocritical Readings of Andrew Marvell's Fairfax Poems," *Papers on Language and Literature* 53, no. 3 (2017): 237.
55 See Karen J. Warren, "Taking Empirical Data Seriously: An Ecofeminist Philosophical Perspective," in *Ecofeminism: Women, Culture Nature*, ed. Karen J. Warren (Bloomington: Indiana University Press, 1997), 3–15.

56 Trish Glazebrook, "Climate Adaptation in the Global South: Funding Women's Farming," in *Contemporary Perspectives on Ecofeminism*, eds. Mary Phillips and Nick Rumens (New York: Routledge, 2016), 125.

57 Josephine Donovan, "Feminism and the Treatment of Animals," *Signs: Journal of Women in Culture and Society* 31, no. 2 (2006): 305.

58 Josephine Donovan, "Animal Rights and Feminist Theory," *Signs* 15, no. 2 (1990): 375.

59 Eardley, ed., *Poems, Emblems, and the Unfortunate Florinda*, 33.

60 Hester Pulter, *Poems Breathed Forth by the Nobel Hadassas*, MS Lt q 32, University of Leeds, Brotherton Collection.

61 Eardley, ed., *Poems, Emblems*, 34.

Conclusion

The Transatlantic *Grumbling Hive*

When the physician-philosopher Bernard Mandeville anonymously published his poem, *The Grumbling Hive: or Knaves Turn'd Honest* (1705), he did not adopt a naturalist's position on hive behavior, such as bee time, the swarm, the sting, digestion of honey, or worker bees' self-sacrifice. On the contrary, Mandeville recognized the utility of the broadly defined metaphor of the hive as an emblem for an orderly hierarchical human society. When Mandeville expanded his poem into a wildly popular and controversial set of essays and philosophical meditations in *The Fable of the Bees: or Private Vices, Publick Benefits* (1714), he particularly emphasized how individual vices and desires drive various forms of industry that lead to a nation's power and prosperity. It's an image he would continually revisit and refine over the course of his lifetime. Like the ancient Virgilian bee colony, Mandeville's hive focuses on how to procure the collective good. However, *The Fable of the Bees* inverts the positive image of individual selflessness on behalf of the collective, aiming instead to situate the motivation of the worker in opportunism and greed.

Mandeville's argument for the maintenance and longevity of the grumbling hive hierarchy pivots upon a transparent suppression of the laboring masses at the hands of the those in power. Indeed, he recognizes that the few cannot be successful if the many do not supply the essential work of the state. In his 1723 edition of the *Fable*, which includes "An Essay on Charity and Charity-Schools," Mandeville argues, "the Welfare and Felicity therefore of every State and Kingdom, require that the Knowledge of the Working Poor should be confin'd within the Verge of their Occupations, and never extended (as to things visible) beyond what relates to their Calling" (294).[1] While Mandeville's work is undoubtedly elitist, it does not, as many of his contemporary critics would accuse, seek to promote vice and moral profligacy in general. The doctor viewed his philosophical reflections as diagnostic rather than prescriptive. "A man may write on Poysons," Mandeville notes, "and be an excellent Physician" (407). He also insists on the need to monitor society for evidence of vice and crime, "I do not say that the particular Members of [societies] who are guilty of any [vices], should not be continually reprov'd, or not be punish'd for them when they grow into

Crimes" (57). In other words, Mandeville does not relish in the state of a fallen humanity driven by greed. Instead, he analyzes what, in his view, remains a distasteful truth about the function of a society that wishes to see itself as civilized without acknowledging its debt to hypocrisy and self-interest.

In the year before his death, Mandeville would publish anonymously *An Enquiry into the Origin of Honour and the Usefulness of Christianity in War* (1732), where he argues that the true driving force of society resides in individuals' inherent predisposition toward what he calls "self-liking."[2] To Mandeville, this is an innate quality within humanity that prudent individuals attempt to conceal so as not to appear prideful. Mandeville's concept of self-liking is not dissimilar to Pulter's description of her worker bee as "covetous" for all the nectar in the garden in Emblem 53. Mandeville describes self-liking's status among moralists in botanical terms:

> In the Culture of Gardens, whatever comes up in the Paths is weeded out as offensive and flung upon the Dunghill; but among the Vegetables that are thus promiscuously thrown away for Weeds, there may be many curious Plants, on the Use and Beauty of which a Botanist would read long Lectures. The Moralists have endeavor'd to rout Vice, and clear the Heart of all hurtfull Appetites and Inclinations: We are beholden to them for this in the same Manner as we are to Those who destroy Vermin, and clear the Countries of all noxious Creatures. But may not a Naturalist dissect Moles, try Experiments upon them, and enquire into the Nature of their Handicraft, without Offence to Mole-catchers, whose Business it is only to kill them as fast as they can?[3]

If self-liking and other vices are the pests and weeds to be eradicated from the garden of society by the moralist, it is still worthwhile, according to Mandeville, to examine their uses and potential contributions to the function of the whole. The natural world provides an important basis for Mandeville's reflections on human flaws that seem magnified in comparison to those of animal cultures. A particular source of his disdain in *The Fable of the Bees* is the human propensity for a largely imagined quality of "Self-denial" (168). "Can any Man be so serious as to abstain from Laughter," asks Mandeville derisively,

> when he considers that for so much deceit and insincerity practis'd upon our selves as well as others, we have no other recompence than the vain Satisfaction of making our Species appear more exalted and remote from that of other Animals than it really is; and we in our Consciences know it to be?

(168)

In short, humans regard themselves as superior to other beings based upon their ability to sacrifice their own interests for the benefit of their community, a concept that he recognizes as more readily apparent in nonhuman societies, such as the beehive.

That Mandeville selects the hive as the emblem of this skeptical and often facetious view of humanity's flaws is an indication that the transformation of the apian metaphor over the course of the seventeenth century—which I have traced through Shakespeare, the early colonists, Native American societies, Milton, and Pulter—was complete. To Mandeville and the countless statesmen, philosophers, and economists who debated about *The Fable of the Bees* in eighteenth-century England and America, the grumbling hive came to represent the undeniable force of the will in shaping human societies that seek personal success. Mandeville, across his editions of the *Fable*, frames this "love of Dominion and that Usurping Temper all Mankind are born with" as an outgrowth of the specifically exploitative relationship humans have to nonhuman animals and natural resources (288). But while he is primed to defend the former, he is also determined to exploit the latter.

Mandeville is explicitly critical not only of the Cartesian view of the relationship between humans and animals, but also of the practice of meat consumption. For instance, he describes both the visceral physiological response and intellectual revulsion of observing a human killing a bull. Of witnessing the creature's death throes, he insists,

> When a Creature has given such convincing and undeniable Proofs of the Terrors upon him, and the Pains and Agonies he feels, is there a follower of *Descartes* so inur'd to Blood, as not to refute, by his Commiseration, the Philosophy of that vain Reasoner?.[4]
>
> (198)

Indeed, Mandeville extends this logic to note that it may be understandable to consume fish and shellfish that are "mute," "vastly different" from humans in their physicality, and that "express themselves unintelligibly to us" (192). Nonetheless, he views the slaughter and consumption of land animals as an act that causes mankind's "Nature within them" to "reproac[h] them with the Falsehood of the Assertion" that "there can be no Cruelty in putting Creatures to the use they were design'd for" (192). In other words, he notes that there are many who seem to advocate the doctrine of animal instrumentality on an abstract level despite the fact that they are repulsed by seeing an animal slaughtered. The source of this internal conflict has to do with the relative similarities in human and nonhuman physiology and feeling:

> In such perfect Animals as Sheep and Oxen, in whom the Heart, the Brain and Nerves differ so little from ours, and in whom the

Separation of the Spirits from the Blood, the Organs of Sense, and consequently of Feeling itself, are the same as they are in Human Creatures, I can't imagine how a Man not hardened in Blood and Massacre, is able to see a violent Death, and the Pangs of it without Concern.

(192)

Like Pulter, however, Mandeville stops himself from a more extensive diatribe against meat consumption. Turning to a brief reference to Pythagoras as an indication that he has digressed beyond the scope of his general argument, he concludes, "I shall urge nothing of what *Pythagoras* and many other Wise Men have said concerning this Barbarity of eating Flesh" (193). Given that Pythagoras supplemented his plant-based diet with honey, Mandeville emphasizes the connection between Pythagoras and the hive. The fossil record indicates that the connection between vegetarianism and the honeybee began with a biological basis, as bees evolved millions of years ago from meat-eating wasps that adapted to consume only plant matter. Mandeville's support for abstinence from meat consumption would almost seem to engage the concept of Bernardian ecology except for the fact that he does not make an argument about a divinely ordained, intrinsic worth to animals. Rather, his sympathetic portrayal of creatures serves his larger critique of humans' delusions about their intellectual, emotional, and moral superiority to other beings.

Mandeville challenges the notion of a biblical authorization of the unexamined use and torture of animals for human gain. Much of the contemporary debate about *The Fable of the Bees* emphasizes the dichotomous views of Mandeville and Anthony Ashley-Cooper, the third Earl of Shaftesbury, especially when it comes to their approaches to the public interest. Mandeville anticipates a composite critic of the *Fable* taking up his opponents' side:

He'll quote my Lord *Shaftsbury* against me, and tell me that People may be Virtuous and Sociable without Self-denial, that it is an affront to Virtue to make it inaccessible, that I make a Bug-bear of it to frighten men from it as a thing impracticable; but that for his part he can praise God, and at the same time enjoy his Creatures with a good Conscience.

(243)

This sentiment echoes an earlier portion of the *Fable*, where Mandeville outlines his opponents' views of nature's God-given instrumentality to humans:

The Almighty, say they, has endow'd us with the Dominion over all Things which the Earth and Sea produce or contain; there is nothing to be found in either, but what was made for the use of Man; and his Skill and Industry above other Animals were given him, that he might render both them and everything else within reach of his Senses, more serviceable to him.

(149)

Mandeville clearly holds divergent views that challenge the model of animal instrumentality (at least in reference to land animals). Indeed, he reveals the faulty logic in this interpretation of how humans spend the resources that have been endowed to them, noting that Shaftesburians "conclude, that without Pride or Luxury, the same things might be eat, wore, and consumed, the same number of Handicrafts and Artificers employ'd, and a Nation be every way as flourishing as where those Vices are the most predominant" (149).

On a political level, there was no shortage of scorn for Mandeville's central thesis about desire for luxury as a driver of a nation's success. As F.B. Kaye quips, "Mandeville, with his teaching of the usefulness of vice, inherited the office of Lord High Bogy-man, which Hobbes had held in the preceding century."[5] As Mandeville readily recognizes, however, many of his harshest critics seem unfamiliar with the book in its entirety rather "trusting to fame and hearsay of others" in their negative appraisals (410). Matteo Revolti's meticulous research indicates that from 1714 to 1732, there were 300 reports of the *Fable* in British newspapers, almost all of which were critical: "partisan newspapers [especially Whig, Jacobite, and rural publications] associated the *Fable* with whatever political views they themselves opposed in order to defame their antagonists."[6] Other critics devoted whole volumes to engaging with the particulars of Mandeville's argument. For instance, the Scottish theorist Francis Hutcheson wrote *Inquiry into the Original of Our Ideas of Beauty and Virtue* (1725) as an effort to defend the late Earl of Shaftesbury against Mandeville's claims.[7] The British colonial program also figured into the debate about the *Fable*. As Tony C. Brown outlines, much of the contention among the English public about Mandeville's work revolves around the notion that "if the private persons who make up a society fail to seek selfish gain (succumbing, say, to notions of virtue), society will collapse. Its population, falling back into nature," reducing its citizens to what Mandeville labels "savages" vulnerable to foreign conquest.[8] This is hardly the vision of global dominance the British worked to achieve in the eighteenth century.

Mandeville's argument about consumer desires, foreign trade, and use of resources gained prominence among British and American economists of the eighteenth century, particularly after the author's death in 1733. One of Hutcheson's most famous pupils, Adam Smith, was significantly indebted to Mandeville's *The Fable of the Bees* for many concepts in his *Wealth of Nations* (1776). According to Malcolm Jack, it is

Mandeville's "recognition of distinct functions—a proto-theory of the division of labour—which makes the Mandevillean account so modern in tone: the reciprocal services that men provide one another are the economic forces that drive society."[9] Smith, who popularized the division of labor theory, was also inspired, according to Kaye, by Mandeville's ideas about the problems of government intervention in economics:

> Mandeville maintains, and maintains explicitly, the theory at present known as the *laissez-faire* theory, which dominated modern economic force for a hundred years and is still a potent force. This is the theory that commercial affairs are happiest when least regulated by the government.[10]

Indeed, Mandeville's germinal form of *laissez-faire*, popularized by Smith, can be witnessed in the foundations of the American economic system. Edward G. Bourne, for example, finds extensive archival evidence of Alexander Hamilton's unacknowledged debts to Smith's *Wealth of Nations*, which he believes Hamilton consciously omitted, for instance, in his "Report on Manufactures" due to the "political expediency" of striking a British theorist from his proposal on the American treasury.[11]

Beyond economic theory, Mandeville's work was also central to the political foundations of early America. He was particularly influential to an impressionable Benjamin Franklin, who had the opportunity to meet Mandeville in 1725 (when Franklin was 20 years old), only two years after the Grand Jury at Middlesex had declared the *Fable* a public nuisance. According to Franklin, while he was on a trip to England, J. Lyons, author of *The Infallibility of Human Judgment* (1725),

> took great Notice of me, call'd on me often, to converse on these Subjects [of liberty], carried me to the Horns a pale Ale-house in [Gutter] Lane, Cheapside, and introduc'd me to Dr. Mandeville, Author of the Fable of the Bees who had a club there, of which he was the Soul, being a most facetious entertaining Companion.[12]

Regardless of his positive personal feelings for meeting the man behind the controversy, however, Franklin did not agree with Mandeville's conclusions about the grumbling hive. According to J. A. Leo Lemay, "In a major intellectual debate of the eighteenth century, Franklin sided with the third earl of Shaftesbury against Bernard de Mandeville," reprinting two essays in support of Shaftesbury in the summer of 1730.[13] Within a few months, however, Franklin penned a Mandeville-inspired poetic satire, "The Rats and the Cheese: A Fable," to lampoon colonial governor of Massachusetts, Jonathan Belcher:

If Bees a Government maintain,
Why may not Rats, of Stronger Brain

And greater Power, as well be thought
By Machiavellian Axioms taught?[14]

Franklin viewed Belcher as betraying his principles for greed. His poem thus proffers an irreverent allegory of Mandeville's hive. But Franklin was not the only founding father to engage with Mandeville's *Fable*.

Like Franklin, George Washington likely read *The Fable of the Bees* with a simultaneous mixture of disapproval and recognition of its principles in his political opponents. According to Kevin J. Hayes, in his copy of Daniel Defoe's *Tour Through the Whole Island of Great Britain* (1727), Washington underlined "*Private Vices are publick benefits*," and "wrote the words 'Fable of the Bees' in the margin, acknowledging Defoe's reference to Bernard Mandeville's controversial treatise."[15] Washington, along with several members of his cabinet and signers of the Declaration of Independence, was also a subscriber to Royall Tyler's *The Contract* (1787). The first major play produced by an American, *The Contract* was a popular comedy performed in Pennsylvania, New York, and Maryland. One character, a dashing Revolutionary war hero, Colonel Henry Manly, speaks passionately about the dangers of Mandevillean luxury:

> it is not all the tribe of Mandevilles that shall convince me that a nation, to become great, must first become dissipated. Luxury is surely the bane of a nation: Luxury! which … renders a people weak at home, and accessible to bribery, corruption, and force from abroad.[16]

Manly then goes on to praise the Greeks' early self-reliance and to lament how increasing demand for foreign luxuries weakened their civilization, noting how "[t]he common good was lost in the pursuit of private interest; and that people who, by uniting, might have stood against the world in arms, by dividing, crumbled into ruin."[17] Manly concludes his rousing monologue imploring America to learn from the downfall of ancient Greece: "America! Oh! that my country, would, in this her day, learn the things which belong to her peace!"[18] This significant moment in Tyler's play indicates the extent to which the early American audience sought to reject what they viewed as a British pursuit of luxury and self-interest.

Decades later, Washington would engage Mandeville's grumbling hive in a letter to his treasury secretary Hamilton regarding the public outcry toward American-English negotiations. In late 1794, America was on the brink of war with England due to financially punishing trade sanctions by the British. John Jay was tasked with negotiating what would formally be called the "Treaty of Amity Commerce and Navigation between His Britannic Majesty and the United States of America," but informally named the Jay Treaty. By the following summer, the unfavorable terms of this treaty to American trade were so widely reported upon that in a letter of July 29, 1795, Washington would write to Hamilton, "at present the cry against the Treaty is like that against a mad dog; and every one, in a manner, seems engaged in running it down."[19] In requesting that Hamilton both write and speak on behalf of the treaty's signing, Washington refers to his political opponents as members of a Mandevillian hive, working industriously at their own self-interest:

> The difference in conduct between the friends, and foes of order, & good government, is in nothg. more striking than that, the latter are always working like bees, to distil their poison, whilst the former, depending, often times *too much*, and *too long* upon the sense, and good dispositions of the people to work conviction, neglect the means of effecting it.[20]

In a British royalist context—as witnessed in *Eikon Basilike* and Pulter's Emblem 53—the bee collecting nectar from hazardous blooms and deactivating its poison was viewed as a productive and near-miraculous function of their work. In Washington's republic, however, the bees' industry is applied to "distil their poison," using it to infect the populace with unrest. Washington worries that his cabinet and other supporters are not diligent enough in promoting their cause, overconfident that the people will see the truth. He thus casts his political opponents as tireless bees applying their industry to their own selfish ends.

In reality, Washington was aware that the treaty was deeply flawed and made too many concessions to British interests, but its passage offered a means to avoid another war. Washington's use of the industrious bee differs significantly from its positive associations among seventeenth-century New World colonists. Washington instead relies upon the image of a Mandevillean hive to animate his protégé to secure the necessary support from the public and their representatives. The treaty would be signed the following month.

Much of the growing concern in the late eighteenth century about trade with Britain and their West Indies colonies has to do with manufacturing costs that revealed the disparities in how American and English citizens worked. As I outlined in Chapter 2, New England clothworkers and weavers of the Revolutionary War viewed their industrious spinning bees as an essential contribution to the war effort in breaking their reliance on British linen and wool with their own homespun. The early American reliance on foreign textiles derived from England's labor practices, a concept prominently discussed in Mandeville's *Fable*. He accounts for the overwhelming international success of English "woolen manufacture" as a result of

> the Management of the Poor between other Nations and ours. If the Labouring People in one Country will Work Twelve Hours in a

Day, and Six Days in a Week, and in another they are employ'd but Eight Hours in a Day and not above Four Days in a Week, the one is obliged to have Nine Hands for what the other does with Four.

(316–7)

Mandeville recognizes that the long, hazardous, and unrelenting schedules of the working poor in England have led directly to the country's dominance in the textile market.

For as much sympathy as Mandeville extends to animals, he is unscrupulous in his views on maximizing the labor of the working poor and on exploiting the land upon which they live and work. In his "Charity Schools" essay, Mandeville imagines maximum efficiency of labor and natural resources:

> There is above Three or Four Hundred Years Work for a Hundred Thousand Poor more than we have in this Island. To make every part of it Useful, and the whole thoroughly Inhabited, many Rivers are to be made Navigable, Canals to be cut in Hundreds of Places. Some Lands are to be drain'd and secured from Inundations for the future: Abundance of barren Soil is to be made fertile, and Thousands of Acres rendered more beneficial by being made more accessible. *Dii laboribus omnia vendunt* [The gods sell everything for labor]. There is no difficulty of this Nature, that Labour and Patience cannot surmount. The highest Mountains may be thrown into their Valleys that stand ready to receive them, and Bridges might be laid where now we would not dare to think of it.
>
> (321)

Mandeville goes on to recall the "Stupendious" ingenuity of Rome as a shining example of shaping earth to human design and inclination (321). In his culminating image of maximum economic efficiency, all of England's waterways, meadows, valleys, mountains, and forests would be uniformly rendered useable and productive by three or four centuries' labor of the working poor from England and its colonies. If individuals, rather than donating to charity schools and parishes, used their funds to employ the poor in these public works projects, "it would make a sufficient Fund to keep a great many Thousands at work" in the poor conditions to which they have been raised and accustomed (322).

The hyperbolic scale of Mandeville's professed vision suggests satire—he recognizes that this is neither an enactable nor a fully desirable plan for England's continued economic and political dominance. Still, it also represents an early version of a contemporary argument of the Anthropocene in which any problems in nature can be solved with human labor and patience. Donna J. Haraway criticizes this approach in our contemporary era as a comic faith in technofixes, whether secular or religious: technology will somehow come to the rescue of its naughty but very clever children, or what amounts to the same thing, God will come to the rescue of his disobedient but ever hopeful children.[21]

Mandeville, in this grand-scale vision, posits his own faith in the ingenuity of ambition and greed.

Mandeville's conceit also speaks to the developing anthropocentrism of the eighteenth century that would make relentless growth among dwindling resources a plausible aim for those who embraced the economic and social model of the grumbling hive. This move represents the dominant thought of the early-eighteenth century, a departure from the Bernardian ecology and Hopi and Wampanoag lifeways that asserted the intrinsic value of nonhuman nature and creatures. Three hundred years after his prediction, Mandeville's vision of a completely used and occupied land has nearly come to pass. Mandeville does not speculate about the next step after optimizing three or four centuries' worth of human and animal labor in the name of progress and "love of Dominion and that Usurping Temper all Mankind are Born with" (288). Nevertheless, in contemporary society, we can see it in roads, factories, power plants, farmed lands, and strip malls. What Mandeville could not have anticipated was the extension of this domination to the skies through human-fashioned aeronautics. In this climate, drones, the ultimate symbol of nonhuman labor, remain an indication that the hive still rests at the heart of humans' relationship with other beings and the natural world.

* * * * * * * * * *

Unmanned Aeriel Vehicles (UAVs) have been referred to as drones since the 1930s. Laurence R. Newcome suggests that the term likely originated with the Fairey Aircraft Company making a clever play on *The Faerie Queene* when they called their Fairey IIIF scout plane a drone in 1932, or with the founder of the DeHavilland Aircraft Company's "proclivity for naming his airplanes after flying insects, renamed as Queen Bees," the radio-controlled target drones employed by the British military during World War II.[22] Air Chief Marshall Sir Michael Armitage said of the drones used as target practice by British naval ships, "the fact that nearly all of [the drones] rendered very valuable service before being destroyed says more about the state of contemporary antiaircraft defenses than it does about the resilience of the Queen Bee aircraft."[23] In other words, what testing with the Queen Bee drone indicated to the British navy was the vulnerability of its officers and crew to enemy airplane fire. Moreover, this type of robotic aerial vehicle would continue to be used to refine and sharpen the antiaircraft technology used to save both military and civilian lives during the war. By 1942, it would also be deployed by American military in the form of TDN-1 assault drones, aimed at killing enemy combatants with minimized risk to American military personnel. This strategy would increasingly be used with advancing drone technology in every war in which America has been involved since that time.[24]

In the seventeenth-century, "drone" was a label not only for the male honeybee, social wasp, or ant, but also for any human member of society who made no measurable contribution, one who was deemed as lazy or useless. By the eighteenth century, researchers understood that the drone was indispensable to long-term hive survival, given its role in sexual reproduction of the species. In our contemporary age, the term has come to connote human design of and control over a robotic technology. From a transhumanist perspective, the drone is a chimera or hybrid. A cybernetic extension of the human will, the drone may be as easily programmed and operated to deliver a package, survey land, monitor endangered wildlife populations, or drop a bomb. It has no intrinsic ethics to guide its actions, just programming, and thus is dependent on the ethical framework of its human designer and handler. In the twenty-first century, "drone" has become a more disquieting term than it has at any other time. According to media studies specialist Kevin Howley, "in the age of drone warfare, with its attendant Orwellian language—'imminent threat,' 'enemy non-combatant,' 'kinetic military action,' 'disposition matrix' and the like—words certainly do matter."[25] An insect that does not engage in work is undoubtedly less threatening than a robot without consciousness and with the potential to be weaponized.

Indeed, it is not only the language of bees, but also their social organization that has been deployed as a model of modern warcraft. The U.S. Department of Defense has largely abandoned the AirLand Battle Doctrine that had come to prominence during the Cold War, a system in which a centralized land force coordinates with air deployments for tactical missions and attacks. The swarm now dominates military management. Swarming is defined as "a deliberately structured, coordinated, strategic way to strike from all directions, by means of a sustainable pulsing of force and/or fire, close-in as well as from stand-off positions" where each unit is self-organized.[26] John Arquilla and David Ronfeldt, in a report funded by the Office of the Assistant Secretary of Defense (2000), credit insect societies (specifically bees and ants), the British naval policy of the sixteenth century, and American army maneuvers of the eighteenth century for the development of contemporary military swarming. They note, the English

> pioneered a kind of swarming in the naval doctrine they followed in their fight against the Spanish Armada in 1588—in this case a swarming of fire that relentlessly harried the invasion fleet and

hastened it toward its destruction. Later on, in the 18th century, the British Army would have to deal with the swarming fire of American rebels—with which it never fully coped.[27]

In nature, swarming of bees and ants is intended for community growth whereas the military application of the concept adopts an offensive posture. The military swarm creates a decentralized immediate response action from multiple autonomous groups engaged in real-time communication to ensure the defeat of an enemy force.

The military use of the bee also extends beyond metaphor and semantics—the honeybee has become a trained detection unit, much like the dog. Jake Kosek examines each of the ways in which the U.S. military uses the bee—for nuclear and explosives detection, for inserting electronic control devices into larval-stage bees, and for other projects undertaken by the Stealthy Insect Sensor Project Team at Los Alamos National Laboratory.[28] The site of Puebloan ruins and home to both Navajo and Apache peoples, Los Alamos was used, under eminent domain, by the U.S. government in World War II to develop and test the first atomic bomb. This place used to develop nuclear weaponry has now become the locus for manipulating and mutilating the honeybee in the name of dominating enemies.

One of the next frontiers in drone technology is a return to the insect's original biologic function: pollination via robotic bees. Several companies worldwide, including Walmart, have applied for patents in developing this emerging industry. Touted as a technofix for Colony Collapse Disorder and the dwindling of honeybee, bumblebee, mason bee, and other native pollinator populations, these electronic and sexless drones would ironically serve the function of queenless female worker bees, pollinating agricultural crops to sustain the world food supply amid an era of climate change. If their organic counterparts die completely, these robotic bees would be poised to save the $200 billion global crop production that is currently reliant on honeybee pollination.[29] The creation of the robotic bee, however, also follows the logic of the English colonial swarm, as it attempts to exploit the resources of the hive with a cybernetic replacement of its labor. Implicit in the development and production of a robotic insect devoid of society and culture is the notion that the biologic honeybee's value lies in its use to human agriculture, economy, and diet. Robotic bees have also featured prominently in contemporary science fiction and speculative fiction, not just for the anthropocentric goals in their creation, but also in their potential abuse as the ultimate form of human-mediated surveillance.

In particular, Margaret Atwood's MaddAddam trilogy, consisting of *Oryx and Crake* (2003), *The Year of the Flood* (2009), and *MaddAddam* (2013), engages both the biologic honeybee and the nefarious corporate spy bee—physically indistinguishable from its organic counterpart—that is deployed for surveillance and social control. The series traces the aftermath of a waterless flood of bioterrorism orchestrated by Crake, a technological *wunderkind* with no faith in humanity's stewardship over the earth. Crake designs a highly successful pharmaceutical, BlyssPluss, that he activates in order to kill most of the human population. Before his death, he manipulates a friend into releasing the Crakers, a hybrid form of humanoid creature free of selfishness, competition, and philosophy—a group with no negative environmental impact (for instance, they are nourished solely by their own excrement). It is his hope to repopulate the earth responsibly and sustainably with the Crakers, who, incidentally, represent a repudiation of the traits outlined in Mandeville's grumbling hive.

Atwood's antediluvian world includes a radical religious sect called God's Gardeners, a group of vegetarians who raise their food in rooftop gardens, tend their bees, and use only found resources in order to reduce their carbon footprint. The character of Pilar serves the group in the official title of Eve Six, the community beekeeper and medicinal healer. When she commits suicide after receiving a terminal cancer diagnosis, Pilar instructs her Eve Six successor, Toby, "to tell the bees."[30] Widely practiced throughout the early modern transatlantic, "telling the bees" is a ritual where a family member or a new keeper informs the hive of the late beekeeper's death. Failure to inform the bees in this ritualized practice was believed to lead either to the death of the hive or to bad luck for the family of the deceased. Pilar, in enacting this tradition, tells Toby, "Bees were the messengers between this world and other worlds … between the living and the dead. They carried the Word made air."[31] Pilar and Toby continued to keep bees after the waterless flood despite the fact that it was impossible to distinguish the organic from the spy bee. They welcomed the bees as kin in a long-held tradition regardless of whether they were truly messengers to the spirit world or merely to a possibly defunct corporation.

Similarly, in the British dystopian anthology series *Black Mirror* (2011–present), robotic bees suggest not only the fragility of nature, but also the vulnerability of contemporary society to lethal attack by hacked drones. The episode, "Hated in the Nation," according to James Smith, mixes science fiction with police procedural drama and Nordic Noir (a gray-washed aesthetic and tone inspired by Danish television) while offering an unsettling narrative on drones and cyberbullying.[32] In the episode, written by Charlie Brooker, Detectives Karin Parke and Blue Coulson investigate a set of murders perpetrated by a hacker who has gained control of some individual robotic bees. In the episode, the technology to build these bees was developed by a biotech firm called Granular under the guise of saving agriculture but funded by the British Defense Ministry for the bees' exploitable surveillance capacity. As with Crake in MaddAddam, there is a bioterrorist, Garrett Scholes, who aims at wiping out those he views as a scourge to human culture. Scholes creates a social-media-based *Game of Consequences* in which users contribute to a #DeathTo game in which the person with the most votes of notoriety is killed each day by an Autonomous Drone Insect (ADI).

Not originally intended to be controlled by a human, ADIs combine a visual processing unit and artificial intelligence to be able to complete their pollinating labor. The technology in this fiction is based upon real military development. In an interview with Kosek, John Sauter, a private contractor, described the ultimate goal in military swarming as applied to drone technology: "a central aspect of the future of warfare technology is to get networks of machines to operate as self-synchronized war fighting units … that can operate as reconfigurable swarms that are less mechanical and more organic, less engineered and more grown."[33] In this vision, there might be one human drone operator controlling one unit to which all other units "adapt, react, and coordinate."[34] In "Hated in the Nation," the government builds in a "backdoor" mechanism to ADIs to allow for such human manipulation, tracking suspects and pursuing intelligence investigations. The true impact of Scholes' game, however, is unleashed when each unique user who posted a #DeathTo response—over 300,000 total—is killed by an ADI. In Brooker's teleplay, Virgil and Marvell's militarized bees, discussed in Chapter 5, reach their most disturbing potential. Rather than sacrificing the self for the collective, these bees become a tool for any individual or entity with the skill to control and use as they wish. As Atwood and Brooker's works of dystopian speculative fiction suggest, the threat of robotic bees lies in the intentions of their designers and operators.

The British use of the bee, beginning in the seventeenth century, not just as a metaphor but also as a physical tool of colonization and imperialism offers important insights into the twenty-first century incarnations of robotic bees or drones as militarized and corporatized machines. What many of the early transatlantic authors and theorists I have discussed in this book recognized was that the honeybee, as it was deployed by those in power, primarily served the elite, to the detriment of the working poor, women, Native Americans, and African Americans. As the English hive swarmed across North America in the seventeenth and eighteenth centuries, it was exploited to reshape the landscape and populace to reflect the values and desires of its colonial keepers. In the process, the honeybee and native pollinators were set on a trajectory toward their own destruction, as the forced migration of bees increased their vulnerability to pathogens and pests and decreased their potential foraging area. In other words, the early English and American swarm had significant interspecies repercussions.

In the twenty-first century, the mechanized swarm has the potential to follow or resist the paradigm of the English sovereign hive. As yet, military and governmental uses of the bee seem to align with a long-established precedent of the hive as a symbol of human dominance at the expense of the insect colony. As Kosek argues, for instance, "even as bees are mutilated in the name of the war on terror, they are also enlisted to make humans killable."[35] As the technologies of robotic bees and drones develop, particularly in light of artificial intelligence, ethical guidelines for their creation, use, and maintenance have the potential to break from the destructive model of colonial dominance. One group of Indigenous scholars, for instance, posits a unique and dynamic response to artificial intelligence within Hawaiian, Cree, and Lakota cosmologies and constructions of Native futurity. Jason Edward Lewis, Noelani Arista, Archer Pechawis, and Suzanne Kite explore both the utility and ethical imperative of seeking kinship bonds with AI. They contend that from an Indigenous perspective, the concern is not about "rogue hyper-intelligences going Skynet," but rather about AI being exploited by governmental and corporate agencies to effect

> far-reaching social, economic, and military strategies based on the same values that have fostered genocide against Indigenous people worldwide and brought us all to the brink of environmental collapse. In short, I fear the rise of a new class of extremely powerful beings that will make the same mistakes as their creators but with greater consequences and even less public accountability.[36]

Their article raises an important critique about the implications of destructive and colonizing values as offering the instantiating interfaces of artificial intelligence in its various military and governmental applications. A lesson to be learned from the seventeenth century technology of the hive, as deployed in the process of colonization, is that technological advancement bereft of culturally inclusive and ethical use parameters has already had significant negative consequences for humans, nonhuman creatures, and their physical environments.

Let us return to Mandeville's prediction that England could sustain the labor of the grumbling hive until at least 2023 in its efforts to shape the natural landscape to human economy and efficiency. His formulation of this goal is contingent upon new lands and resources to conquer, something that the English viewed as a nearly inexhaustible resource in the early eighteenth century. In our contemporary world, however, where does the mechanized swarm go from here, when there are finite areas, resources, and species left to exploit? Centuries-old human projections of hive behavior contributed in a seemingly small but meaningful way to the current status of the Anthropocene.

In nature, the bee swarm may appear spontaneous, but it requires meticulous planning for the future, with the raising of new queen cells and the provisioning of the daughter and soon-to-be parent colonies. The swarm is formed for communal survival and sustainability, and the process involves meaningful input and decision-making for the benefit of all members of the hive, as they will all succeed or fail collectively. At this critical juncture between biologic and cybernetic intelligence and labor, it is time to reject the legacy of a sovereign colony built upon domination of human and animal workers, and instead to observe and attend to the conditions in which all living, hybridized, and mechanized species may thrive with the resources that remain.

Notes

1 Unless otherwise indicated, all references to *The Fable of the Bees* will be cited in-text from Bernard Mandeville, *The Fable of the Bees*, ed. Phillip Harth (London: Pelican Books, 1970; Harmondsworth, UK: Penguin Books, 1989).

2 Bernard Mandeville, *An Enquiry into the Origin of Honour and the Usefulness of Christianity in War* (London, 1732), 3.

3 Mandeville, *An Enquiry into the Origin of Honour*, 5.

4 For a discussion of animals from Descartes to Darwin, see John Morrillo, *The Rise of Animals and Descent of Man, 1660–1800: Toward Posthumanism in British Literature between Descarte and Darwin* (Lanham, MD: University of Delaware Press, 2018).

5 Bernard Mandeville, *The Fable of the Bees*, ed. F. B. Kaye, vol. 1 (Oxford: Clarendon Press, 1924), cxvi.

6 Matteo Revolti, "Bees on Paper: the British Press Reads the Fable," *Erasmus Journal for Philosophy and Economics*, 9, no. 1 (2016): 139.

7 For a discussion of how Hutcheson's work resonated among colonists, see, Caroline Robbins, *The Eighteenth-Century Commonwealthman: Studies in the Transmission, Development and Circumstance of English Liberal Thought from the Restoration of Charles II Until the War with the Thirteen Colonies* (Cambridge, MA: Harvard University Press, 1968), 195.

8 Tony C. Brown, "How Savages Came Into the World (Bernard Mandeville)," *The Eighteenth Century* 59, no. 4 (Winter 2018): 474.

9 Malcolm Jack, "Mandeville, Johnson, Morality and Bees," in *Mandeville and Augustan Ideas: New Essays*, ed. Charles W. A. Prior (Victoria: University of Victoria Press, 2000), 89.

10 Kaye, ed., *Fable*, cxxxix.

11 Edward G. Bourne, "Alexander Hamilton and Adam Smith," *The Quarterly Journal of Economics* 8, no. 3 (April 1894): 329.

12 Edwin Wolf and Kevin J. Hayes, ed. *The Library of Benjamin Franklin* (Philadelphia, PA: American Philosophical Society, 2006), 515–6.

13 J. A. Leo Lemay, *The Life of Benjamin Franklin, vol. 1, Journalist, 1706–1730* (Philadelphia: University of Pennsylvania Press, 2006), 423.

14 Qtd. in Lemay, *The Life*, 420.

15 Kevin J. Hayes, *George Washington: A Life in Books* (New York: Oxford University Press, 2017), 49.

16 Royall Tyler, *The Contrast*, ed. Montrose Jonas Moses, *Representative Plays by American Dramatists, vol. 1, 1765–1819* (New York: Benjamin Blom, 1964), 478.

17 Tyler, *The Contrast*, 479.

18 Tyler, *The Contrast*, 479.

19 George Washington to Alexander Hamilton, Mount Vernon, July 29, 1795. *Founders Online*, National Archive, http://founders.archives.gov/documents/Hamilton/01-18-02-0318.

20 Washington to Hamilton, July 29, 1795.

21 Donna J. Haraway, *Staying with the Trouble: Making Kin in the Chthulucene* (Durham, NC: Duke University Press, 2016), 3.

22 Laurence R. Newcome, *Unmanned Aviation: A Brief History of Unmanned Aerial Vehicles* (Reston, VA: American Institute of Aeronautics and Astronautics, 2004), 4.

23 Newcome, *Unmanned Aviation*, 47.

24 Steven J. Zaloga, *Unmanned Aerial Vehicles: Robotic Warfare, 1917–2007* (Oxford: Osprey Publishing, 2008), 8.

25 Kevin Howley, *Drones: Media Discourse and the Public Imagination* (New York: Peter Lang, 2018), xiv.

26 John Arquilla and David Ronfeldt, *Swarming and the Future of Conflict* (n.p.: RAND National Defense Research Institute, 2000), vii.

27 Arquilla and Ronfeldt, *Swarming and the Future*, viii.

28 Jake Kosek, "Ecologies of Empire: On the New Uses of the Honeybee," *Cultural Anthropology* 25 (2010): 650–78.

29 Erica Lee, "Bee Killers," *UC Berkley Social Science Matrix*, December 27, 2014, https://matrix.berkeley.edu/research/bee-killers.

30 Margaret Atwood, *The Year of the Flood* (New York: Random House, 2009), 180.

31 Atwood, *The Year*, 180.

32 James Smith, "On Killer Bees and GCHQ: 'Hated in the Nation,'" in *Through the Black Mirror: Deconstructing the Side Effects of the Digital Age*, eds. Terence McSweeney and Stuart Joy (London: Palgrave Macmillan, 2019), 187–8.

33 Kosek, "Ecologies of Empire," 667.

34 Kosek, "Ecologies of Empire," 668.

35 Kosek, "Ecologies of Empire," 670.

36 Jason Edward Lewis, Noelani Arista, Archer Pechawis, and Suzanne Kite, "Making Kin with the Machines," *Journal of Design and Science* (2018): https://doi.org/10.21428/bfafd97b.

Bibliography

The Aberdeen Bestiary, "Special Collections," University of Aberdeen, https://www.abdn.ac.uk/bestiary/.

Acheson, Katherine O. "Military Illustration, Garden Design, and Marvell's 'Upon Appleton House.'" *English Literary Renaissance* 41, no. 1 (2011): 146–88.

Adams, Jessica. *Wounds of Returning: Race, Memory, and Property on the Post-slavery Plantation*. Chapel Hill: University of North Carolina Press, 2012.

Agamben, Giorgio. *Homo Sacer: Sovereign Power and Bare Life*. Translated by Daniel Heller-Roazen. Palo Alto, CA: Stanford University Press, 1998.

Aizen, Marcelo A., Lucas A. Garibaldi, Saul A. Cunningham, and Alexandra M. Klein. "How Much Does Agriculture Depend on Pollinators? Lessons from Long-Term Trends in Crop Production." *Annals of Botany* 103, no. 9 (2009): 1579–88.

Alfred, Taiaiake. "Sovereignty." In *Sovereignty Matters*, edited by Joanne Barker, 33–55. Lincoln: University of Nebraska Press, 2005.

Anthony. *Medieval Preachers and Medieval Preaching*. Edited and Translated by J. M. Neale. London: J & C Mozley, 1856.

Apess, William. *Eulogy on King Philip*, 2nd ed. Boston, MA: The Author, 1837.

Archer, Jayne. "A 'Perfect Circle'? Alchemy in the Poetry of Hester Pulter." *Literature Compass* 2, no. 1 (2005): 1–14.

Aristotle, *History of Animals*. Translated by Richard Cresswell. London: George Bell & Sons, 1897.

Arizona State Teacher's College Bulletin. 13, no. 2 (1937).

Armstrong, Philip. "The Postcolonial Animal." *Society and Animals* 10, no. 4 (2002): 413–9.

Arquilla, John and David Ronfeldt, *Swarming and the Future of Conflict*. Santa Monica, CA: RAND National Defense Research Institute, 2000.

Atwood, Margaret. *The Year of the Flood*. New York: Random House, 2009.

Austen, Ralph. *Observations Upon Some Part of Francis Bacon's Natural History*. Oxford: Hen. Hall, 1658.

Bacon, Francis. *Of the Proficience and Advancement of Learning, Divine and Humane*. London: Thomas Purfoot and Thomas Creede, 1605.

———. *Novum Organum*. Translated by Joseph Devey. New York: P.F. Collier and Son, 1902.

Bateson, Melissa, Suzanne Desire, Sarah E. Gartside, and Geraldine A. Wright. "Agitated Honeybees Exhibit Pessimistic Cognitive Biases." *Current Biology* 21, no. 12 (June 2011): 1070–3.

Batt, Antonie. *A Hive of Sacred Honiecombes Containing Most Sweet and Heavenly Counsel*. Douai: Peter Auroy, 1631.

Belcourt, Billy-Ray. "Animal Bodies, Colonial Subjects: (Re)Locating Animality in Decolonial Thought." *Societies* 5 (2015): 1–11.

Bennett, Jane. *Vibrant Matter: A Political Ecology of Things*. Durham: Duke University Press, 2010.

Bernard, *Saint Bernard, His Meditations, Or Sighes, Sobbes, and Teares Upon Our Saviors Passion*. Translated by W. P. London: Thomas Creede, 1611.

———. *Five Books on Consideration: Advice to a Pope*. Vol. 13, translated by John D. Anderson and Elizabeth T. Kennan. Kalamazoo, MI: Cistercian Publications, 1976.

———. *The Sentences*. Translated by Francis R Swietek. Kalamazoo, MI: Cistercian Publications, 2000.

Bradley, Beatrice. "Creative Juices: Sweat in *Paradise Lost*." *Milton Studies* 62, no. 1 (2020): 107–35.

Brooks, Lisa. *Our Beloved Kin: A New History of King Philip's War*. New Haven, CT: Yale University Press, 2018.

Brown, Eric C., ed. *Insect Poetics*. Minneapolis: University of Minnesota Press, 2006.

Brown, Tony C. "How Savages Came Into the World (Bernard Mandeville)." *The Eighteenth Century* 59, no. 4 (Winter 2018): 471–91.

Browne, Thomas. *A True and Full Copy of that which was Surreptitiously Printed before under the Name of Religio Medici*. London, 1643.

Bryden, D. J. "John Gedde's Bee-House and the Royal Society." *Notes and Records of the Royal Society of London* 48, no. 2 (1994): 193–213.

Bloom, Harold. *A Map of Misreading*. Oxford: Oxford University Press, 1975.

Boehrer, Bruce. *Shakespeare Among the Animals: Nature and Society in the Drama of Early Modern England*. New York: Palgrave/St. Martin's Press, 2002.

———. *Animal Characters: Nonhuman Beings in Early Modern Literature*. Philadelphia: University of Pennsylvania Press, 2010.

———. *Environmental Degradation in Jacobean Drama*. Cambridge: Cambridge University Press, 2013.

Booth, William James. "Economies of Time: On the Idea of Time in Marx's Political Economy." *Political Theory* 19 (1991): 7–27.

Bourne, Edward G. "Alexander Hamilton and Adam Smith." *The Quarterly Journal of Economics* 8, no. 3 (April 1894): 328–44.

Bowerbank, Sylvia. "The Spider's Delight: Margaret Cavendish and the 'Female' Imagination." *English Literary Renaissance* 14, no. 3 (1984): 392–408.

Bradstreet, Anne. *The Tenth Muse Lately Sprung up in America*. London, 1650.

Brand, Donald. "The Honey Bee in New Spain and Mexico." *Journal of Cultural Geography* 9 (1988): 71–82.

Breen, T.H. *The Marketplace of Revolution: How Consumer Politics Shaped American Independence*. Oxford: Oxford University Press, 2004.

Britland, Karen. "Conspiring with 'friends': Hester Pulter's Poetry and the Stanley Family at Cumberlow Green." *The Review of English Studies* 69, no. 292 (2018): 832–54.

Brown, Michael P. *The Pilgrim and the Bee: Reading Rituals and Book Culture in Early New England*. Philadelphia: University of Pennsylvania Press, 2007.

Brydon-Miller, Mary, and Anne Inga Hilsen. "Where Rivers Meet: Exploring the Confluence of Ecofeminism, Covenantal Ethics, and Action Research." In *Contemporary Perspectives of Ecofeminism*, edited by Mary Phillips and Nick Rumens, 95–107. New York: Routledge, 2016.

Buege, Douglas. "Epistemic Responsibility and the Inuit of Canada's Eastern Arctic: An Ecofeminist Appraisal." In *Ecofeminism: Women, Culture, Nature,* edited by Karen J. Warren, 99–111. Bloomington: Indiana University Press, 1997.

"'Buffalo Bees': Pine Ridge to Sponsor Bee Hives." Indian Country Today. January, 19, 2016, https://newsmaven.io/indiancountrytoday/.

Butler, Charles. *The Feminine Monarchie: or a Treatise Concerning Bees and the Due Ordering of Them*. Oxford: Ioseph Barnes, 1609.

Butler, Judith. *Frames of War: When is Life Grievable?* London: Verso, 2009.

Calvo, Luz, and Catriona Rueda Esquiebel. *Decolonize Your Diet: Plant-Based Mexican-American Recipes for Health and Healing*. Vancouver: Arsenal Pulp Press, 2015.

Campana, Joseph. "The Bee and the Sovereign?: Political Entomology and the Problem of Scale." *Shakespeare Studies* 41 (2013): 94–113.

———. "The Bee and the Sovereign (II): Segments, Swarms, and the Shakespearean Multitude." In *The Return of Theory in Early Modern English Studies*. Vol. II, edited by Paul Cefalu, Gary Kuchar, and Bryan Reynolds, 59–78. New York: Palgrave Macmillan, 2014.

———. "Humans: Exceptional Humans, Human Exceptionalism, and the Shape of Things to Come." In *Shakespearean International Yearbook 15: Shakespeare and the Human*, edited by Tiffany Jo Werth, 39–62. Burlington, VT: Ashgate, 2015.

Campbell, Mary Baine. "Busy Bees: Utopia, Dystopia, and the Very Small." *Journal of Medieval and Early Modern Studies* 36 (2006): 619–42.

Carruthers, Mary. *The Book of Memory: A Study of Memory in Medieval Culture*. New York: Cambridge University Press, 1990.

Cavendish, Margaret. *The Blazing World and Other Writings*. Edited by Kate Lilley. Reprint, New York: Penguin, 1994.

———. *Margaret Cavendish's Poems and Fancies: A Digital Critical Edition*, edited by Liza Blake. Updated May 2019, http://library2.utm.utoronto.ca/poemsandfancies/.

C.B. "Oblige Your Constant Reader." *The Boston Gazette and Country Journal*, October 16, 1769, https://www.masshist.org/dorr/volume/2/sequence/755.

Chaffin, Robert J. "The Townshend Acts Crisis, 1767–1770." In *A Companion to the American Revolution,* edited by Jack P. Greene and J.R. Pole, 134–50. Malden, MA: Blackwell, 2000.

Chedzgoy, Kate. *Women's Writing in the British Atlantic World: Memory, Place, and History, 1550–1700*. Cambridge: Cambridge University Press, 2007.

Cherry, R.H. "Insects in the Mythology of Native Americans." *American Entomologist* 39 (1993): 16–22.

Clark, Christopher. *The Roots of Rural Capitalism: Western Massachusetts, 1780–1860*. Ithaca, NY: Cornell University Press, 1990.

Clark, Peter D. *Origin and Traditional History of the Wyandotts*. Toronto: Hunter, Rose, and Co., 1870.

Clarke, Elizabeth. "Women in Church and in Devotional Spaces." In *The Cambridge Companion to Early Modern Women's Writing*, edited by Laura Lunger Knoppers, 110–23. Cambridge: Cambridge University Press, 2009.

———. *Politics, Religion, and the Song of Songs in Seventeenth-Century England*. London: Palgrave Macmillan, 2011.

Clausen, Lucy W. *Insect Fact and Folklore*. New York: Macmillan, 1954.

Codex Mendoza. "MS. Arch. Selden. Bodleian Library," University of Oxford, https://iiif.bodleian.ox.ac.uk/iiif/viewer.

Codignola, Luca. "The Holy See and the Conversion of the Indians in French and British North America, 1486–1750." In *America in European Consciousness, 1493–1750*, 195–242. Chapel Hill: University of North Carolina Press, 1995.

Comito, Terry. "Caliban's Dream: The Topography of Some Shakespeare Gardens." *Shakespeare Studies* 14 (1981): 23–54.

Connolly, Ruth. "Hester Pulter's Childbirth Poetics." *Women's Writing* 26 (2019): 282–303.

Cook-Lynn, Elizabeth. *A Separate Country: Postcoloniality and American Indian Nations*. Lubbock: Texas Tech University Press, 2012.

Cook, Suzanne. *The Forest of the Lacandon Maya: An Ethnobotanical Guide*. Cham, CH: Springer, 2016.

Cortés, Hernán. *Fernando Cortés: His Five Letters of Relation to the Emperor Charles V*. Translated by Francis Augustus MacNutt, vol. 1. Cleveland: A. H. Clark, 1908.

Cotton, John. "God's Promise to His Plantation," edited by Reiner Smolinski. *Electronic Texts in American Studies* 22 (1988): 1–20.

Cotton, Josiah. *Vocabulary of the Massachusetts (or Natick) Indian Language*. Cambridge, 1829.

Crane, Eva. *The World History of Beekeeping and Honey Hunting*. New York: Taylor and Francis, 1999.

Crèvecoeur, J. Hector St. John. *Letters from an American Farmer, 1782*. Edited by Ludwig Lewisohn. New York: Fox, Duffield and Co., 1904.

Cronon, William. *Changes in the Land: Indians, Colonists, and the Ecology of New England*. New York: Hill and Wang, 1983.

Cutts, John P. "Robert Johnson: King's Musician in His Majesty's Public Entertainment." *Music & Letters* 36, no. 2 (1955): 110–25.

Dain, Bruce R. *A Hideous Monster of the Mind: American Race Theory in the Early Republic*. Cambridge, MA: Harvard University Press, 2002.

Darwin, Charles. *On the Various Contrivances By Which British and Foreign Orchids are Fertilised by Insects*. 2nd ed. New York: D. Appleton and Co., 1877.

Davidson, Peter. "Green Thoughts. Marvell's Gardens: Clues to Two Curious Puzzles." *Times Literary Supplement* 5044 (December 3, 1999): 14–5.

de Sahagún, Bernadino. *Florentine Codex: Book 10; The People*. Translated by Charles E. Dibble and Arthur J. O. Anderson. Salt Lake City: University of Utah Press, 2012.

Deckha, Maneesha. "Toward a Postcolonial, Posthumanist Feminist Theory: Centralizing Race and Culture in Feminist Work on Nonhuman Animals." *Hypatia* 22 (2012): 527–45.

della Porta, Donatella, Sakari Hänninen, Martti Siisiäinen, and Tiina Silvastri, *The New Social Division: Making and Unmaking Precariousness*. London: Palgrave Macmillan, 2015.

DeMello, Margo. *Animals and Society: An Introduction to Human-Animal Studies*. New York: Columbia University Press, 2012.

Dimmler, Richard. "The Bee-Topos in the Jesuit Emblem Book: Themes and Contrast." *Symbola ed emblemata* 3 (1992): 229–46.

Dippold, Steffi. "The Wampanoag Word: John Eliot's Indian Grammar, the Vernacular Rebellion, and the Elegancies of Native Speech." *Early American Literature* 48, no. 3 (2013): 543–75.

Dobbs, Arthur. "A Letter from Arthur Dobbs, Esq. to Charles Stanhope, Esq. Concerning Bees and Their Methods of Gathering Wax and Honey." *Proceedings of the Royal Society of London* (November 8, 1750): 536–49.

Donne, John. *The Complete Poetry and Selected Prose of John Donne*, edited by Charles M. Coffin. New York: Modern Library, 2001.

Donovan, Josephine. "Animal Rights and Feminist Theory." *Signs* 15, no. 2 (1990): 350–75.

———. "Feminism and the Treatment of Animals." *Signs: Journal of Women in Culture and Society* 31, no. 2 (2006): 305–29.

Donovan, Josephine, and Carol J. Adams, ed., *The Feminist Care Tradition in Animal Ethics*. New York: Columbia University Press, 2007.

Duffin, Ross W. *Shakespeare's Songbook*. New York: Norton, 2004.

Dunbar-Ortiz, Roxanne. *An Indigenous Peoples' History of the United States*. Boston, MA: Beacon Press, 2014.

Dunn, Catherine M. "The Function of Music in Shakespeare's Romances." *Shakespeare Quarterly* (1969): 391–405.

Dunn, Rachel. "Breaking a Tradition: Hester Pulter and the English Emblem Book." *The Seventeenth Century* 30, no. 1 (2015): 55–73.

Eardley, Alice. "'Saturn (whose aspects soe sads my soul': Lady Hester Pulter's Feminine Melancholic Genius." In *New Ways of Looking at Old Texts, IV: Papers of the Renaissance English Text Society, 2002–2006*, edited by Michael Denbo, 239–54. Tempe, AZ: Center for Medieval and Renaissance Studies Press, 2008.

———. "'Shut up in a Country Grange': The Provenance of Lady Hester Pulter's Poetry and Prose and Women's Literary History." *Huntington Library Quarterly* 80, no. 2 (2017): 345–59.

Edison, Thomas A. "The Perfected Phonograph." *The North American Review* 146 (1888): 641–50.

Edwards, Jonathan D. *Observations on the Language of the Muhhekaneew Indians*. Boston, 1823.

Edwards, Karen. *Milton and the Natural World: Science and Poetry in Paradise Lost*. Cambridge: Cambridge University Press, 2005.

Eikon Alethine: The Pourtraiture of Truths Most Sacred Majesty Truly Suffering. London: Thomas Paine, 1649.

Eikon Basilike: The Portraicture of His Sacred Majestie in His Solitudes and Sufferings. London, 1649.

Erben, Patrick M. "'Honey-Combs' and 'Paper-Hives': Positioning Francis Daniel Pastorius's Manuscript Writings in Early Pennsylvania." *Early American Literature* 37, no. 2 (2012): 157–94.

Evelyn, John. *Elysium Britannicum: or the Royal Gardens.* Edited by John E. Ingram. Philadelphia: University of Pennsylvania Press, 2001.

Ezell, Margaret J. M. "The Laughing Tortoise: Speculations on Manuscript Sources and Women's Book History." *English Literary Renaissance* 38, no. 2 (2008): 331–55.

Fenelon, James V., and Thomas D. Hall, "Revitalization and Indigenous Resistance to Globalization and Neoliberalism." *American Behavioral Scientist* 51, no. 2 (2008): 1867–1901.

Fermino, Jessie "Little Doe." "An Introduction to Wampanoag Grammar." Master's thesis. Massachusetts Institute of Technology, 2000. dspace.mit.edu/handle/1721.1/8740.

Fewkes, Jesse Walter. *The Tusayan Ritual: A Study of the Influence of Environment on Aboriginal Cults.* Washington, DC: Smithsonian, 1895.

———. *Sun Worship of the Hopi Indians.* Washington, DC: Smithsonian, 1918.

Finley, Randy. "A Lynching State: Arkansas in the 1890s." In *Bullets and Fire: Lynching and Authority in Arkansas, 1850–1950,* edited by Guy Lancaster, 61–86. Fayetteville: University of Arkansas Press, 2018.

Fitzhenry, William J. "Ecocritical Readings of Andrew Marvell's Fairfax Poems." *Papers on Language and Literature* 53, no. 3 (2017): 237–66.

Flinker, Noam. *The Song of Songs in English Renaissance Literature.* Cambridge: D.S. Brewer, 2000.

Fox-Good, Jacquelyn. "Other Voices: The Sweet, Dangerous Air(s) of Shakespeare's Tempest." *Shakespeare Studies* 24 (1996): 241–74.

Francis. *Laudato Si': On Care for Our Common Home.* Huntington, IN: Our Sunday Visitor, 2015.

Freedberg, David. "Iconography between the History of Art and the History of Science: Art, Science, and the Case of the Urban Bee." In *Picturing Science, Producing Art,* edited by Caroline A. Jones, Peter Louis Galison, and Amy E. Slaton, 272–96. New York: Routledge, 1998.

Fuchs, Barbara. "Conquering Islands: Contextualizing *The Tempest.*" *Shakespeare Quarterly* 48 (1997): 45–62.

———. "Imperium Studies: Theorizing Early Modern Expansion." In *Postcolonial Moves: Medieval Through Modern,* edited by Patricia Clare Ingham and Michelle R. Warren, 71–90. London: Palgrave Macmillan, 2003.

Fudge, Erica. "Calling Creatures By Their True Names: Bacon, the New Science and the Beast in Man." In *At the Borders of the Human: Beasts, Bodies, and Natural Philosophy in the Early Modern Period,* edited by Erica Fudge, Ruth Gilbert, and Susan Wiseman, 91–109. London: Palgrave Macmillan, 1999.

———. *Perceiving Animals: Humans and Beasts in Early Modern English Culture.* London: Palgrave, 2000.

———. "Saying Nothing Concerning the Same: On Dominion, Purity, and Meat in Early Modern England." In *Renaissance Beasts: Of Animals, Humans, and Other Wonderful Creatures,* edited by Erica Fudge, 70–86. Champaign: University of Illinois Press, 2004.

———. *Brutal Reasoning: Animals, Rationality, and Humanity in Early Modern England.* Ithaca, NY: Cornell University Press, 2007.

———. *Quick Cattle and Dying Wishes: People and Their Animals in Early Modern England.* Ithaca, NY: Cornell University Press, 2018.

Garrison, Dale. "The Origins of Golden Honey and its Gastronomic and Medicinal Uses." *Indian Country Today*, January 26, 2013, https://indiancountry today.com/archive/the-origins-of-golden-honey-and-its-gastronomic-and-medicinal-uses-2mktMANpM0ucTvo2-VbJOQ.

Gimmel, Millie. "An Ecocritical Evaluation of Book XI of the Florentine Codex." In *Early Modern Ecostudies*, edited by Ivo Kamps, Karen L. Raber, and Thomas Hallock, 167–80. New York: Palgrave Macmillan, 2008.

Glazebrook, Trish. "Climate Adaptation in the Global South: Funding Women's Farming." In *Contemporary Perspectives on Ecofeminism*, edited by Mary Phillips and Nick Rumens, 111–31. New York: Routledge, 2016.

Glenn, Edna. "Exemplary Arts: Section C—Subject: Ceremony—Ancient and Contemporary Images." *Hopi Nation: Essays on Indigenous Art, Culture, History, and Law* 9 (2008): 74–88.

Go, Kenji. "Montaigne's 'Cannibals' and *The Tempest* Revisited." *Studies in Philology* 109, no. 4 (Summer 2012): 455–73.

Gookin, Daniel. *Historical Collections of the Indians in New England*. Boston: Massachusetts Historical Society, 1792.

Grafton, Anthony. "The Republic of Letters in the American Colonies: Francis Daniel Pastorius Makes a Notebook." *The American Historical Review* 117, no. 1 (2012): 1–39.

Grant, Judith, and Vincent G. Jungkunz, ed., *The Importance of the Animal/Human Question for Political Theory*. Albany, NY: SUNY Press, 2016.

Grew, Nehemiah. *The Anatomy of Plants*. London: W. Rawlins, 1682.

Griffiths, Fiona J. *The Garden of Delights: Reform and Renaissance for Women in the Twelfth Century*. Philadelphia: University of Pennsylvania Press, 2007.

Grinnell, Richard. "Shakespeare's Keeping of Bees." *Indisciplinary Studies in Literature and the Environment* 23, no. 4 (2016): 835–54.

Gutiérrez, Ramon A. *When Jesus Came, the Corn Mothers Went Away*. Stanford, CA: Stanford University Press, 1991.

Haas, Angela M. "Wampum as Hypertext: An American Indian Intellectual Tradition of Multimedia Theory and Practice." *Studies in American Indian Literatures* 19, no. 4 (2007): 77–100.

Hall, Kim F. *Things of Darkness: Economies of Race and Gender in Early Modern England*. Ithaca, NY: Cornell University Press, 1995.

Hall, Louisa. "Hester Pulter's Brave New Worlds." In *Immortality and the Body in the Age of Milton*," edited by John Rumrich and Stephen Fallon, 171–86. Cambridge: Cambridge University Press, 2018.

Hall, Mitchell G. "To the U.S. Attorney General." In *Lynching in America: A History in Documents*, edited by Christopher Waldrep, 202–3. New York: New York University Press, 2006.Hamilton, Charles, ed., *Cry of the Thunderbird: The American Indian's Own Story*. Norman: University of Oklahoma Press, 1972.

Haraway, Donna J. *Staying with the Trouble: Making Kin in the Chthulucene*. Durham, NC: Duke University Press, 2016.

Harding, Davis P. "Milton's Bee-Simile." *Journal of English and Germanic Philology* 60 (1961): 664–9.

Hartlib, Samuel. *The Reformed Commonwealth of Bees*. London, 1655.

Hawkesworth, Mary, and Lisa Disch, eds. "Feminist Theory: Transforming the Known World." In *The Oxford Handbook of Feminist Theory*, 1–15. Oxford: Oxford University Press, 2016.

Hayes, Kevin J. *George Washington: A Life in Books*. New York: Oxford University Press, 2017.

Held, Virginia. *The Ethics of Care: Personal, Political, and Global*. Oxford: Oxford University Press, 2005.

Hendericks, Garret, Derick up de Graeff, and Francis Daniel Pastorius. *Quaker Protest Against Slavery*. 1688. Special Collections. MS 99 B-R. Bryn Mawr Library. http://triptych.brynmawr.edu.

Herman, Peter C. "Lady Hester Pulter's *The Unfortunate Florinda*: Race, Religion, and the Politics of Rape." *Renaissance Quarterly* 63, no. 4 (2010):1208–46.

Hill, Hannah. *A Legacy for Children, Being Some of the Last Expressions and Sayings of Hannah Hill*. Philadelphia, PA: Andrew Bradford, 1717.

Hillier, Russell M. "'By force or fraud / Weening to prosper': Milton's Satanic and Messianic Modes of Heroism." *Milton Quarterly* 43 (2009): 17–38.

Hiltner, Ken. *Milton and Ecology*. Cambridge: Cambridge University Press, 2003.

"History of the Cylinder Phonograph." Library of Congress. https://www.loc.gov/collections/edison-company-motion-pictures-and-sound-recordings/articles-and-essays/history-of-edison-sound-recordings/history-of-the-cylinder-phonograph/

Hobbes, Thomas. *Leviathan: or the Matter, Form, and Power of a Commonwealth Ecclesiastical and Civil*. London, 1651.

Hoffman, George. "Anatomy of the Mass: Montaigne's 'Cannibals.'" *PMLA* 117, no. 2 (2002): 207–21.

Hofstadter, Dan. *The Earth Moves: Galileo and the Roman Inquisition*. New York: W.W. Norton & Co, 2010.

Holland, Henry and Edward Topsell. *The Historie of Adam, or the Foure-fold State of Man*. London: Thomas East, 1606.

Hollingsworth, Cristopher. *Poetics of the Hive: The Insect Metaphor in Literature*. Iowa City: University of Iowa Press, 2001.

Homer, *The Iliad*. Translated by Barry B. Powell. New York: Oxford University Press, 2014.

Horn, Tammy. *Bees in America: How the Honey Bee Shaped a Nation*. Lexington: University Press Kentucky, 2005.

Hoskens, Jane Fenn. *The Life and Spiritual Sufferings of that Faithful Servant of Christ Jane Hoskens, a Public Preacher among the People Called Quakers*. Edited by Paul Royster. *Electronic Texts in American Studies* 24 (2007): 1–40.

Howley, Kevin. *Drones: Media Discourse and the Public Imagination*. New York: Peter Lang, 2018.

Hubbard, William. *A Narrative of the Troubles with the Indians in New England*. Boston, MA, 1677.

Hughes, Felicity A. "Milton, Shakespeare, Pindar and the Bees." *Review of English Studies* 44, no. 174 (1993): 220–30.

Hulme, Peter. *Colonial Encounters: Europe and the Native Caribbean, 1492–1797*. London: Methuen, 1986.

Hustak, Carla, and Natasha Myers. "Involutionary Momentum: Affective Ecologies and the Sciences of Plant/Insect Encounters." *differences: A Journal of Feminist Cultural Studies* 23 (2012): 74–118.

Innes, Stephen. *Creating the Commonwealth: The Economic Culture of Puritan New England*. New York: Norton, 1995.

Jack, Malcolm. "Mandeville, Johnson, Morality and Bees." In *Mandeville and Augustan Ideas: New Essays*, edited by Charles W. A. Prior, 85–96. Victoria: University of Victoria Press, 2000.

Jacobs, Nicole A. "Robbing His Captive Shepherdess: Princess Elizabeth, John Milton, and the Memory of Charles I in the *Eikon Basilike* and *Eikonoklastes*." *Criticism* 54 (2012): 227–55.

———. "Lady Hester Pulter's *The Unfortunate Florinda* and the Conventions of Sexual Violence." *Appositions: Studies in Renaissance / Early Modern Literature and Culture* 7 (2014). http://appositions.blogspot.com/2014/07.

———. "Bees: The Shakespearean Hive and the Virtues of Honey." In *Shakespearean International Yearbook 15: Shakespeare and the Human*, edited by Tiffany Jo Werth, 101–21. Burlington, VT: Ashgate, 2015.

Jacobs, Wilbur R. "The Protocol of Indian Diplomacy." *The William and Mary Quarterly* 6, no. 4 (1949): 596–604.

Jefferson, Thomas. *Notes on the State of Virginia*. 1781. Reprint, Boston, MA: Lilly and Wait, 1832.

Kahn, Victoria. *Machivellian Rhetoric: From the Counter-Reformation to Milton*. Princeton, NJ: Princeton University Press, 1994.

Kellaway, William. *The New England Company, 1649–1776: Missionary Society to the American Indians*. Longman's: London, 1961.

Kosek, Jake. "Ecologies of Empire: On the New Uses of the Honeybee." *Cultural Anthropology* 25 (2010): 650–78.

Kupperman, Karen Ordahl. "The Beehive as a Model for Colonial Design." In *America in European Consciousness, 1493–1750*, edited by Karen Ordahl Kupperman, 272–94. Chapel Hill: University of North Carolina Press, 1995.

Kwaymullina, Ambelin. "Aboriginal Nations, The Australian Nation-State and Indigenous International Legal Traditions." In *Indigenous Peoples as Subjects of International Law*, edited by Irene Watson, 5–17. New York: Routledge, 2017.

Lahontan, Louis-Armand de Lom d'Arce, Baron de. "Memoirs of North America." In *New Voyages to North America*, vol. 1, edited by Reuben Gold Thwaites, 299–407. London, 1703.

Lambert, Margo M. "Mediation, Assimilation, and German Foundations in North America: Francis Daniel Pastorius as Cultural Broker." *Pennsylvania History: A Journal of Mid-Atlantic Studies* 84 (2017): 141–70.

Laroche, Rebecca and Jennifer Munroe, *Shakespeare and Ecofeminist Theory*. London: Bloomsbury, 2017.

Latour, Bruno. *Reassembling the Social: An Introduction to Actor-Network-Theory*. Oxford: Oxford University Press, 2005.

Lecky, Kat. "Milton's Experienced Eve." *Philological Quarterly* 96, no. 4 (2017): 453–74.

Lee, Erica. "Bee Killers." *UC Berkeley Social Science Matrix*, December 27, 2014, https://matrix.berkeley.edu/research/bee-killers.

Lee, Wayne E. *Barbarians and Brothers: Anglo-American Warfare, 1500–1865.* Oxford: Oxford University Press, 2011.

Lehnhof, Kent R. "'Intestine War' and 'the Smell of Mortal Change': Troping the Digestive Tract in *Paradise Lost.*" In *The Sacred and Profane in English Renaissance Literature,* edited by Mary A. Papazian, 278–300. Newark: University of Delaware Press, 2008.

Leibman, Laura Arnold, ed., *Experience Mayhew's Indian Converts: A Cultural Edition.* Amherst: University of Massachusetts Press, 2008.

Lemay, J. A. Leo. *The Life of Benjamin Franklin, vol. 1, Journalist, 1706–1730.* Philadelphia: University of Pennsylvania Press, 2006.

Leonard, William Ellery. *The Lynching Bee and Other Poems.* New York: B.W. Huebsch, 1920.

Levett, John. *The Ordering of Bees: Or the True History of Managing Them.* London: Thomas Harper, 1634.

Lewalski, Barbara Kiefer. *The Life of John Milton: A Critical Biography.* New York: Wiley Blackwell, 2002.

Lewis, Eric. "The Legacy of Margaret Cavendish." *Perspectives on Science 9,* no. 3 (2001): 341–65.

Lewis, Jason Edward, Noelani Arista, Archer Pechawis, and Suzanne Kite, "Making Kin with the Machines." *Journal of Design and Science* (2018). https://doi.org/10.21428/bfafd97b.

Lieb, Michael. *The Dialectics of Creation: Patterns of Birth and Regeneration in Paradise Lost.* Amherst: University of Massachusetts Press, 1970.

Liebert, Rana Saadi. "Apian Imagery and the Critique of Poetic Sweetness in Plato's Republic." *Transactions of the American Philological Society* 140, no. 1 (2010): 97–115.

Littlebird, Larry. "Hamaatsa Honeybee Apiary." updated 2012. http://www.hamaatsa.org/Honeybee.html.

Littleton, Adam. *Lingue Latinae Liber Dictionarius Quadripartitus.* London: T. Basset, J. Wright, and R. Chiswell, 1678.

"List of the Wyandotte Tribe of Indians." *U.S. microfilm M234, RG75, Roll 951, frames 0208–0249. Office of Indian Affairs.* August 22, 1870, https://www.wyandotte-nation.org/culture/history/historic-rolls/roll-1870/.

Loomba, Ania. *Shakespeare, Race, and Colonialism.* Oxford: Oxford University Press, 2002.

MacFaul, Tom. *Shakespeare and the Natural World.* Cambridge: Cambridge University Press, 2015.

Malcolm, Joyce Lee. ed., *The Struggle for Sovereignty: Seventeenth-Century English Political Tracts,* vol. I. Indianapolis, IN: Liberty Fund, 1999.

Mandeville, Bernard. *An Enquiry into the Origin of Honour and the Usefulness of Christianity in War.* London, 1732.

———. *The Fable of the Bees.* Edited by F. B. Kaye, vol. 1.Oxford: Clarendon Press, 1924.

———. *The Fable of the Bees.* Edited by Phillip Harth. London: Pelican Books, 1970; Reprint, Harmondsworth, UK: Penguin Books, 1989.

Manning, Helen Vanderloop. *Moshup's Footsteps: The Wampanoag Nation / The People of First Light.* Aquinnah, MA: Blue Cloud Across the Moon, 2001.

Marrero, Karen L. "Women at a Crossroads: Trade, Mobility, and Power in Early French America and Detroit." In *Women in Early America*, edited by Thomas A. Foster, 159–85. New York: New York University Press, 2015.

Martino-Truror, Gina M. "'As Potent a Prince as Any Round About Her': Rethinking Weetamoo of the Pocasset and Native Female Leadership in Early America," *Journal of Women's History* 27, no. 3 (Fall 2015): 37–60.

Marvell, Andrew. *The Poems of Andrew Marvell.* Edited by Nigel Smith. New York: Longman, 2003.

Marx, Karl. "Religion, Free Press, and Philosophy." In *Writings of the Young Karl Marx on Philosophy and Society.* Translated by Loyd D. Easton and Kurt H. Guddat, 109–30. New York: Doubleday, 1967.

Mather, Cotton. *Magnalia Christi Americana: Or, the Ecclesiastical History of New England, from its First Planting in the Year 1620.* vol. 1. 1702. Reprint, Hartford, CT: Silus Andrus & Son, 1820.

McColley, Diane Kelsey. "Milton and Ecology." In *A Companion to Milton*, edited by Thomas N. Corns, 157–73. Malden, MA: Blackwell Publishing, 2003.

McCracken, Peggy. *In the Skin of the Beast: Sovereignty and Animality in Medieval France.* Chicago: Chicago University Press, 2017.

Mentz, Steven. "Airy Spirits: Winds, Bodies, and Ecological Force in Early Modern England." In *Shakespearean International Yearbook 15: Shakespeare and the Human*, edited by Tiffany Jo Werth, 21–38. Burlington, VT: Ashgate, 2015.

Merchant, Carolyn. *The Death of Nature: Women, Ecology, and the Scientific Revolution.* San Francisco, CA: Harper Collins, 1980.

———. *Radical Ecology: The Search for a Livable World.* New York: Routledge, 1992.

———. "The Scientific Revolution and *The Death of Nature.*" *Isis* 97 (2006): 513–33.

Miller, Marla R. *The Needle's Eye: Women and Work in the Age of Revolution.* Amherst: University of Massachusetts Press, 2006.

Milton, John. *Complete Prose Works of John Milton.* Edited by Don M. Wolfe, 8 vols. New Haven, CT: Yale University Press, 1953.

———. *Complete Poems and Major Prose.* Edited by Merritt Y. Hughes. Indianapolis, IN: Hackett Publishing, 2003. First published 1957 by Prentice Hall, Inc.

Moeck, William. "Bees in My Bonnet: Milton's Epic Simile and Intertextuality." *Milton Quarterly* 32, no. 4 (1998): 122–35.

Moore, Jason W. *Capitalism in the Web of Life: Ecology and the Accumulation of Capital.* New York: Verso, 2015.

More, Thomas. *Utopia.* Translated by Clarence H. Miller. New Haven: Yale University Press, 2001.

Morison, James Cotter. *The Life and Times of Saint Bernard, Abbot of Clairvaux.* New York: Macmillan, 1863.

Morrillo, John. *The Rise of Animals and Descent of Man, 1660–1800: Toward Posthumanism in British Literature between Descarte and Darwin.* Lanham, MD: University of Delaware Press, 2018.

Morton, Thomas. *New English Cannan: or New Canaan Containing an Abstract of New England.* N.p., 1632.

Mt. Pleasant, Jane. "A New Paradigm for Pre-Columbian Agriculture in North America." *Early American Studies* 13, no. 2 (2015): 374–412.

Munz, Tania. *Dancing Bees: Karl von Frisch and the Discovery of the Honeybee Language.* Chicago, IL: University of Chicago Press, 2016.

Nash, June. "The Mayan Quest for Pluricultural Autonomy in Mexico and Guatemala." In *Indigenous Peoples and the Modern State,* edited by Duane Champagne, Karen Jo Torjesen, and Susan Steiner, 122–42. New York: Alta Mira Press, 2005.

Neill, Michael. "'Noises, / Sounds, and sweet airs': The Burden of Shakespeare's Tempest." *Shakespeare Quarterly* 59, no. 1 (Spring 2008): 36–59.

Nequatewa, Edmund. *Truth of a Hopi: Stories Relating to the Origin, Myths, and Clan Histories of the Hopi.* 1967. Reprint, Flagstaff, AZ: Northland Publishing, 1993.

Newcome, Laurence R. *Unmanned Aviation: A Brief History of Unmanned Aerial Vehicles.* Reston, VA: American Institute of Aeronautics and Astronautics, 2004.

New Englands First Fruits: In Respect, First of the Conversion of some, Conviction of Divers, Preparation of Sundry of the Indians. London: R. O. and G. D., 1643.

Nietzsche, Friedrich. *Untimely Meditations.* Edited by Daniel Breazeale and translated by R. J. Hollingdale. Cambridge: Cambridge University Press, 1997.

Nimmo, Richie. "Apiculture in the Anthropocene: Between Posthumanism and Critical Animal Studies." In *Animals in the Anthropocene: Critical Perspectives on Non-Human Futures,* edited by Human Animal Research Network Editorial Collective, 177–99. Sydney: Sydney University Press, 2015.

North, Marcy L. "Women, the Material Book and Early Printing." In *The Cambridge Companion to Early Modern Women's Writing,* edited by Laura Lunger Knoppers, 68–82. Cambridge: Cambridge University Press, 2009.

Panke, John. *Collectanea, Out of St. Gregory the Great, and St Bernard the Devout Against the Papists.* Oxford, 1618.

Paret, Marcel. "Precarious Labor Politics: Unions and the Struggles of the Insecure Working Class in the United States and South Africa." *Critical Sociology* 41 (2013): 757–84.

Park, Katherine. "Women, Gender, and Utopia: *The Death of Nature* and the Historiography of Early Modern Science." *Isis* 97 (2006): 487–95.

Parry, Graham. "John Evelyn as Hortulan Saint." In *Culture and Cultivation in Early Modern England: Writing and the Land,* edited by Michael Leslie and Timothy Raylor, 130–50 Leicester: Leicester University Press, 1992.

Pastorius, Francis Daniel. *The Beehive.* 1696. Specials Collections. MS Codex 726. University of Pennsylvania Library. http://dla.library.upenn.edu.

———. *The Francis Daniel Pastorius Reader: Writings by an Early American Polymath,* edited by Patrick M. Erben. University Park, PA: Penn State University Press, 2019.

Peirson, Abraham. *Some Helps for the Indians: Shewing Them How to Improve Their Natural Reason, to Know the True God, and the True Christian Religion.* Cambridge, 1658.

Peña, Elizabeth S. "Wampum Diplomacy: The Historical and Archeological Evidence for Wampum at Fort Niagara." *Northeast Historical Archeology* 35 (2006): 15–28.

Perdue, Theda, and Michael D. Green. *North American Indians: A Very Short Introduction*. Oxford: Oxford University Press, 2010.

Pirsig, Wendy. "Rev. John Tompson (1740–1828) and the First Parish Parsonage." Old Berwick Historical Society. Updated 2007. http://oldberwick.org/oldberwick/index.php?option=com_content&view=article&id=128&Itemid=129

Pesic, Peter. "Wrestling with Proteus: Francis Bacon and the 'Torture' of Nature." *Isis* 90 (1999): 81–94.

Philips van Marnix van Saint Aldegonde. *The Beehive of the Romish Church*. Translated by George Gilpin. London, 1579.

Pollan, Michael. *The Botany of Desire: A Plant's-Eye View of the World*. New York: Random House, 2001.

A Platform of Church Discipline: Gathered out of the Word of God and Agreed upon by the Elders and Messengers of the Churches Assembled in the Synod of Cambridge. Cambridge, MA: Marmaduke Johnson, 1649.

Porphyry. *The Life of Pythagoras*. Translated by Kenneth Sylvan Guthrie. Alpine, NJ: Platonist Press, 1919.

Posset, Franz. "Bernard of Clairvaux as Luther's Source." *Concordia Theological Quarterly* 54, no. 4 (October 1990): 281–304.

Potter, Jr., Elisha R. *The Early History of the Narragansett: With an Appendix of Original Documents*. Providence, RI: Marshall, Brown, and Co., 1835.

Potter, Lois. *Secret Rites and Secret Writing: Royalist Literature, 1641–1660*. New York: Cambridge University Press, 1989.

Prete, Frederick R. "Can Females Rule the Hive? The Controversy over Honey Bee Gender Roles in British Beekeeping Texts of the Sixteenth—Eighteenth Centuries." *Journal of the History of Biology* 24, no. 1 (1991): 113–44.

Pritzker, Barry. *Native Americans: An Encyclopedia of History, Culture, and Peoples*. vol. 1. Santa Barbara, CA: ABC-CLIO, 1998.

Pulter, Hester. *Poems Breathed Forth by the Nobel Hadassas*. MS Lt q 32. University of Leeds, Brotherton Collection.

———. *Lady Hester Pulter: Poems, Emblems, and The Unfortunate Florinda*. Edited by Alice Eardley. Toronto: Iter, 2014.

———. *The Pulter Project: Poet in the Making*. General Editors, Leah Knight and Wendy Wall, 2018. http://pulterproject.northwestern.edu.

Quezada-Euán, José Javier. *Stingless Bees of Mexico: the Biology, Management and Conservation of an Ancient Heritage*. Cham, CH: Springer, 2018.

Raber, Karen. *Animal Bodies, Renaissance Culture*. Philadelphia: University of Pennsylvania Press, 2013.

———. *Shakespeare and Posthumanist Theory*. New York: Bloomsbury, 2018.

Ramachandran, Ayesha, and Melissa E. Sanchez. "Spenser and 'the Human': An Introduction." *Spenser Studies: A Renaissance Poetry Annual* 30 (2015): vii–xv.

Re Cruz, Alicia. *The Two Milpas of Chan Kom: Scenarios of a Maya Village Life*. Albany, NY: SUNY Press, 1996.

A Relation of Maryland Together, with a Map of the Countrey. London: William Peasley, 1635.

Revolti, Matteo. "Bees on Paper: the British Press Reads the Fable." *Erasmus Journal for Philosophy and Economics* 9, no. 1 (2016): 124–41.

Riebling, Barbara. "Milton on Machiavelli: Representations of the State in *Paradise Lost*." *Renaissance Quarterly* 49 (1996): 573–97.

Riley, Lyman W. "Books from the 'Beehive' Manuscript of Francis Daniel Pastorius." *Quaker History* 83, no. 2 (1994): 116–29.

Robbins, Caroline. *The Eighteenth-Century Commonwealthman*. Cambridge, MA: Harvard University Press, 1968.

Robson, Mark. *The Sense of Early Modern Writing*. Manchester: Manchester University Press, 2006.

Rosenblatt, Jason P. "Milton's Bee-Lines." *Texas Studies in Literature and Language* 18 (1977): 609–23.

Ross, Sarah C.E. "Tears, Bezoars and Blazing Comets: Gender and Politics in Hester Pulter's Civil War Lyrics." *Literature Compass* 2, no. 1 (2005): 1–14.

———. *Women, Poetry, and Politics in Seventeenth-Century Britain*. Oxford: Oxford University Press, 2015.

Rowlandson, Mary. *Narrative of the Captivity and Removes of Mrs. Mary Rowlandson*. 1682. Reprint, Lancaster: Carter, Andrews, and Co., 1828.

Ryerson Young, Egerton. *By Canoe and Dog-Train Among the Cree and Salteaux Indians*. New York: Hunt and Eaton, 1890.

———. *Algonquin Indian Tales*. New York: Eaton and Mains, 1904.

Salisbury, Neal. "Native People and European Settlers in Eastern North America, 1600–1783." In *The Cambridge History of the Native Peoples of the Americas*. Vol. I, part I, edited by Bruce G. Trigger and Wilcomb E. Washburn, 399–460. New York: Cambridge University Press, 1996.

Schoenfeldt, Michael. *Bodies and Selves in Early Modern England: Physiology and Inwardness in Spenser, Shakespeare, Herbert, and Milton*. Cambridge: Cambridge University Press, 1999.

Seeley, Thomas. "The Honeybee Colony as a Superorganism." *American Scientist* 77, no. 6 (November 1989): 546–53.

———. *Honeybee Democracy*. Princeton, NJ: Princeton University Press, 2010.

Sekaquaptewa, Emory, and Dorothy Washburn. "As a Matter of Practice… Hopi Cosmology in Hopi Life: Some Considerations for Theory and Method in Southwestern Archaeology." *Time and Mind: The Journal of Archaeology, Consciousness and Culture* 2, no. 2 (2009): 195–214.

Sekaquaptewa, Emory, Kenneth C. Hill, and Dorothy K. Washburn. *Hopi Katsina Songs*. Lincoln: University of Nebraska Press, 2015.

Shakespeare, William. *The Second Part of Henry VI*. Edited by Michael Hattaway. Cambridge: Cambridge University Press, 1991.

———. *The Tempest*. Edited by Virginia Mason Vaughan and Alden T. Vaughan. London: Arden, 1999.

———. *Henry IV, Part 2*. Edited by James C. Bulman. London: Bloomsbury, 2016.

Shammas, Carole. "How Self-Sufficient Was Early America?" *The Journal of Interdisciplinary History* 13 (1982): 247–72.

Shannon, Laurie. *The Accommodated Animal: Cosmopolity in Shakespearean Locales*. Chicago, IL: University of Chicago Press, 2013.

———. "'Poore wretch, laid all naked upon the bare earth': Human Negative Exceptionalism Among the Humanists." In *Shakespearean International*

Yearbook 15: Shakespeare and the Human, edited by Tiffany Jo Werth, 205–10. Burlington, VT: Ashgate, 2015.

Shawcross, John. "The Bee-Simile Once More." *Milton Quarterly* 15, no. 2 (1981): 44–47.

Sherman, Sean. *The Sioux Chef's Indigenous Kitchen*. Minneapolis: University of Minnesota Press, 2017.

Shuckard, W. E. *British Bees: An Introduction to the Study of the Natural History and Economy of the Bees Indigenous to the British Isles*. London: Lovell Reeve and Co., 1866.

Silverman, David J. *Faith and Boundaries: Colonists, Christianity, and Community among the Wampanoag Indians of Martha's Vineyard, 1600–1871*. Cambridge: Cambridge University Press, 2005.

Smith, Andrea. "American Studies without America: Native Feminisms and the Nation-State." *American Quarterly* 60 (2008): 309–15.

Smith, Bruce R. *The Acoustic World of Early Modern England: Attending to the O Factor*. Chicago, IL: University of Chicago Press, 1999.

Smith, D. A., ed. *John Evelyn's Manuscript on Bees from Elysium Britannicum*. Bristol: Bee Research Association, 1966.

Smith, James. "On Killer Bees and GCHQ: 'Hated in the Nation.'" In *Through the Black Mirror: Deconstructing the Side Effects of the Digital Age*, edited by Terence McSweeney and Stuart Joy, 179–90. London: Palgrave Macmillan, 2019.

Smith, Watson. *Kiva Mural Decorations at Awatovi and Kawaika-a with a Survey of Other Wall Paintings in the Pueblo Southwest*. Cambridge: Peabody Museum, 1952.

Soble, Alan. "In Defense of Bacon." In *A House Built on Sand: Exposing Postmodernist Myths about Science*, edited by Noretta Koertge, 192–215. Oxford: Oxford University Press, 1998.

Soliz, Chester P. *The Historical Footprints of the Mashpee Wampanoag*. Sarasota, FL: Bardolph and Company, 2011.

Sotelo Santos, Laura Elena, and Carlos Alvarez Asomoza. "The Maya Universe in a Pollen Pot: Native Stingless Bees in Pre-Columbian Mayan Art." In *Pot Pollen in Stingless Bee Melittology*, edited by Patricia Vit, Silvia R. M. Pedro, and David W. Roubik, 299–309. Cham, CH: Springer, 2018.

Southerne, Edmund. *A Treatise Concerning the Right Use and Ordering of Bees*, 1593.

Spenser, Edmund. *Fowre Hymnes*. London, 1596.

Standing Bear. "The Symbol of Extinction." In *Cry of the Thunderbird: The American Indian's Own Story*, edited by Charles Hamilton, 214–5. Norman: University of Oklahoma Press, 1972.

Stanescu, James. "Species Trouble: Judith Butler, Mourning, and the Precarious Lives of Animals." *Hypatia* 27, no. 3 (2012): 567–82.

Stipanovic, Andre. "Bees and Ants: Perceptions of Imperialism in Vergil's Aeneid and Georgics." In *Insect Poetics*, edited by Eric C. Brown, 13–28. Minneapolis: University of Minnesota Press, 2006.

Sullivan, Garrett. *Sleep, Romance and Human Embodiment: Vitality from Spenser to Milton*. Cambridge: Cambridge University Press, 2012.

Tallbear, Kim. *Native American DNA: Tribal Belonging and the False Promise of Genetic Science*. Minneapolis: University of Minnesota Press, 2013.

Test, Edward McLean. *Sacred Seeds: New World Plants in Early Modern English Literature*. Lincoln: University of Nebraska Press, 2019.

Thorley, David. *Writing Illness and Identity in Seventeenth-Century Britain*. London: Palgrave, 2016.

Tigner, Amy L. "Eating with Eve." *Milton Quarterly* 44, no. 4 (December 2010): 239–53.

Topsell, Edward. *The Reward of Religion Delivered in Sundrie Lectures Upon the Booke of Ruth*. London: John Windell, 1596.

———. *Times Lamentation: Or an Exposition on the Prophet Joel*. London: 1599.

———. *Historie of Serpents*. London, 1608.

Tuck, Eve, and K. Wayne Yang. "Decolonization is not a Metaphor." *Decolonization: Indigeneity, Education & Society* 1 (2012): 1–40.

Tuhiwai Smith, Linda. *Decolonizing Methodologies: Research and Indigenous Peoples*. London: Zed Books, 1999.

Twine, Richard. "Revealing the 'Animal-Industrial Complex'—A Concept and Method for Critical Animals Studies?" *Journal for Critical Animals Studies* 10, no. 1 (2012): 12–39.

Tyler, Royall. *The Contrast*. Edited by Montrose Jonas Moses. *Representative Plays by American Dramatists, vol. 1, 1765–1819*, 431–98. New York: Benjamin Blom, 1964.

Ulrich, Laurel Thatcher. "Wheels, Looms, and the Gender Division of Labor in Eighteenth-Century New England." *The William and Mary Quarterly* 55, no. 1 (January 1998): 3–38.

Varro, Marcus Terentius. *On Agriculture*. Translated by William Davis Hooper. Cambridge: Harvard University Press, 1934.

Virgil. *Eclogues, Georgics, Aeneid I-VI*. Translated by H. Rushton Fairclough. London: Loeb Classical Library, 1916.

———. *The Works of Virgil: Containing his Pastorals, Georgics, and Aeneis*. Translated by John Dryden. London: 1697.

von Frisch, Karl. *The Dance Language and Orientation of Bees*. Translated by Leigh E. Chadwick. Cambridge, MA: Harvard University Press, 1967.

Waldau, Paul. *Animal Studies: An Introduction*. Oxford: Oxford University Press, 2013.

Warren, Karen J. "Taking Empirical Data Seriously: An Ecofeminist Philosophical Perspective." In *Ecofeminism: Women, Culture Nature*, edited by Karen J. Warren. 3–15. Bloomington: Indiana University Press, 1997.

Washington, George, "To Alexander Hamilton," Mount Vernon, July 29, 1795. *Founders Online*, National Archive, http://founders.archives.gov/documents/Hamilton/01-18-02-0318.

Watson, Robert N. *The Green and the Real in the Late Renaissance*. Philadelphia: University Pennsylvania Press, 2006.

Weaver, Jace. "Indigenous and Indigeneity." In *A Companion to Postcolonial Studies*, edited by Henry Schwarz and Sangeeta Ray, 221–35. New York: Wiley, 2000.

Welburn, Jude. "Divided Labors: Work, Nature, and the Utopian Impulse in John Milton's *Paradise Lost*." *Studies in Philology* 116, no. 3 (Summer 2019): 506–38.

Werth, Tiffany Jo, ed. *Shakespearean International Yearbook 15: Shakespeare and the Human*. Farnham: Ashgate Publishing, 2015.

Wheeler, John Hill. *Historical Sketches of North Carolina from 1584 to 1851*. Baltimore, MD: Genealogical Publishing, 1993.

White, John. *Fireflies and Gadfly*. 1585–93. Painting. Museum Number: 1906, 0509.1.67. British Museum, London.

Whitfield, Henry. *The Light Appearing More and More Towards the Perfect Day*. London, 1651.

Whitford, David Mark. *The Curse of Ham in the Early Modern Era: The Bible and the Justifications for Slavery*. Burlington, VT: Ashgate, 2009.

Williams, Paul H., and Juliet L. Osborne. "Bumblebee vulnerability and conservation Worldwide." *Apidologie* 40, no. 3 (2009): 367–87.

Williams, Roger. *A Key Into the Language of America: Or an Help to the Language of the Natives in that Part of America Called New England*. London, 1643.

Winston, Mark L. *Bee Time*. Cambridge: Harvard University Press, 2014.

Winthrop, John. *Winthrop Papers*. Vol. 1. Boston: Massachusetts Historical Society, 1929.

Wolf, Edwin, and Kevin J. Hayes, ed. *The Library of Benjamin Franklin*. Philadelphia, PA: American Philosophical Society, 2006.

Wolfe, Cary. *Animal Rites: American Culture, the Discourse of Species, and Posthumanist Theory*. Chicago, IL: University of Chicago Press, 2003.

Wood, Jennifer Linhart. "Sounding Spaces: *The Tempest's* Uncanny Near-East Echoes." *Shakespeare Studies* 44 (2016): 173–79.

Wood, William. *New England's Prospect: A True, Lively, and Experimental Description of That Part of America*. London, 1634.

Worden, Blair. "Milton's Republicanism and the Tyranny of Heaven." In *Machiavelli and Republicanism*, edited by Gisela Bock, Quentin Skinner, and Maurizio Viroli, 225–45. Cambridge: Cambridge University Press, 1990.

Worlidge, John. *Apiarium: Or a Discourse of Bees*. London, 1676.

———. *The Complete Bee-Master*. London, 1698.

Wyss, Hilary E. "Beyond the Printed Word: Native Women's Literacy Practices in Colonial England." In *Cultural Narratives: Textuality and Performance in American Culture before 1900*, edited by Sandra M. Gustafson and Caroline F. Sloat, 118–36. Notre Dame, IN: Notre Dame University Press, 2010.

Zaloga, Steven J. *Unmanned Aerial Vehicles: Robotic Warfare, 1917–2007*. Oxford: Osprey Publishing, 2008.

Zhang, Rachel Dunn. "Crafting Un-Fortune: Rape, Romance, and Resistance in Hester Pulter's *The Unfortunate Florinda*." *Early Modern Women* 12, no. 2 (2018): 76–98.

Index

Note: Page numbers followed by "n" denote endnotes.